BREAKING
THE RULES

BUREAUCRACY AND REFORM
IN PUBLIC HOUSING

ENVIRONMENT, DEVELOPMENT, AND PUBLIC POLICY

A series of volumes under the general editorship of
Lawrence Susskind, *Massachusetts Institute of Technology*
Cambridge, Massachusetts

CITIES AND DEVELOPMENT

Series Editor: Lloyd Rodwin, *Massachusetts Institute of Technology*
Cambridge, Massachusetts

THE ART OF PLANNING
Selected Essays of Harvey S. Perloff
Edited by Leland S. Burns and John Friedmann

BREAKING THE RULES
Bureaucracy and Reform in Public Housing
Jon Pynoos

CITIES OF THE MIND
Images and Themes of the City in the Social Sciences
Edited by Lloyd Rodwin and Robert M. Hollister

THE FUTURE OF HOUSING MARKETS
A New Appraisal
Leland S. Burns and Leo Grebler

HERE THE PEOPLE RULE
Selected Essays
Edward C. Banfield

MAKING-WORK
Self-Created Jobs in Participatory Organizations
William Ronco and Lisa Peattie

NEIGHBORHOODS, PEOPLE, AND COMMUNITY
Roger S. Ahlbrandt, Jr.

Other subseries:

ENVIRONMENTAL POLICY AND PLANNING
Series Editor: Lawrence Susskind, *Massachusetts Institute of Technology*
Cambridge, Massachusetts

PUBLIC POLICY AND SOCIAL SERVICES
Series Editor: Gary Marx, *Massachusetts Institute of Technology*
Cambridge, Massachusetts

BREAKING THE RULES

BUREAUCRACY AND REFORM IN PUBLIC HOUSING

Jon Pynoos

University of Southern California
Los Angeles, California

PLENUM PRESS • NEW YORK AND LONDON

Library of Congress Cataloging in Publication Data

Pynoos, Jon.
  Breaking the rules.

  (Environment, development, and public policy. Cities and development)
  Bibliography: p.
  Includes index.
  1. Public housing — United States — Management — Case studies. 2. Housing
authorities — United States — Officials and employees — Case studies. 3. Boston Hous-
ing Authority — Management — Case studies. I. Title. II. Series.
HD7288.78.U5P96   1986   363.5′8   86-18703
ISBN 0-306-42302-2

© 1986 Plenum Press, New York
A Division of Plenum Publishing Corporation
233 Spring Street, New York, N.Y. 10013

Printed in the United States of America

Preface

This is a study of how a bureaucracy allocates a commodity or a service—in this case, public housing. In the broadest sense, it seeks to understand how bureaucrats try to resolve two often conflicting goals of regulatory justice: equity (treating like cases alike on the basis of rules) and responsiveness (making exceptions for persons whose needs require that rules be stretched). It analyzes the extent to which such factors as bureaucratic norms, the task orientation of workers, third-party pressure, and outside intervention affect staff members' use of discretion. Many of the rules under consideration were intended by federal officials to achieve such programmatic objectives as racial desegregation and housing for the neediest; in this regard, the study is also an examination of federal-local relationships. Finally, the study examines how the use of discretion changes over time as an agency's mission shifts and reforms are attempted.

This book is directed at the audience of administrators of programs who offer services to the public and struggle with how to allocate them. The book is also intended for those concerned with housing policy, particularly the difficult problems of whom to house. Finally, it is hoped that students of public management, social welfare, government, and urban planning, who are interested in how public policy is administered through a bureaucracy, will find the book insightful.

The case chosen for study is the Boston Housing Authority. This agency, like many of its counterparts across the country, has been beset with financial, management, and legal problems over the past twenty years. The study's purpose, however, is not to promote yet another reform, but rather to help understand the difficulties in setting policy and carrying it out in an urban bureaucracy that serves the poor.

What emerges is a struggle for power between the Boston Housing Authority's office staff and its project managers, between outside agencies and office staff, and between existing tenants and applicants with different incomes and racial backgrounds. In a broader sense, the study analyzes an agency, with inadequate resources to create sound, financially solvent, and safe communities, which is nevertheless charged with the broad responsibility of housing needy low-income people and promoting racial integration.

The Boston Housing Authority (BHA) was chosen for investigation because it represents a large public agency whose policies have an important impact on its clients in terms of where they live and when they obtain housing. Morever, the BHA incorporates several important structural characteristics typical of its counterparts in larger cities such as Chicago, St. Louis, and Newark. These characteristics include large size, functional complexity, differentiation of projects, large minority residential population, and prior reform efforts. In 1970, the BHA employed over 800 people. Its size, therefore, led to specialization of functions which, in turn, mitigated against the possibility that any one person was making all-important decisions. Moreover, the complexity resulted in a multilayered organization in which central office staff, as well as frontline workers or "street-level" bureaucrats, also played an important role. This structure allowed the investigation of the effects of bureaucratic norms and positions of responsibility. The BHA housing stock included approximately 14,000 units scattered throughout the city. The authority housed over 50,000 residents, or almost one-tenth of the city's population. Because of its scale and importance, it was expected that, given Boston's history, politics was likely to have some impact on tenant selection and assignment. Finally, when the study began, the BHA had already been the target of reform for almost ten years. Much of the reformers' efforts centered on establishing rules for tenant selection and assignment.

A major problem with any case study is the generalizability of its findings. It is well known, for example, that Boston is a city with deep racial and ethnic antagonisms, and these issues have had a major impact on decision making in the housing authority. However, although it may appear to be at the far end of the spectrum in terms of race relationships, the experience of other authorities in large cities, such as Providence or New Haven, indicates that Boston is not alone in terms of these problems. What may be more true of the BHA than of some other authorities is the extent to which the administrative system failed in terms of carrying out certain tasks. But even housing authorities such as the one in New

York, in which a follow-up study was conducted, face many of the problems that will be discussed in this book.

The field research for this study took place during two time periods: from 1970 to 1972 and from 1980 to 1985. It represents extensive interviews with BHA staff, board members, political and agency staff, federal officials, and other professionals, as well as participant observations of activities. Many internal BHA documents were reviewed. Initial access to the BHA was provided by Elaine Werby, the Assistant to the Director, who broached the subject with the authority's board which subsequently gave its approval. As a result, I was permitted to interview personnel and to inspect internal files and documents. After several weeks of reading material, interviews were conducted with the Tenant Selection Department's seventeen staff members to find out what they did, how they had come to work there, what the work conditions were like, how they made decisions, what they regarded as the pressures on them, and how they interpreted the rules. For several months the tenant selection and assignment process was observed, during which time discussions were also held with the staff and tenant assignment data was collected. To protect confidentiality, names of staff members are not used in this study.

During the initial period of participant observation in the central office, it became clear that a great deal of resistance to the tenant and assignment rules came from project managers. Two projects were then selected for study and, with the approval of the Assistant Director of Management, a research assistant was sent to study the role of the managers in tenant selection. Each project was observed for approximately three weeks.

In an attempt to explore the influence of outside parties on decision making, about twenty people were interviewed including agency workers, politicians, and other BHA staff who interacted with the Tenant Selection Department; ex-employees of the BHA; and regional officials of the Department of Housing and Urban Development (HUD). These interviews were particularly helpful as a check regarding the validity of earlier interviews with tenant selection staff. HUD audit reports on tenant selection and assignment procedures were also reviewed at that time. Following the series of interviews with outside parties, more extensive interviews were conducted with ten key decision makers in the tenant selection department. These interviews, which usually took place out of the office, lasted approximately two hours each and centered on the officials' views of reform, outside intervention, and agency policy.

At the end of phase one, staff and officials, at both the Department of

Housing and Urban Development and the National Association of Housing and Redevelopment, who were involved in the rule controversies, were interviewed in Washington. Both organizations allowed me to read correspondence and memoranda relevant to the study. Shortly thereafter, several months were spent at the New York Housing Authority in an attempt to determine whether conditions there differed from those in Boston.

In phase two of the study, during the period from 1980 to 1985, research was again conducted at the Boston Housing Authority. By this time, some issues had changed radically whereas others were still the same. As one observer commented, Boston moved from an independently operated agency to the frying pan of a master appointed by the court and, finally, into the fire of a court-appointed receiver responsible for running the authority without a board. Nevertheless, issues of whom to house and what degree of discretion staff should have in decision making remained high on the agenda of both the BHA and other interested parties. In fact, if anything, these issues became more visible in terms of political debate and press coverage than they had been since the mid-1960s. During the second phase of research, interviews were conducted with the judge in charge of the case, staff of the master's office, and BHA staff under the receivership. Again, agency documents were reviewed and interviews were conducted with key staff in the central office and at HUD.

James Q. Wilson of Harvard University followed the study from its inception and provided assistance in formulating basic questions and the research strategy. He was instrumental in helping me generalize from my particular findings and clarify the broad themes in my work. His willingness to read rough drafts and to help smooth these chapters into final products made my work much easier. No matter how busy, and even while on sabbatical, Professor Wilson was always accessible and took the time to scrutinize my manuscript. Michael Lipsky of MIT deserves special thanks. Although overloaded with students from his own university, he generously took me on as his advisee. His conceptual grasp of theoretical and policy issues opened up many new avenues of thought for me, especially concerning the concept of street-level bureaucrats. His ability to see how sections of my work could be rearranged and rewritten contributed much to the clarity of my arguments. In addition, his encouragement and confidence in me helped immeasurably.

A number of friends read my manuscript in its early form and provided me with information and ideas: Cathy Donaher, Rob Hollister, Ken

Geiser, John Mollenkopf, Maureen Power, Art Solomon, and Chester Hartman. Jeffrey Prottis, who did the project fieldwork, which he later incorporated as part of his own thesis, deserves special thanks as does Bob Schafer, who assisted me with the computer analysis. Betty Mulroy, Bill Sota, and Lisa Hamburger were especially helpful in tracking down information for the 1980–85 period. My friend Marc Older, who helped me secure the photographs for the book, was extremely generous with his time. In addition, I owe special thanks to Lisa Peattie, who recommended the manuscript for publication, as well as to Lloyd Rodwin of MIT, the editor of this Plenum series, for his patient support and constructive suggestions. Langley Keyes, who read an early draft of the manuscript, kindly provided me with a number of useful recommendations which guided later additions and revisions.

Of course, this study could not have been possible without the cooperation of the BHA and agencies with which it is connected. I am very grateful to Harry Spence, John Washek, Louise Elving, John Murphy, Joseph Vera, and Judge Paul Garrity among others for sharing both information and their views with me in spite of the press of work. I am certain that there are many points in the manuscript on which these persons would disagree; the final responsibility for the accuracy of the data, analysis, and conclusions rests solely with me.

I would also like to thank The Boston Globe, the Boston Housing Authority, Cymie Paine, and Goody, Clancy and Associates, Inc., for providing the photographs that are used in this book.

A researcher needs funds for his work. I am indebted to the Joint Center for Urban Studies, the Ford Foundation, and the Sloan Foundation for their financial support.

The preparation of a manuscript is always an anxiety-producing ordeal. Fortunately, my early chapters were in the good hands of Sara Jane Woodward and later ones were overseen by Marie Mandel. I also wish to thank Donna Deutchman for her meticulous editing of all the chapters, which greatly added to the clarity and consistency of the final document. In addition, I want to thank Irv Borstein for his constant advice, support, and encouragement. Finally, I would like to dedicate this book to my family—my family of origin, my parents Rita and Morris Pynoos as well as my brother Robert; and the family which Elyse and I have created together, composed of Jessica, Rebecca, and Joshua. All of these persons will be somewhat relieved as well as pleased that this study, which spanned almost twelve years, is finished and in print.

Contents

CHAPTER EIGHT: THE LATER YEARS: COURT-INITIATED REFORM EFFORTS   157

CHAPTER NINE: SUMMARY AND IMPLICATIONS   187

BIBLIOGRAPHY   205

INDEX   213

CHAPTER ONE

Bureaucracy and Public Housing

Despite its many well-known problems, public housing is still the government's major housing program for low-income Americans.[1] More than three million people live in its units; and most large cities maintain long waiting lists with names of those applicants anxious for apartments.[2] Un-

---

[1]For a review of the financial problems see Frank de Leeuw, *Operating Costs in Public Housing—A Financial Crisis* (Washington, D.C.: The Urban Institute, 1970). Criticisms of overall policy are found in Eugene J. Meehan, *The Quality of Federal Policy Making: Programmed Failure in Public Housing* (Columbia: University of Missouri Press, 1979) and Raymond J. Struyk, *A New System for Public Housing: Salvaging A National Resource* (Washington, D.C.: The Urban Institute, 1980). Architectural failings are noted in Albert Mayer, "Public Housing Architecture," *Journal of Housing*, 19 (1962): 446–456. The politics surrounding site selection isolation are discussed in Martin Meyerson and Edward Banfield *Politics, Planning, and the Public Interest* (New York: Free Press, 1955). Managerial problems are discussed in J. Mulvihill, "Problems in the Management of Public Housing," *Temple Law Quarterly*, (Winter 1962): 163–194; and George Schermer Associates and Kenneth Jones, *Changing Concepts of the Tenant Management Relationship* (Washington, D.C.: National Association of Housing and Redevelopment Officials, 1967). Public housing's declining image is discussed in Chester Hartman, "Social Values and Housing Orientations," *Journal of Social Issues*, 19 (April 1963): 113–131. Also see Seymour Bellin and Louis Kriesberg, "Relations Among Attitudes, Circumstances, and Behavior: The Case of Applying for Public Housing," *Sociology and Social Research*, 52 (1967): 453–469, and Richard Coleman, "Explorations in the Contemporary Images of Housing" (Cambridge: MIT-Harvard Joint Center for Urban Studies, mimeographed, 1972).

[2]Data on units is available in the U.S. Department of Housing and Urban Development, *Statistical Yearbook* (Washington, D.C.: GPO, 1978). Waiting lists which were reported infrequently, however, do not accurately indicate demand, since demand would be much higher if people felt they had a good chance of getting in.

derstandably, with the demand for public housing so great and the supply so limited, the process by which vacancies are allocated is a vital issue.

The policies and practices whereby people become aware of and apply for public housing, are assigned to particular developments, may be transferred among them, and in a few cases evicted out of them influence many aspects of housing authority operations. They determine the patterns of integration or segregation found in projects; they influence the security and community aspects of developments; and they determine who has access to the financial benefits inherent in public housing.

The procedure by which public housing is distributed, like that of other social welfare programs, raises issues of equity: given the differences in needs even among subgroups such as the poor, who should receive available public housing units? This volume examines the public housing allocation process with an eye to its fairness, describes the organizational mechanisms that affect decisions, and assesses the potential for designing and implementing rules capable of preventing inequities.

Until the 1960s most local public housing authorities used their extensive legal powers to select intact working-class families as tenants and to segregate whites from nonwhites. By the 1960s, however, the number and proportion of minority and very poor applicants had increased, due, in part, to urban renewal and highway dislocation. With these qualitative and quantitative shifts in public housing applicants, reformers attempted to control bureaucratic discretion to insure that the new clients were housed and to integrate projects racially.

The reformers advanced two main strategies to insure the equitable distribution of units: the right of appeal and the adoption of general rules. Those supporting the right of appeal argued that applicants who felt they had been unjustly treated were best protected by a formal adjudicatory process before an impartial board.[3]

Advocates of general rules, on the other hand, argued that case-by-case adjudication occurred without sufficient guidelines; besides, very few people ever filed complaints under rights of appeal.[4] They therefore

---

[3]For experiential accounts regarding right of appeal procedures see Richard Lempert and Kiyoshi Ikeda, "Evictions from Public Housing: The Effects of Independent Review," *American Sociological Review*, 35 (1970): 852–860, and Leon Mayhew, *Law and Equal Opportunity: A Study of the Massachusetts Commission Against Discrimination* (Cambridge: Harvard University Press, 1968).

[4]Theodore Lowi, *The End of Liberalism* (New York: Norton, 1969), especially pp. 299–301.

supported the adoption of general rules as the best means to insure fairness and achieve organizational objectives. These rules were to be known beforehand by all parties, clarified through illustrations, and applied to specific cases. The resulting system of policy implementation through rules was expected to produce regulatory justice in which persons in the same categories were treated equally.

Lawrence Friedman[5] has contended that welfare programs such as public housing are the ideal context for simple allocation rules such as first come, first serve because the staff have no reason to favor some applicants over others. Moreover, in a client-oriented bureaucracy rule adherence protects the staff from charges of discrimination and unfairness.

Friedman's argument about rule effectiveness in public housing is based on his finding that "if there were abuses, no one in government seemed to have heard of them." Indeed, the theoretical assumption underlying Friedman's analysis is the Weberian notion that a bureaucracy, like a machine, can and should function in a predictable manner which treats like cases alike. A bureaucracy can be made to apply general rules to particular cases without succumbing to political pressures, personal biases, and other external influences which are specifically excluded from its specialized calculus.

In spite of Friedman's claim, however, some critics of bureaucratic behavior have argued that rule adherence itself may be an undesirable goal, whereas others have contended that regulatory justice based on rules alone is unattainable. For example, the unwillingness of agency staff to distinguish between cases is often cited as the cause of undue hardship on clients who may have special needs. The resulting outcry is that bureaucrats are inhumane, rule-bound, faceless, and unresponsive. The other side of the problem is represented by those who contend that the Weberian ideal of regulatory justice is only a theoretical construct and, in fact, bureaucrats have too many sources of discretion and strong incentives to exercise it, thereby potentially treating recipients unfairly and undermining policy objectives and the intent of the rules. From this perspective, the key goal is to understand how officials exercise their discretion and to create mechanisms, incentives, or sanctions, in addition to rules, that restrict or govern this discretion so that the rights and interests of recipients are protected.[6] As Lipsky has pointed out, public

---

[5]Lawrence Friedman, "Public Housing and the Poor: An Overview," *California Law Review* (May 1966): 687.

[6]Joel Handler, *Protecting the Social Service Client: Legal and Structural Controls on Official Discretion* (New York: Academic Press, 1979).

service reform is, overall, a dialectic search for the appropriate balance between compassion and flexibility (responsiveness) on the one hand and impartiality and rigid rule adherence (equity) on the other.[7]

This volume is primarily a study of the implementation of public policy through a bureaucracy. It examines the problems that occur in attempting to apply general rules to specific cases (i.e., regulatory justice) in a bureaucracy. It therefore should be viewed as part of a small but growing number of case studies of policy implementation.[8] It is part of an emerging body of literature in a field that seeks to understand what takes place between the formal enactment of a program and its intended or unintended outcomes. Its major methodological contributions derive from examining the stages in the policy process (e.g., the design, monitoring, and evaluation of the rules at the federal level and implementation at the local level) as well as its quantitative analysis of outcomes. The study also examines the behavior of individuals at different levels of the bureaucracy in order to better understand how staff in different positions exercise discretion in implementing rules. And, finally, it looks at the policy process over time to shed light on how changing conditions affect bureaucratic behavior as well as policy implementation and reformulation.

The activity under investigation is the selection and assignment of public housing tenants, a routine activity of public housing authorities scattered across the country.[9] The rules governing tenant selection and

---

[7]Michael Lipsky, *Street-Level Bureaucracy: Dilemmas of the Individual in Public Services* (New York: Russell Sage Foundation, 1980).

[8]Several recent studies of policy implementation relevant to this study are: Stephen Bailey and Edith Mosher, *ESEA: The Office of Education Administers a Law* (Syracuse: Syracuse University Press, 1968); Jeffrey Pressman and Aaron Wildavsky, *Implementation* (Berkeley: University of California Press, 1972); Martin Rein and Francine Rabinowitz, "Toward a Theory of Implementation" (Cambridge: Joint Center for Urban Studies, mimeographed, 1974); Frederick Wirt, *Politics of Southern Equality* (Chicago: Aldine, 1970); and Daniel Mazmanian and Paul Sabatier, eds., *Effective Policy Implementation* (Lexington, MA: Lexington Books, 1981).

[9]A first-hand examination of tenant selection is Irwin Deutscher. "The Gatekeeper in Public Housing," in *Among the People,* ed. Irwin Deutscher and Elizabeth Thompson (New York: Basic Books, 1968): pp. 38–52. Deutscher perceptively examined the criteria (race, family constellation, and demeanor) that one bureaucrat used to judge applicants and the factors (situational and political) that limited her authority. He did not, however, study the process.

Elizabeth Huttman, "Stigma and Public Housing: A Comparison of British and American Policies and Experience," diss., University of California at Berke-

assignment are often intended not only to insure fairness but also to achieve higher-order policy objectives, such as racial integration or housing the neediest, that are often set by federal regulations and implemented through local agencies. Hence, the study also explores the issue of whom public housing should house and the extent to which federal objectives, as reflected in guidelines and rules, are followed at the local level.[10] The study examines bureaucratic decision making over a forty-year time period, permitting an analysis of how changes in socioeconomic conditions and program priorities influence attempts to limit or increase staff discretion and, in turn, how staff members respond to altered bureaucratic incentives and agency missions.

USES OF DISCRETION

A major question in policy implementation is why rules do not lead to expected results or, in more positive terms, what conditions under which rules lead to desired outcomes. The key conceptual issue in the implementation of rules and procedures is bureaucratic discretion. Handler defines discretion as the opposite of fixed, clearly defined, and precisely stated eligibility rules and conditions.[11] Discretion, he says, gives officials choices. It is therefore important to understand what accounts for the availability of discretion as well as to analyze what factors affect how staff use it. The following variables have been identified as influencing the implementation of rules and will be examined in more depth in later chapters: (1) the clarity of the statutes or rules themselves; (2) the role of frontline workers and their power *vis à vis* upper-level managers and officials; (3) the norms of the staff; (4) the interest in and the ability of outside parties to influence staff decisions; (5) the extent to which outside

---

ley, June 1969, deals in general terms with issues regarding assignment priorities. Another study, focusing on site selection, more specifically touches on issues of tenant selection and assignment policies: Frederick Lazin, "Public Housing in Chicago, 1963–1971. Gautreux v. Chicago Housing Authority: A Case Study of the Cooptation of a Federal Agency by Its Local Constituency," diss., University of Chicago, March 1973.

[10]For two opposing views of whom public housing should serve see Roger Starr, "Which of the Poor Shall Live in Public Housing?" *The Public Interest*, 23 (1971): 116–124, and Al Hirshen and Vivian Brown, "Too Poor For Public Housing: Roger Starr's Poverty Preferences," *Social Policy*, (May/June 1972): 228–232.

[11]Handler, *Protecting the Client*, Chapter 1.

organizations monitor decisions and employ sanctions or incentives to induce compliance; and (6) the extent to which the objectives underlying the rules are eroded over time by the emergence of conflicting policies or changes in the relevant socioeconomic conditions.

FEDERAL-LOCAL RELATIONSHIPS: CLARITY OF RULES

Major social programs such as public housing have their basis in enabling legislation that creates the authority for administrative units to carry out specified missions. Theoretically, discretion can be narrowed, and client equity achieved, through the passage of clear statutes followed by the promulgation of specific administrative guidelines and rules that instruct program administrators and staff. However, statutes themselves and subsequent administrative guidelines and rules are often vague, unspecific, and even contradictory, allowing a substantial amount of interpretation at all levels.

Government faces major obstacles in the formulation of clear and specific statutes, rules, and guidelines primarily due to conflicting interests and the difficulty involved in applying specific rules to diverse situations. Federal legislation, for example, often deals only in generalities, especially when conflicting values come into question. Since the federal government has to reconcile very diverse interests, it has often left difficult allocation choices to state and local agencies.[12] Federal government stipulation is often constrained by the necessity to obtain program participation. Since lower-level government might refuse programs or grants if unacceptable conditions are known to be strictly enforced, the federal government must make these programs attractive. Nevertheless, it is not uncommon for the federal legislative or administrative branch to define goals in addition to (and often in conflict with) agency missions because various committees or departments have their own viewpoint on priorities. Hence, in public housing we see issues of equal opportunity and racial integration imposed on other objectives, such as housing the neediest or financial solvency. Even in instances wherein goals are clearly agreed upon, specific guidelines are still a rarity. This may be because the legislative or administrative branch does not know how to achieve the

---

[12]See Martha Derthick, *The Influence of Federal Grants* (Cambridge: Harvard University Press, 1970).

stated ends or because the situations in communities are so diverse that single approaches to identified problems are inappropriate. Therefore, federal policy statements, as a practical matter, tend to be general, ambiguous, and even contradictory, leaving a great deal of latitude to more local administrative agencies which encounter similar problems in defining goals but, unlike the federal level, are faced with day-to-day decisions regarding allocation of resources to clients.

THE TASK ORIENTATION OF STREET-LEVEL BUREAUCRATS

Ambiguous or conflicting rules, as well as the large span of control in many organizations, create opportunities for lower-level staff to exercise discretion in performing critical tasks of the organization. Lipsky refers to such operators in public service agencies who have interaction with clients as *street-level bureaucrats*.[13] Several features of their jobs create the opportunity for the use of discretion. First, they often encounter situations which are too complex for the application of simple rules. Second, street-level bureaucrats often work in situations in which the public wants them to respond to individual circumstances. But the overriding concern for policy implementation is that these staff may not necessarily share the objectives of their superiors because of either personal needs or the positions they occupy within their organizations (or both). Therefore, even if the rules are clearly defined, and certainly in cases wherein there is either ambiguity or conflict, they might choose not to comply fully in order to maximize their own autonomy and/or client processing and control goals. Their power to undermine upper-level directives derives partly from their command of such organizational resources as information and expertise and partly from the dependence of upper-level staff upon their performance. This reciprocal relationship challenges the traditional theory of policy implementation, which theorizes that influence flows from upper to lower levels in an organization and that all staff perceive common organizational objectives. Instead, it is possible that, in certain organizational settings and in certain circumstances, street-level bureaucrats make policy simply through their behavior.

[13]Lipsky, *Street-Level Bureaucracy*, pp. 3–28.

THE NORMS OF THE STAFF

On the basis of rules, agency staff are expected to treat clients in similar situations alike. However, from the picture that will emerge in this volume, it should be clear that rules by themselves may be only general guides rather than detailed prescriptions for behavior. It has often been thought that in such situations professional ethics might define the parameters within which agency staff make decisions about clients. However, from an organizational viewpoint, individual decisions based on professional norms can run counter to overall agency objectives. Moreover, if client loads are large, professional norms about which clients need what types of help and how much time and effort to exert on their behalf may still be subject to the stereotyping and simplifications characteristic of less professional street-level bureaucrats. Finally, there are many frontline workers such as tenant selection staff and housing managers who would qualify as professionals only in the loosest sense of the term. Therefore, concerns remain regarding bias based on staff perception of client attributes such as moral worth or racial characteristics.

Traditionally, we have looked for the roots of worker bias in the backgrounds of the staff. When such bias existed, the answer has been to change the attitudes of the staff, reduce the discretion open to them, alter the incentives, or impose sanctions, the ultimate form of which is to remove them from their positions. However, when such behavior continues, even in the presence of reform and regardless of the backgrounds of staff, the reasons for such apparent bias actually may lie in the work conditions, which may be more difficult to change. From a supervisory and client perspective, the concern with worker bias is even more complicated because individual staff may define their roles, the perceived mission of the agency, and the needs of clients differently. Hence, some staff may choose to be advocates for certain clients while others may sit on the sidelines, content to rely on the rules as best they can for processing clients. As a result, interactions with staff as well as outcomes may still vary depending upon the staff with whom clients come into contact.

THE INFLUENCE OF THIRD PARTIES

Rules are intended, among other objectives, to insulate bureaucrats from outside third parties who might attempt to influence their decisions.

Some scholars have assumed that the influence of third parties in public housing is a moot issue because they have little interest in such welfare programs owing to the low status of their residents.[14] However, the issue of who gets what might interest a broad group of actors because of its potential implications, particularly in the case of public housing. For example, applicants to public housing are clearly affected in the matters of whether they are admitted, the depth of the subsidy they receive, when they get in, and the condition and location of the units they are offered. Such decisions affect the quality of the apartment, available services such as shopping, schools and safety, and the nature of the neighbors with whom they will interact. In turn, existing tenants in public housing will potentially be affected by the behavior and life-styles of new neighbors. Social workers and politicians may also have concerns because client or constituent housing problems are among the most difficult to solve. Finally, housing managers may be affected by the extent to which new tenants pay their rent on time, complain, or cause problems with other tenants.

The extent to which interested parties are effective advocates for applicants depends, of course, on the amount of discretion available to staff members in the first place. Where discretion exists, third-party influence on staff decisions may be related to a variety of other factors such as the extent to which they share norms regarding the special needs of the applicant, the third party's role as a reference group, and how a decision in favor of the client makes the staff person's job easier rather than more difficult.

OUTSIDE INTERVENTION, CHANGING CONDITIONS, AND REFORM

A potential countervailing force to staff bias, third-party influence, and the power of street-level bureaucrats lies in the actions of upper-level managerial staff at the agency level and of officials at the federal and state levels responsible for monitoring and rule compliance. Their ability and/or willingness to reform the system so that rules are carried out is contingent, however, on a variety of factors. For example, effective monitoring is dependent on knowledge of the process and measurement of outcomes. As has been pointed out earlier, however, much of the

[14]Friedman, "Housing and the Poor," p. 687.

process occurs in interactions between frontline staff and clients or between staff and third parties, both of which are difficult to observe. Additionally, outcomes of goods and services related to who gets what are difficult to measure because of the variability in the product. Therefore, even if upper-level staff are aware of noncompliance, they may not know where or how to intervene because links between bureaucratic behavior and outcomes cannot be clearly articulated. Whether appropriate sanctions or incentives exist to alter behavior in order to provide corrective action is potentially just as troublesome an issue. Finally, reform may depend not only on knowledge of how well outputs conform with original intent but also on socioeconomic conditions which vary over time and affect the interest in and the strength of staff and constituent support for change.[15]

SUMMARY

This study examines the history of rule allocation and adherence in the Boston Housing Authority. Its purpose is to explore the possibility of introducing predictability and fairness into the allocation process of a major public bureaucracy. The discretion, rule adherence, and power of those involved at various levels of the bureaucracy, from policy makers to clients, will be examined as well as the outcomes of various relationships between these levels. From this, an attempt will be made to draw implications for the future equity and efficiency of rule-based programs in bureaucratic agencies of this type.

[15]See Paul Sabatier and Daniel Mazmanian, "The Implementation of Public Policy: A Framework of Analysis" in Mazmanian and Sabatier, pp. 3–35, for a discussion of the influence of changing conditions on policy implementation.

CHAPTER TWO

The Emergence of Rules

Public housing began as a response to economic problems: In order to increase employment and provide low income housing, the federal Public Works Administration (PWA) in 1934 started to build and manage housing projects. The 1,018-unit Old Harbor Village in South Boston (later renamed the Mary Ellen McCormick project) was one of the first of these developments. The role of the PWA was short-lived, however. After several court decisions denied the federal government eminent domain to acquire and clear slum property, the PWA extricated itself from the program. Since that time, the federal government's role has been to provide debt financing to localities for the purpose of building projects, operating subsidies, and guidelines for construction and management through the Public Housing Administration.[1]

The Housing Act of 1937 allowed local governments to create independent authorities that could float tax-exempt bonds without endangering local debt limits or burdening local tax rates. Advocates of the 1937 act felt that such authorities would be free from the abuses of big-city political machines. As one study explained:

> An independent citizen governed agency would be more efficient and public regarding, less corrupt and subject to political influence than any other agency form, such as a department directly under the control of the mayor or local governing body. The notion was that men of probity and wisdom, imbued with concern for the public welfare but not necessarily possessing any expertise other than sound

---

[1]See discussions of this period in Charles Abrams, *The City Is the Frontier* (New York: Harper & Row, 1965); Leonard Freedman, *Public Housing: The Politics of Poverty* (New York: Holt, Rinehart and Winston, 1969): Lawrence Friedman, *Government and Slum Housing* (Chicago: Rand McNally, 1968).

general knowledge and common sense, would be the best repository for certain kinds of public welfare programs.[2]

In spite of this clear intent, local politicians controlled the Boston Housing Authority (BHA) upon its creation in 1937. Under the Massachusetts enabling legislation, mayors appointed four of the five local housing authority board members for staggered terms. The value of passing out board appointments to one's friends was evident in a political system in which the mayor's election was based on a loyal following[3] and where, as in Massachusetts, board members were well paid.[4] Moreover, BHA Board members controlled a substantial reservoir of jobs, contracts, and housing units. By 1970, the authority employed 800 persons, had an annual budget of over $8 million exclusive of new construction, and managed over 14,000 housing units.[5] Although the subsidized units varied considerably in amenity and location, all were much sought after.

LOCALLY ORIGINATED RULES

The Happy Years: Patronage and Screening

From 1937 through the early 1950s, a period one commentator has referred to as the "happy years" of public housing, the authority selected tenants with a free hand.[6] The only restriction, enforced by the PHA, required observance of the statutory income limits demanded by real

[2]Chester Hartman and Gregg Carr, "Housing Authorities Reconsidered," *Journal of the American Institute of Planners* (January 1969). Some of the reform-machine dynamics surrounding public housing are described in Meyerson and Banfield, *Politics, Planning, and the Public Interest.*

[3]See Arnold Howitt, "Strategies of Governing: The Executive Behavior of Mayors in Philadelphia and Boston," Ph.D. diss. Harvard University, 1974.

[4]In 1970 authority members were allowed $40 per day and the chairman $50 per day with annual maximums of $10,000 and $12,000 respectively. This payment technically was given for management of state-financed public housing and thus sidesteped the federal prohibition of salaries for board positions. The same individuals, of course, directed both state and federal projects.

[5]Breakdown of the BHA housing stock in 1970 was as follows: 3,841 state-aided units, 11,600 federally aided conventional units, and 3,000 federally aided leased housing units. Boston Housing Authority, *Annual Report* (Boston: BHA, 1970).

[6]Richard Scobie, *Problem Tenants in Public Housing: Who, Where, and Why Are They* (New York: Praeger, 1975), p. 2.

estate interests in order to prevent public housing from competing with private housing. The authority received thousands of applications for apartments. To select tenants it investigated the family composition and living conditions of those who met the income limits[7] and then screened applicants to avoid potentially troublesome families and to assure stable working class tenants. A list of fifteen grounds for rejection was implemented which included excessive use of alcohol, unmarried couples, out-of-wedlock children, unsanitary housekeeping, and obnoxious conduct or behavior in connection with the processing of an application.[8] According to Elizabeth Wood, a prominent national housing figure who was executive director of the Chicago Housing Authority, "The original tenants included many families, middle class as to living standards but caught in the depression and with low incomes. They used the projects well and happily."[9]

Those applicants who passed the screening were supposed to be selected according to need as reflected in their prior housing condition; but political patronage, rather than need, often determined the priority of assignment. In the early years of public housing, political patronage had two components: cost and access. Veteran BHA employees reported that sometimes tenants had to make illegal payments to obtain apartments. Accounts of such shakedowns are also found in newspaper articles. For example, in 1951, city council members alleged that "money must be passed to get into housing projects."[10] The BHA board chairman, however, denied the charge: "As far as I know it's idle talk. The BHA is putting the most needy persons in the projects and when one tries to do a good job it is maddening to have people make such statements."[11]

Even more widespread than stories of the illegal fees were accounts that politicians controlled assignments. In a typical controversy involving assignments to a new project, a parish priest claimed he "had been in-

---

[7]*Boston Globe*, January 4, 1951.

[8]See May Hipshman, *Public Housing at the Crossroads: The Boston Housing Authority* (Boston: Citizens Housing and Planning Association, 1967), p. 27.

[9]*Boston Globe*, January 30, 1963. Robert Fischer has noted that early tenants were only temporarily poor. See Robert Fischer, *Twenty Years of Public Housing* (New York: Harper & Row, 1959), p. 164. Friedman refers to these tenants as "the submerged middle class." See Friedman, *Government and Slum Housing*, pp. 20–21.

[10]*Boston Globe*, May 1, 1951.

[11]*Ibid.*

formed that Boston politicians were being allotted 30 apartments apiece for which they could 'name' the future tenants."[12] The priest, who had worked months to get the new project built, did not, however, condemn the process on principle; rather, he argued that he "should be able to name a few of the people who will occupy the project."[13] Apparently, his list of 30 worthy families, including a Gold Star mother and a disabled veteran, had been ignored. The priest also objected to the housing authority's failure to publicize detailed eligibility requirements and to inform applicants whether or not they were accepted or rejected after investigations. The board chairman responded that the authority received "literally thousands of requests from people in public, private, and religious life."[14] He claimed that it was only a coincidence that many of those being housed had such letters of approbation from outsiders and said that such support was "not the determining factor in whether the family was rehoused or not."[15] Regardless of the chairman's public protestations, in interviews, veteran staff confirmed that political patronage had been a way of life at the BHA. Moreover, screening and political patronage combined to insure a working-class and middle-class clientele, which was highly desirable to BHA staff.

The Middle Years: Segregating New Clients

By the middle 1950s several new forces impinged on the tenant composition of public housing. Many whites, who earlier might have desired project living, purchased their own homes with the aid of rising incomes and government mortgage insurance programs or moved into private sector rental units. In addition, many public housing tenants who were now over the income limits were required to vacate their units.[16] As public housing was losing its old clientele, it was also attracting a new set of tenants. The urban renewal section of the Housing Act of 1949 gave preference to those displaced by slum clearance for placement in public housing. Most of these high priority applicants had very low incomes, and an increasing number of them were black. Moreover, increased migration

---

[12]*Boston Globe,* January 4, 1951.
[13]*Ibid.*
[14]*Ibid.*
[15]*Ibid.*
[16]Friedman, "Public Housing and the Poor."

from the South added to the number of minority citizens on the waiting list. Although screening was still an important strategy used to limit the entrance of these families, it could no longer be totally effective. The authority therefore developed a strategy for segregating its new, largely black clientele from its traditionally white working-class tenants.

Unlike many other large cities, Boston public housing projects were constructed with little neighborhood resistance; large projects can be found in Charlestown, Roxbury, the South End, South Boston, East Boston, Jamaica Plain, and Columbia Point. The acceptance of projects is partly explained by the circumstances that prevailed in the early period. Political patronage and screening kept out undesirable white tenants. Neighborhoods had little fear of black tenants because Boston's minority population was small and segregation was an accepted policy. In 1940, Lenox Street, in the South End, was the first project to accept blacks and was completely segregated. Orchard Park, the second project open to black tenants, had certain buildings known as "the colored section" designated for black occupants. As black applicants increased in number, they were gradually allowed to inhabit projects in the expanding black ghetto. As a result, by 1960 the racial pattern was clear:

> [Thirteen] of 25 projects were more than 96 percent white; of these, 7 were exclusively occupied by whites. Of the 1,733 Negro families in 15 federally aided projects, 98.6 percent were in 7 projects, two of which were entirely black. Discrimination was even more evident in the ten state-aided projects—3.6 percent of 3,675 units were occupied by Negroes. Of these, 122 Negro families were concentrated in 4 projects, one of which was entirely Negro. That the pattern of segregation was neither accidental nor a matter of location is vividly evidenced by two projects across the street from each other—Mission Hill is 100 percent white while Mission Hill Extension is 80 percent Negro.[17]

Not only were projects highly segregated, but, according to one study, the authority concentrated a disproportionate number of families identified as having problems according to BHA standards in a few projects.[18] The report pointed out that in several projects the majority of children were fatherless and half the families were receiving some sort of welfare aid.

[17]Hipshman, *Public Housing at the Crossroads,* p. 29.
[18]*Boston Globe,* January 29, 1963.

Reform: Desegregating the Projects

Although individuals had leveled sporadic charges against the BHA's policies of screening, patronage, and segregation, the civil rights movement made the first concerted effort to change tenant selection and assignment. In 1962, the National Association for the Advancement of Colored People (NAACP) and the Congress on Racial Equality (CORE) filed complaints with the Massachusetts Commission Against Discrimination (MCAD) alleging that "the recent statistics obtained from public information indicate an apparent pattern of discrimination."[19] The NAACP noted that some projects were strictly for nonwhites whereas others were strictly for whites. This charge was labeled "absurd" with "absolutely no truth to it" by the BHA chairman. He added:

> I personally have never had a complaint from anyone claiming they were being discriminated against. If it (the NAACP) has any specific cases in mind, I know nothing about them. You must remember people choose their projects. They make application and usually state the projects they prefer to go into. We try to house them where they want to go. The most searching investigation will fail to disclose any pattern of discrimination. Applications make no reference to color.[20]

Faced with BHA resistance, three liberal groups broadened their pressure on the BHA and the mayor: the Massachusetts Committee on Discrimination in Housing (MCDH), which represented twenty civil rights groups including the NAACP and CORE: the United Community Services Committee on Public Housing (UCS), a social agency coalition; and the Tenant Association Council (TAC), a group of tenants from seven predominantly black public housing projects.[21] While the NAACP and CORE bolstered their case before the MCAD with new data and a survey of tenants indicating discrimination on the part of BHA officials,[22] in 1963

[19]*Boston Globe,* May 30, 1962.

[20]*Ibid.*

[21]Parts of the discussion on early reform are drawn from Richard Scobie, "The BHA's Department of Tenant and Community Relations, 1964–1968" (Boston: BHA, mimeographed, n.d.), and Philip MacDonnell, "The Process of Change at the Boston Housing Authority," unpublished undergraduate thesis, Harvard College, April 1971. Both Scobie and MacDonnell worked for the BHA. MacDonnell and I conducted several interviews with BHA staff.

[22]Greater Boston Committee on Racial Equality (CORE), "Report on CORE's Public Housing Survey" and "Segregation in the Boston Public Housing Projects" (n.p., both mimeographed, 1963).

the coalition groups seized an opportunity to push their causes more actively.

The BHA was without an executive director; the board had been administering the authority on its own for three years. Critics charged that board administration of the authority had resulted in a "five-headed monster." A *Boston Globe* editorial pointed out that the BHA needed a director with requisite imagination and training for "building new public housing units for low-income families, and for others being relocated." Furthermore, the editorials charged, "nothing has been done to explore rehabilitation housing. New paths must be broken toward small and attractive projects."[23] As the pressure increased, the board attempted to promote a maintenance superintendent, reportedly one of Mayor Collins's school chums, to the position of executive director. Tipped off by a sympathetic board member, the liberal groups converged on the meeting at which the board was going to discuss the candidate. The director of CORE read a statement at that meeting which clearly indicated that the groups considered the superintendent unqualified:

> We believe the new director must be the best we can find. There has been no public indication that the Mayor has done anything to stimulate an intensive search for the best qualified candidate. The BHA chairman has apparently refused to submit any names—except the man he favors—to other members for their consideration. Urban renewal displaces hundreds of families, most of them poor and most of them Negroes, and now it is time for bold leadership.[24]

This statement also linked the appointment of an appropriate director to desegregation: "If a new director is appointed without a firm public commitment to end isolated racial and economic ghettoes then second ratism will become further established in a significant sector of the community."[25] The liberal groups then recommended a new search and an agreement that no director would be appointed who did not pledge full support for a program of open, unsegregated public housing. Toward the end of the meeting, a representative of the American Veterans Committee asked for copies of agendas for future meetings which city hall reporters, invited by the reform groups, had earlier been unable to obtain. The chairman told the audience that it was not possible to learn in advance when the

[23]*Boston Globe*, February 6, 1963.
[24]*Boston Globe*, March 28, 1963.
[25]*Ibid.*

appointment of an executive director would next arise on the agenda. The reform groups therefore packed the meetings for several successive weeks.

In an atmosphere of civil rights militancy, school boycotts, and sit-ins, and amid rumors that housing was going to be the next target, Mayor Collins himself, rather than the board, responded to the reform pressure. Even though the board had the formal power of appointment, Collins announced that Ellis Ash, a deputy to Edward Logue, director of the Boston Redevelopment Authority and a public housing professional with close ties to civil rights groups and housing reformers, was to be acting administrator of the BHA. The board contented itself with resentful acquiescence and formally hired Ash.

New Rules and Regulations

Ash accepted the position of acting director with Mayor Collins's understanding that he was to "take care of that NAACP business."[26] In his initial move, Ash privately invited the board to endorse a press statement he had drafted as the basis for an agreement with the civil rights groups before he released it to the press. The statement promised non-discrimination in all practices and the achievement and maintenance of integrated housing developments through the establishment of an equitable tenant selection system, the hiring of an intergroup relations officer, and the creation of an advisory committee (whose membership would be agreeable to the NAACP and CORE as well as to the authority) to confer on issues of desegregation and race relations.[27] Such a policy, if effective, would strip the board of much of its patronage and reduce its power. According to an insider, the board grudgingly signed the statement, "hoping it would serve to buy some time; they had no intention of acting on it."[28]

In late 1963, after this agreement with the NAACP and CORE was made final, Ash formulated the operating procedures of his program in more detail. However, due to board procrastination, it was not until 1965 that new tenant selection and assignment procedures were finally adopted. The new procedures attempted to move the BHA toward ra-

[26]MacDonnell, "Process of Change at BHA," p. 46.
[27]*Boston Globe*, June 20, 1963.
[28]Scobie, "BHA, 1964–1968," p. 2.

tional and predictable operation based on written rules that limited staff discretion in the key areas of eligibility, priority, and assignment.[29]

The 1965 resolution discarded the list of fifteen exclusionary factors previously used to screen applicants. In its place, the resolution defined an unacceptable family as one whose composition or behavior constituted:

1. a danger to the health, safety, or morals of other tenants;
2. a seriously adverse influence upon sound family and community life;
3. a source of danger or damage to the property of the Authority;
4. a source of danger to the peace and comfort of other families; or
5. in any other sense, a nuisance.[30]

Being broad, and leaving much room for subjectivity, these standards could be used restrictively—especially by veteran staff wedded to past practices. Ash therefore turned these sensitive decisions over to a newly formed Department of Tenant and Community Relations. This department, an outgrowth of the concept of an intergroup relations officer, was composed of hand-picked, recently recruited staff loyal to Ash. Committed to serving applicants rather than excluding them, these welfare professionals defined an unacceptable family as one that demonstrated severe antisocial behavior as indicated in a major criminal conviction (e.g., drug addiction, child abuse, breaking or entering, assault and battery, prostitution) within the last two years; illegitimacy of more than one child the youngest of whom is less than two years old; a poor rent-paying record; property destruction; or harassment of neighbors while previously a BHA tenant.

Under the revised rules, the staff of the old Tenant Selection Department weeded out unacceptable applicants and forwarded their case folders to the staff of the new Department of Tenant and Community Relations for further evaluation. Despite the definitive restrictions, the social workers receiving rejected applications in the new department found the tenant selection staff misinterpreting the definitions and excluding applicants who were qualified. For example, many rejected refer-

[29]Boston Housing Authority, "Resolution Establishing Policies and Standards Governing Occupancy of Federally Aided Developments" (n.p., mimeographed, November 1965).
[30]*Ibid.*, p. 9.

rals had court records earlier than the two-year limit, had been charged with crimes but not convicted, or were women with illegitimate children older than two years. All of these referrals were returned to the Tenant Selection Department for housing. Overall, about 95 percent of the referrals were judged eligible under the revised rules and review.[31]

The 1965 resolution also established an assignment priority for those applicants who qualified for public housing. Priority depended on three factors: rent level, need, and statutory requirements. Rent level was an efficiency factor introduced to insure a balanced operating budget. While the authority stated that recipients of public assistance would not be excluded, the number of very low income tenants had to be limited so that "an excessive number of families at the bottom of the income scale would not jeopardize solvency."[32] Staff were therefore instructed to select families alternately from upper and lower rent ranges so that the authority could meet its operating expenses. Within rent ranges, staff were next to give highest priority to applicants in the worst housing condition. Relative housing need was determined by a weighted scoring system based on whether applicants were without housing, about to be without housing, or living in unsafe, unsanitary, or overcrowded conditions.[33] In all three need categories, "objective and uniform consideration" was also given to personal factors such as chronic health problems and disability. If two applicants had the same score, priority went to the family with the greatest number of minor children that the vacancy would accommodate. If families had an equal number of children, priority was accorded to veterans and those displaced by public action. Finally, if all factors were still equal, the earliest filed case had precedence. Ash and the reform groups were very optimistic about the benefits of the new procedures. One staff member indicated, for example, that determining

[31]Boston Housing Authority, Department of Tenant and Community Relations, "Follow-up Study of a Selected Group of Tenants Identified During Application Process as Potential Problem Families" (n.p., mimeographed, July 1967).

[32]Very low income tenants threatened solvency primarily because they paid less rent (rent was based on a formula combining income and family size) but also because their rent payment record was worse than that of higher-income tenants. Boston Housing Authority, "Resolution Establishing Policies and Standards Governing Occupancy of Federally Aided Developments," (Boston: BHA, 1965), p. 14.

[33]Such point schemes form the basis for applicant priority in English council housing. See J. B. Cullingworth, *Housing and Local Government* (London: Allen and Unwin, 1966), pp. 124–129.

priority based on need represented "a real change—the first lowering of the door in terms of patronage."

The tenant selection staff carried out the necessary procedures to categorize applicants. Nonetheless, the new policy often had little bearing on decisions because Ash could not exert control over the chief of the Tenant Selection Department, described by one staff member as being "a king in his own kingdom."[34] According to a student of the organization during this period, the chief exemplified a traditional lack of cooperation with the executive director:

> The five member Board has historically headed the organization and department heads still ignore the Administrator or perform end-runs around him to the Board.[35]

A staff member explained:

> Some department heads want to act big and go directly to Board members or politicians. They and the Board make things really hard for Ash.[36]

As a practical matter, the executive director lacked the power and prestige to implement his priorities, especially in regard to primary project assignments. As Ash later recalled, the board disregarded rent level, need, and statutory requirements and continued to base priority on political patronage:

> The actual assignment of tenants to units, or who got what, was done in the Chairman's office. Vacancies did not go to Tenant Selection but to the Chairman. When one long-awaited project of 100 or so units was ready for occupancy, there followed hours upon hours of individual judgements as to who would get the units during which the wishes of the Mayor, Council members, certain legislators and each Authority member had to be satisfied. As a result, the project was not opened up for two months after it was ready despite the obvious need and the waiting list.[37]

---

[34]Quoted in Lewis Popper, "The Boston Housing Authority: A Study of Conflict in Bureaucracy," unpublished undergraduate thesis, Harvard College, 1968, p. 40. Popper worked as Ash's assistant while doing his research.

[35]*Ibid.*

[36]Quoted *Ibid.*

[37]Quoted in Citizens Housing and Planning Association, *A Struggle for Survival: The Boston Housing Authority, 1969–1973* (Boston: Citizens Housing and Planning Association, 1973), p. iv–10.

Ash's new policy for determining assignment location, designed to end segregation in BHA projects, also ran into interference. According to the procedures, staff had to assign applicants in a manner

> consistent with a positive policy of integation and racial balance, the need for a careful selection of "pioneer" families and the promotional effort that is involved in initial integration stages and in situations where the objective is to arrest or reverse "tipping" trends. The placement pattern in individual developments over a period of time should tend to reflect the racial balance of the total racial ratio existing throughout all the developments maintained by the Authority.[38]

Thus, racial integration was to become a major constraint on what the authority had previously claimed was the main determinant in locating tenants: applicant preference. Applicants were no longer supposed to choose projects, only areas of the city; and even those choices might be disallowed if they conflicted with the policy of integration. The staff was to disapprove applicant preference altogether when it was based on "like or dislike" of a project's racial composition. In a situation in which an applicant refused a project assignment (the inverse of preference) for reasons of racial prejudice, he or she was then to be placed below all other eligible applicants in priority. If the applicant refused an assignment for unbiased reasons, such as health, that were documented and supported in writing, then his or her priority status was reevaluated.

Ash did not leave the actual integration effort to the Tenant Selection Department but turned it over to the newly formed Department of Tenant and Community Relations. However, in order to place black applicants in projects, the department's staff had to know when and where vacancies were available. Thus, managers were able to thwart the policy's implementation by refusing to cooperate with the social welfare staff. Instead of advising the new department of openings, they phoned their vacancies to the chairman of the authority who then selected his own assignees. Ash and the reformers in the Department of Tenant and Community Relations were therefore forced to bypass the regular system in assigning black applicants by setting up a parallel system. For example, they created an informal network with sympathetic tenants who would call them to report vacant units. With the help of the NAACP, the staff also recruited "pioneer" black families willing to move in to white pro-

[38]Boston Housing Authority, "Resolution," p. 19.

jects. According to one staff participant, the first four families to move into Mary Ellen McCormick and Old Colony in South Boston did so amid rumors that "100 niggers were going to be sweeping into the place." At that time, blacks neither lived in the area's private housing nor attended the local high school. The black pioneer families were met by sympathetic neighbors and plainclothesmen who were stationed nearby to protect them. In several other projects where a similar strategy was undertaken, reformers made a specific attempt to create an image of the stable black family (i.e., two parents) in order to ease the strain. The advisory committee hoped to have black families occupy 10 percent of the units in formerly all-white projects within three years, with a long range goal of 25 percent.

The integration effort relied in part on outside support. Reformers made an effort to elicit the aid of the Catholic Church, a powerful force in most of Boston's white areas. However, according to a BHA staff member, Cardinal Cushing was unwilling to issue a statement asking his pastors to back integration, claiming privately that he might lose one-half of his parishioners by such an action. Nonetheless, one monsignor did visit the neighborhood to help alleviate tension when trouble broke out at D Street in South Boston. The rector in the Jamaica Plain area not only gave a sermon on the moral imperative of equality and integration but placed 1,000 copies of the document under the doors of project residents. Interviewers were then sent out to see if the mood of the tenants had changed. According to one of the BHA staff participants, the prevailing feeling "seemed to be like something from a white Citizens Council in the South: 'They (the blacks) have their project, why do they want ours?' " In spite of the Department of Tenant and Community Relations efforts, this resistance continued and many civil rights leaders were unhappy with the results.

In late 1965, the NAACP charged that the BHA had "failed to initiate an effective tenant selection program which would integrate and desegregate all existing federally subsidized housing developments as set forth in the agreement."[39] In a similar vein, in early 1966, the spokesman for the Massachusetts Advisory Commission to the United States Commission on Civil Rights charged the BHA with having "broken its solemn promise to carry out desegregation in public housing."[40] Although the advisory com-

---

[39]*Boston Globe*, October 13, 1965.
[40]*Boston Globe*, February 16, 1966.

mission acknowledged the authority's effort to diminish discriminatory tenant selection practices, they voiced dissatisfaction with the progress. They urged federal agencies to investigate the agency and, if necessary, to withhold funds to effect compliance. A *Boston Globe* editorial further suggested that two projects, Mission Hill (96 percent white) and Mission Hill Extension (88 percent black), be integrated by shifting families from one project to the other.[41]

Criticism of Ash's plan continued to increase. By 1967, people who had until then supported the integration policy began to express uncertainty about the operation. The policy succeeded in increasing the number of black public housing residents from 2,137 (15.2 percent) in 1962 to 3,736 (25.9 percent) in 1967. In addition, virtually all developments at that time contained some blacks. However, eight projects were still over 95 percent white and five others over 90 percent white. Moreover, in several projects where blacks had become predominant the racial balance had worsened. As more blacks moved into projects, whites tended to leave, and new white applicants refused to accept assignments. The administration faced the choice of moving in only black families or leaving apartments empty; the waiting list was over 50 percent black by this time. Noting these trends, one analyst concluded that "efforts to promote integration have run into the discouraging reality that most families of both races are reluctant to live in projects where they are a conspicuous minority."[42]

Black families, in particular, became increasingly reluctant to isolate themselves in white areas where they not only were subject to harassment by project residents but felt unwelcome in adjoining bars, stores, restaurants, and churches. When many of the original pioneers requested transfers to projects in black areas, civil rights groups became disenchanted with the strategy and hesitant to recruit new applicants. As an alternative approach, the reformers suggested sending blacks to white projects in larger numbers and, at the same time, moving whites into black projects. Such a strategy, however, could not win the necessary support from either the board or Mayor Collins, who by this time was withdrawing even his nominal support for integration. According to one of his aides, "the Mayor felt he would be 'politically' dead if he became that strong a liberal." Although the reformers stood by their integrationist

---

[41]*Boston Globe*, February 17, 1966.
[42]Hipshman, *Public Housing at the Crossroads*, p. 31.

platform, their voices became much more subdued. They had achieved a degree of integration, but not nearly their goal of 25 percent minority tenancy in previously all white projects. They had failed to change the attitudes of most white tenants and staff, and, as one activist pointed out, the integration effort had lost its popularity: "The days of 'we shall overcome' were ending." While the reformers had not achieved their integration objectives, the chief of the Department of Tenant and Community Relations nevertheless felt that they had made progress in some other areas:

> With continued resistance form the Board and only a partial thaw in relationships with management, the progress was not spectacular, but certain inroads were made with the tenant selection process, some of the most notorious staff were identified and isolated, some new points of view were brought to bear on old problems of development.[43]

NATIONALLY ORIGINATED RULES

Federal Intervention

While local integration efforts slackened, a major new assignment plan was emerging at the national level. Until the 1960s the federal government imposed only income eligibility guidelines on tenant selection procedures. The effect, however, was hardly benign: by leaving site selection and assignment procedures to local authorities, in effect, the government stance supported separate and sometimes unequal projects, thus giving no encouragement for integration and ample latitude for segregation.[44] Furthermore, the Supreme Court school desegregation decision (*Brown* v. *Board of Education of Topeka*, 1954) had little immediate impact on the situation.[45]

---

[43]Scobie, "BHA, 1964–1968," p. 8.

[44]For the general implications of federalism for racism see William Ricker, *Federalism* (Boston: Little, Brown, 1964), pp. 142–145.

[45]I am indebted for the chronology of events to Dorothy Willis's "Briefing Paper on Tenant Selection and Assignment Policies" (Washington, D.C.: HUD, mimeographed, 1969). For early histories see Jordan Luttrell, "The Public Housing Administration and Discrimination in Federally Assisted Low-Rent Housing," *Michigan Law Review* (March 1966): 871–889, and Jordan Luttrell, "Public

According to one analyst, the lack of federal administrative policy was due to the absence of statutory guidance from higher government levels combined with the practical necessity of deference to the political power of segregationists in Congress; because public housing was the least popular and the most politically vulnerable of the housing programs, it was essential to keep the support of southern congressmen.[46] In addition, the existence of public housing units depended on the voluntary initiative of local governments. If the federal agency pursued integration, many communities would be reluctant to build units and therefore the main goal of the program—to provide housing for low-income citizens—would be in jeopardy. In spite of the obstacles, in 1962 the national counterparts of the civil rights groups that produced change at the BHA began to lobby for a federal policy opposing housing segregation. Their efforts produced President Kennedy's Executive Order 11603 on equal opportunity in housing which charged executive agencies with eliminating discrimination in publicly subsidized housing. The President's Committee on Equal Opportunity in Housing, established under the executive order, recommended general policies and procedures to implement the order and to check on progress.

Although the creation of the president's committee strengthened the federal enforcement powers, its presence was far from an attack on segregation since it had no legislative backing. According to one scholar, if the legislative gates were to be raised to overcome southern opposition, "an intense majority opinion had to crystallize."[47] This necessary climate was created by a remarkable series of events during the 1960s which included the election of two presidents who provided strong leadership for civil rights, the assassination of one whose death was transformed into a

---

Housing and Integration: A Neglected Opportunity," *Columbia Journal of Law*, 6 (1970): 253–279. For a general discussion of the federal role in desegregating public housing in Chicago during this period, see Frederick Lazin, "The Failure of Federal Enforcement of Civil Rights Regulations in Public Housing, 1963–1971: The Cooptation of a Federal Agency by Its Local Constituency," *Policy Science:* 4 (1973), 263–273.

[46]See Davis McEntire, *Residence and Race* (Berkeley: University of California Press, 1960), pp. 319–321.

[47]Wirt, *Politics of Southern Equality*, p. 64. For a detailed description of the origins of the Civil Rights Act see Gary Orfeld, *The Reconstruction of Southern Education: The Schools and the 1964 Civil Rights Act* (New York: Wiley-Interscience, 1969).

crusade for new laws, the election of even larger majorities in both houses giving control to both parties' liberal wings, and the swelling of protests to end southern discrimination. One result was the Civil Rights Act of 1964 which gave the president's committee the power to review agency rules and regulations and authorized the federal housing agency to withhold funds from subsidized institutions that practiced discrimination.

The Housing and Home Finance Agency (the HHFA, HUD's precursor) responded to the Civil Rights Act in 1965 by issuing regulations prohibiting discrimination in low-rent housing on the basis of race, color, or national origin. In a more specific thrust to promote nondiscrimination, the HHFA recommended that the public housing authorities adopt a free choice plan that allowed applicants to designate which projects they desired to live in. Proponents of the free choice plan felt that such a strategy would afford the optimum balance between what some have viewed as two conflicting objectives: allowing an individual to live near and associate with those he chooses, yet permiting minorities to secure access to all housing accommodations. If, after a housing authority assumed a neutral stance, projects remained segregated, the result could then be attributed to the desires of different races to live among their own people. By 1965, however, the BHA had already dropped its equivalent of a free choice plan in favor of a more affirmative program. The HHFA, recognizing the desegregation goals behind the 1965 resolutions, allowed the BHA to continue with its alternate plan.

In April 1966, the National Committee Against Discrimination in Housing (NCDH), a civil rights group composed of 46 cooperating religious, labor, and civic reform organizations, presented a report to the White House accusing the administration of permitting an attitude of "amiable apartheid" in federal housing programs. The groups demanded that President Johnson take more affirmative action to "bring about desegregation of the racially impacted ghettoes and to affirmatively advance patterns of racial and economic integration."[48] Among its 17 charges, the report claimed:

> Contrary to Executive Order 11063, the Public Housing Administration (now the Housing Assistance Administration) has taken no meaningful action to desegregate existing public housing projects[49]

---

[48]*Washington Post*, February 9, 1967.

[49]National Committee Against Discrimination in Housing, *How the Federal Government Builds Ghettos* (Washington, D.C.: National Committee Against Discrimination in Housing, February 1967).

and went on to recommend that

> HUD should require every local public housing authority to work
> with regional representatives of the Division of Civil Rights in devel-
> oping and executing plans for the desegregation of all presently seg-
> regated public housing projects in the United States. Approval of
> additional public housing units should be conditioned on the local
> public housing authority's implementation of desegregation plans, as
> determined by the Division of Civil Rights.[50]

In February 1967, the NCDH complained that it had received no
response from the White House and made public its report, *How the
Federal Government Builds Ghettoes.* The NCDH attacked Secretary
Robert Weaver of HUD[51] at a press conference, accusing Weaver, a black
man who had once headed NCDH, of shirking his responsibility to carry
out an affirmative housing desegregation program; in addition, they urged
President Johnson to force Weaver to act.

In the meantime, however, Weaver's staff had been working on a
plan to desegregate public housing projects. According to one HUD official, the "NCDH had forced Dr. Weaver's hand and he had to develop a
policy. Hot summers and civil rights marches were coming together leading the federal government to do something." Although Weaver publicly
called the NCDH statements "inaccurate and unfair,"[52] on the day of
their press conference he took the opportunity to reveal the nucleus of his
new tenant assignment plan:

> Applicants will be assigned in numerical order, on the basis of date of
> application, need, and family size. Any suitable vacancy in the lo-
> cality's public housing will be offered to an applicant. Where there
> are vacancies in several projects, the unit in a project with the largest
> number of vacancies will be preferred. If, after three offers, the
> applicant declines to accept any of them, he will go the bottom of the
> list of eligibles.[53]

Apparently, Weaver had accepted the reports of several HUD field inspections that free choice plans not only failed but had actually been used
to promote discrimination.

[50]*Ibid.*
[51]*Washington Post*, February 9, 1967.
[52]*Ibid.*
[53]Robert Weaver, Secretary, U.S. Department of Housing and Urban Development, "Statement" (n.p., mimeographed, February 8, 1967).

Under these plans, the entire burden for expressing a choice of project or location was upon the individual applicants, who were to make this choice in many communities in which segregated housing patterns have been traditional. In such situations, for various reasons such as community mores, fear of reprisals, types of neighborhoods, inducement by local authority staff—whether by subtle suggestion, manipulation, persuasion, or otherwise—such freedom of choice plans, in their operation, did not provide applicants with actual freedom of access to, or full availability of, housing in all projects or locations.[54]

In contrast to free choice, Weaver's scheme, known as first come, first serve or the 1–2–3 plan, was automatic with respect to offers. It attempted to take the burden off the applicant and removed discretion from the bureaucrats. Moreover, by tying offerings to projects with the highest vacancies, the 1–2–3 plan would prevent situations in which HUD discovered authorities holding open vacancies in white projects while blacks remained on waiting lists.[55] Such policies were violations not only of the Civil Rights Act but of the economy and efficiency requirements of the U.S. Housing Act of 1937.

Response to the HUD Plan

Weaver's plan, published in more detail in the federal register, drew strong adverse reactions from local housing authorities, the National Association of Housing and Redevelopment Officials, and even from the Housing Assistance Administration, the public housing sector of HUD. Executive Director Ash, for example, requested that the BHA be granted permission to continue its existing tenant selection plan which he claimed had produced a measurable change in a long-established pattern of segregated occupancy and which would result in a greater degree of integration than HUD's new plan.[56] Ash, who had come to his position of executive director as a result of pressure by local civil rights groups, therefore found

[54]Statement of the basis for *Low Rent Housing Manual*, Section 102.1, Exhibit 2, Requirements of Low Rent Housing Programs under Title VI of the Civil Rights Act of 1964. The local CORE had already noted these problems in Boston in 1963. See Footnote 24 above.

[55]Weaver himself had noted in 1948 that housing authorities had kept vacancies reserved for whites while blacks remained on the waiting list. See Robert Weaver, *The Negro Ghetto* (New York: Harcourt Brace Jovanovich, 1948).

[56]See letter from Ellis Ash to Herman Hillman, Assistant Regional Administrator for Housing Assistance, September 28, 1967.

himself opposing Weaver's proposal. Ash contended that although the 1–2–3 policy might desegregate southern projects, it would only cause whites to flee projects in Boston, leaving more vacancies and creating black ghettoes that would not appeal to either white or black families.[57] He also felt that the policy would prevent the BHA from assigning applicants to projects where there were fewer vacancies and less problem of racial balance. One of Ash's aides summarized his view of the 1–2–3 rule: "Any money earned by filling vacancies at the cost of creating ghettoes is not worth a tinker's damn."[58]

Housing Assistance Administration (HAA) staff felt that the 1–2–3 plan was designed by upper-level HUD officials, overprotective of other programs such as urban renewal, to scapegoat the local housing authorities.[59] They had apparently been bypassed when Weaver's staff drew up the plan in order to avoid lobbying that would make the procedures less restrictive. In addition to this expected overall criticism of the plan, HAA staff also had specific criticisms. For example, the head of the public housing section complained to her divisional chief that adoption of the plan would be

> the first time to our knowledge that the Federal Government will be saying that unless a low-income family, particularly a low-income Negro family in desperate need of decent housing, accepts the units in the projects with the most vacancies, it must continue to live in the slums. This position would be taken as against the position taken by a housing authority that its interpretation of the non-discrimination requirements of Title VI and of the Constitution requires it to give applicants their choice as to where they prefer to live anywhere in the city after the applicant has been fully informed as to the status of vacancies and the waiting list at various locations, and that it considered it abhorrent to impose the penalty of denial of housing to those who refuse to accept what the authority is willing to offer. We seriously question whether the federal government can sustain the burden of directing that a housing authority impose this penalty on the poor as the price that must be paid for whatever consideration is

---

[57]*Boston Globe*, April 19, 1969.

[58]Archer O'Reilly, quoted *ibid.*

[59]HUD public housing staff felt Weaver was "out to get" public housing authorities, especially in the South. In his 1948 book, Weaver had acknowledged that public housing had a positive racial policy in relation to equitable participation of minority tenants but had attacked it as "an instrument for the spread of segregation." See Weaver, *The Negro Ghetto*, p. 164.

involved on the other side, including utilization of vacancies and the promotion of integration.[60]

She then suggested that, in places where the first come, first serve plan had been tried, the plan fostered segregation rather than mitigating it:

> The basic reason for this, no matter how deplorable, is that the supply of public housing relative to the need is so small, the number and desperate needs of Negro families relative to white families is so great, and private housing is so much less available to Negro families than whites that a greater proportion of Negro families apply and are willing to accept public housing. No housing authority to our knowledge and none of the groups advocating the abolition of freedom of choice, have come up with an acceptable plan of maintaining racial mix under these typical circumstances. Furthermore, the usual result is the vicious circle that, as the waiting lists and the projects become more and more Negro occupied, less and less whites apply.[61]

A HUD official rebutted this line of argument, arguing that:

> If white people really are "public housing material" they will remain in public housing because they won't be able to afford anything else. In the South, particularly in cities where segregation has been openly practiced, more integration will have to take place; not every white person can move out.[62]

He then commented that if public housing became all black it would be justified on the basis that minority groups needed it more than whites.

The National Association of Housing and Redevelopment Officials (NAHRO) supported the BHA and other local housing authorities on the grounds that a rigid, mechanistic formula was not suitable given variation in actual conditions among cities. However, Weaver would not budge. At a meeting with NAHRO officials in November 1967, he pointed out that HUD must have

> some objective criteria. We cannot open it up for discussion or dialogue with practically every local housing authority, or we will be

[60]Memo from Marie McGuire, Housing Assistant, to Donald Hummel, Assistant Secretary of HUD, "Policy Governing Equal Opportunity in HUD Operations and Programs," February 8, 1967.

[61]*Ibid.*

[62]Quoted in *Christian Science Monitor*, March 25, 1969.

engaged in a dialogue forever. The local housing authorities have had
3 years in which to produce, and the time has come for action.[63]

He added that negotiating individual plans with each local housing authority would overburden HUD's staff and would be an impediment to
the regional office staff's primary daily functions (such as dealing with
authorities on housing production) in which a good working relationship
had to be maintained. Weaver apparently mistrusted the federal staff and
feared that they would be co-opted by local public housing authorities.

On advice from the Justice Department, however, HUD relented
and provided for alternate plans. To avoid their widespread use, HUD set
up requirements that only a handful of small authorities could meet: the
average vacancy rate in each of the projects during the preceding twelve
months could not exceed 5 percent and every project had to demonstrate
a substantial degree of desegregation (at least 15 percent black occupancy
in each project). Since the BHA had not succeeded in attaining integration sufficient to make the required showing, its 1965 plan was rejected in
August 1968. During the next three months, Ash worked to develop a
plan which would be acceptable, while retaining as many current policies
as possible. In November, however, HUD sent the BHA a telegram
stating that

> failure to comply would place into effect a deferral policy that would
> affect project applications for new construction, acquisition, moderni-
> zation, turnkey and leasing, as well as any applications dealing with
> amendments for financial assistance under prescribed circum-
> stances.[64]

The next week Ash sent a memo to the BHA Board indicating that he saw

> no other choice than to adopt the changes proposed. The degree to
> which the federal agency may cut off funds is speculative. I trust that
> I have made clear as a matter of principle that the literal effect of the
> changes proposed might well be a step backward for us assuming we
> choose to preserve integration goals.[65]

---

[63]HUD notes on meeting between Robert Weaver and NAHRO, November 24,
1967.

[64]Telegram from Joseph Kohler, Director of Tenant and Operations Services,
HUD Regional Office in New York to the Boston Housing Authority, November
5, 1968.

[65]Ellis Ash, Memo to Boston Housing Authority Board, November 13, 1968.

Finally, after another plea to HUD for a special exception and a subsequent rejection, in December 1968, the BHA adopted the HUD plan that allowed applicants to be assigned only to the three projects with the highest vacancies.

ANOTHER REFORM: LEADERSHIP

While Ash was losing his battle with HUD, local reformers, frustrated by the board's intransigence and lack of change, began a new attack on the BHA. In preparation for the mayoral election of 1967, MCDH, UCS, and the newly formed Citizens Housing and Planning Association (CHPA) sponsored an in-depth study of the authority. This report, researched by a MIT graduate student and assistants from the League of Women Voters, contained a large number of recommendations about personnel, maintenance, administration, and management. In regard to tenant selection, the report suggested:

> Tenant selection, assignment and transfer policies are still in need of clarification and improvement to insure that available public housing units go to families strictly on the basis of relative need and order of application. This is largely an administrative matter, implementation of which awaits full acceptance of these principles by Housing Authority personnel at all levels, from project managers to the Commissioners themselves. Improved appeals procedures for rejected applicants and continual communication between the Authority and the families regarding status of their applications are intrinsic parts of a more rational and just tenant selection system.[66]

While calling on the authority to proceed with racial integration on more than a token basis, the reformers were now concluding that a precondition for any such change was a new board: "By making competent appointments [the Mayor] can promote a strong housing program; by making weak appointments, he can insure an ineffective program."[67] The

[66]Chester Hartman, Introduction to Hipshman, *Public Housing*, p. xviii.

[67]*Ibid.* Mayor Collins's reluctance to push reform was partly based on his use of the BHA as a major source for political patronage. Other areas such as the Boston Redevelopment Authority had dried up by this time. When Edward Logue took charge of the Boston Redevelopment Authority in 1959, he obtained a pledge from Collins that the mayor's office would not interfere with personnel decisions. See MacDonnell, "Process of Change," p. 99.

reformers suggested that new appointees be "men and women who dis-
play a great awareness of the changing role public housing must play and
who will be more aggressive advocates and interpreters of the public
housing program to the community at large."[68]

The reformers circulated their report to all mayoral candidates as a
recommended action program for improving public housing. Kevin
White, a mayoral candidate seeking liberal and black support, endorsed
the findings. After winning the election, White accepted the major recommendation and, early in 1968, appointed Julius Bernstein, a long-time
civil rights and housing reform activist, to fill a board vacancy. A year
later, the governor followed suit and appointed John Connolly, a tenant,
to fill another empty board seat.[69] However, two new board members
could not change policy on a five-member board. Therefore, in early
1969, the director of CHPA wrote the board urging them to:

> state clearly that it is Mr. Ash who must handle all administrative
> functions in the future. It is clear . . . that Mr. Ash cannot manage
> without clear delegation of management powers to him by the Board.
> No administrator can work competently if his policy-making Board
> continually short-circuits his authority by allowing department heads
> and others to bypass the administrator and report directly to the
> Board.[70]

Predictably, the board would neither relinquish its power nor change its
philosophy. Later that year Ash resigned. He concluded that he had

> reached the point of diminishing returns on the value of staying on.
> Maybe my resignation will force a facing up to key issues and what
> must be done. Now the authority can fish or cut bait as far as I'm
> concerned.[71]

Finally, when a third board seat became vacant in 1970, the mayor created a new majority by appointing another tenant, Doris Bunte.

After acquiring control, the new majority issued a statement of objectives committing themselves to a hands-off policy in selecting tenants:

[68]Chester Hartman, Introduction to Hipshman, *Public Housing*, p. xiv.
[69]Reform groups had successfully lobbied in ihe state legislature to void a law that
forbade tenants to serve on local housing authority boards.
[70]*Boston Globe*, February 20, 1969.
[71]*Boston Globe*, June 19, 1969.

> Political considerations have traditionally played an important role in
> tenant selection at the Boston Housing Authority. This is intolerable,
> in the light of the housing crises we face in Boston. We intend to
> introduce a tenant selection procedure that responds to human
> needs, rather than political pressure.[72]

In addition, they hired a new executive director to whom they delegated
the authority's daily operation and personnel hiring. The new director
soon elevated the veteran tenant selection chief to another position and
replaced him with a more reform-oriented appointee. Thus, after eight
years of struggle, a reform-oriented board, a powerful director, and a new
tenant selection chief were finally secured. It appeared to be the right
combination to implement the previously disregarded tenant priority
rules and to test the HUD assignment procedures.

CONCLUSION

The 1960s represents a period when several factions fought for control of the Boston Housing Authority. A major source of the conflict
concerned issues of whom public housing should serve and procedures
which would govern tenant selection. Much of the turmoil was related to
matters of class and race, the latter having been precipitated by the civil
rights movement.

What was most surprising about the era was not so much the local
struggles, but rather the extent of federal involvement in issuing specific
rules and regulations. Whereas previous policy statements had been
somewhat general and ambiguous, leaving a great deal of latitude to local
agencies, during the 1960s the Public Housing Administration took a
much more activist stance due, in part, to external pressure from the civil
rights movement, strong executive leadership, and a liberal Congress.

The most important influence was the Civil Rights Act of 1964, which
required the federal government to withhold funds from federally subsidized programs that practiced segregation. But the adoption of a goal is
not equivalent to implementation. If a minority group manages to force
the passage of legislation such as the Civil Rights Act to control federal
agency behavior, its opponents can still circumvent it in the writing of the

[72]Julius Bernstein, Doris Bunte, and John Connelly, "Statement of Objectives,"
April 26, 1971.

agency regulations, which frequently become a burial ground for reformers' ideals. The Civil Rights Act was general and vague—it gave little
direction to agencies wishing to implement its goals. Federal departmental regulations are generally developed through consultation with constituent groups, especially the affected federal agencies. Therefore compromises are effected that conform to what the agency feels is acceptable but
which are broad and vague enough to win support from constituent local
agencies.

Predictably, the Public Housing Administration made no significant
move on its own to implement the Civil Rights Act by eliminating segregation in its projects. But by 1966, the Department of Housing and Urban
Development had been formed as an executive department and Robert
Weaver, the first black cabinet member and a long-time civil rights housing advocate, was appointed as its secretary. Weaver was particularly
vulnerable to adverse publicity and pressure from the National Committee Against Discrimination in Housing, an organization that in many ways
was his reference group. He therefore attempted to integrate public
housing.

One might still have expected Weaver's objectives to be diluted in
the guideline development stage of policy formulation. However, Weaver
successfully avoided co-optation. Contrary to tradition, Weaver's staff
developed both the initial concept and the guidelines of their program
independent of the usual interest groups. They did not accommodate the
desires of the local housing authorities or the PHA to water down the
guidelines. Upper-echelon HUD officials viewed local housing authorities, especially in the South, as racist institutions. Compromise
would have been surrender. Neither did HUD design individual
schemes, similar to HEW school desegregation plans, for each authority
because there was insufficient staff to oversee the enforcement and the
top HUD officials believed the existing staff to be pawns of the local
agencies they were supposed to regulate. Therefore, instead of performance criteria that spelled out objectives for each authority, HUD pre-
scribed specific priority and assignment rules that were to apply to all
situations. HUD staff considered these rules simple, fair, feasible, and
enforceable. Weaver's departure from traditional practices can be explained both by the political pressure that brought him to the cabinet
office and the highly politicized and confrontational environment that
surrounded the civil rights movement during this period. As a result,
HUD promulgated a set of specific rules for allocating units at the local
level.

CHAPTER THREE

Breakdown of the Rule System

Priority and assignment procedures arose in response to charges of discrimination on the part of BHA staff. Since the discrimination appeared to be the result of bureaucratic norms and pressures where discretion was great, reformers attempted to decrease discretion by imposing strict rules and regulations on bureaucratic behavior.

The Tenant Selection Department was responsible for processing cases. Each day the staff received about forty applications but were able to place only about twenty families; therefore, the waiting list, which stood at about 6,000 in 1970, was constantly growing. To determine the priority of those on the waiting list, the staff scored each applicant's housing need. According to the severity of need and the date of application, prospective tenants were called in for assignment and were offered a choice of units at only the three projects with the highest number of vacancies. This priority and assignment scheme, like earlier ones, failed. The importance of housing need in this bureaucratic equation declined in significance as the inspections and scoring procedures proved to be unreliable indicators of client need. An emergency classification for applicants without homes was retained, but all other standards of need were ignored in determining priority. Moreover, the Department's heavy workload made even the more readily accepted first come, first serve standard hard to implement. Finally, client antipathy and the rule's questionable efficacy led staff members to relax their enforcement of the 1–2–3 assignment plan. Thus, the combined effect of these problems led to the breakdown of this set of rules.

MEASUREMENT PROBLEMS

In order to implement the priority system successfully, the tenant selection staff categorized applicants by need. This practice generated several waiting lists, each containing clients with comparable need. Cases were therefore pulled from each classification to match vacancy types. for example, if a two-bedroom unit became available, a staff member would select the two-bedroom case with the greatest need. If two cases had the same need, the earlier application had priority.

Hypothetically, according to this rule system, assignment priorities among eligible applicants based on need alone were to be ranked as follows: (1) a family that was actually without housing due to no fault of its own; (2) a family that was about to be without housing due to no fault of its own; and (3) a family living in unsafe, unsanitary, or overcrowded housing conditions as determined by an objective scoring system and based on relative housing need. The first two categories were verified by an appropriate outside agency, such as the courts in the case of eviction or the Red Cross in the case of burnouts. An evaluation of existing housing conditions was made through physical inspection of the applicant's living conditions by Tenant Selection Department field staff. This inspection followed completion of the application and a preliminary determination of eligibility. The inspection was arranged by mail and took about twenty minutes. The inspector evaluated the housing's location, structural condition, water supply, sewerage, toilet and bath facilities, kitchen, lighting, heating system, and degree of overcrowding. Observations were recorded on a form; the following is an example of a typical section.

Location of Dwelling
    Does the location of unit constitute a major hazard with respect to
Fire? Yes_____ No_____
Health? Yes_____ No_____
Safety? Yes_____ No_____
Other deficiencies_____

    Does the location of unit constitute a minor hazard with respect to
        Fire, Health, Safety? Yes_____ No_____
        Is play space adequate? Yes_____ No_____
        Is the environment detrimental? Yes_____ No_____

At the central office another staff member scored the findings according to an intricate weighting system. Major hazards such as fire, health, and safety were given 25 points; minor hazards were scored 15 points. Inadequate play space or detrimental environment were given 3 points.

Persons paying over 50 percent of their income for rent were given an additional score of 25 points. Overall scores on housing quality ranged from 0 to 385 points. Persons without housing were automatically given 500 points and those about to be without housing, 450 points. Applicants were then categorized as follows:

A—Without housing	500 points
B—About to be without housing	450 points
—Housing quality	
C-1	308–385 points
C-2	231–307 points
C-3	154–230 points
C-4	77–153 points
C-5	25–76 points
C-6	less than 25 points

In spite of the effort that went into designing this inspection schedule (it was much more extensive than that carried out by the U.S. Bureau of the Census at the time) and despite its long history of use by the department, scores had little bearing on decisions. One staff member admitted that although inspections were carried out and scored, "they were meaningless because the information was not used," and he attributed this neglect to measurement problems that made the system practically unworkable.

Imprecise definitions were an inherent problem in determining housing need. For example, terms indicating the extent of defects— *major, minor, inadequate, low, usable, excessive, poor, detrimental,* and *faulty*—were hardly operational.[1] One staff member pointed out that because of the generality of terms scoring actually relied on the housing inspectors' personal standards:

> It depended on the person doing the interview. You could go into a place and give a major hazard score on fire safety while I might give it

---

[1]Problems of definition and enumerator variability have plagued the U.S. Census of Housing and eventually led to the elimination of categories of structural condition in the decennial census. For a discussion of the problems, see U.S. Bureau of the Census, *Measuring the Quality of Housing: An Appraisal of Census Methods and Procedures* (Washington, D.C.: GPO, 1967).

a minor hazard. And the ten point difference in the total score might
make a year's difference in getting an apartment. In fact the applicant
might never get an apartment.

In addition to imprecise definitions, there was little agreement on
weighting of factors. When asked whether he would advocate using the
housing need criterion if the definitions were tighter, one staff member
commented:

> No. A person can't get into public housing unless she lives in a bad
> housing situation. But a bad housing situation is more than just hous-
> ing condition. Like the person who is living in a house on a limited
> income and her rent has gone from $100 a month to $160 a month:
> maybe the house isn't a torn down shack, but it is just a matter of time
> until they are going to throw her out. Income is only one of fourteen
> categories. If that is the only thing that sets the person off, she will
> have a low score, even though she is going to lose her home.

This sentiment was also reflected in a staff report suggesting the abolition
of the housing-need criterion.[2] It pointed out, for example, that a family
paying a large percentage of its income for a house, thereby depriving
itself of food and clothing, could have a low score because the rent–
income ratio was not heavily weighted. Another family, paying a small
percentage of its income for rent, might have a relatively high total score
because of the heavy weighting given to structural conditions for the
house.[3]

[2]Boston Housing Authority, "Proposal to Abolish the Tenant Selection Scoring
System" (Boston: Mimeographed, July 29, 1971).
[3]Abner Silverman has observed that the weighting scheme in the British scoring
system for council housing is also troublesome: "Obviously excessive weighting
for special aspects such as health, length of residence, or time on the waiting list
can vitiate the statutory mandate to give a reasonable preference to persons who
are occupying insanitary or overcrowded houses, have large families, or are living
in unsatisfactory housing conditions." Abner Silverman, *Selected Aspects of Administration of Publicly Owned Housing*, Housing and Home Finance Agency
(Washington, D.C.: GPO, 1961), p. 56.
    Studies during the early 1970s such as the one conducted by the Joint
Center for Urban Studies have suggested that the nature of housing deprivation
is shifting away from problems associated with the structure itself and in the
direction of problems associated with the cost of a unit relative to the household's
ability to pay for it. See Joint Center for Urban Studies of MIT and Harvard,
America's Housing Needs: 1970 to 1980 (Cambridge: Joint Center for Urban
Studies, 1973).

In addition to complaints concerning definitions and weighting, the staff also argued that the categories were not inclusive enough to reflect an applicant's needs and priorities. For example, one staff member suggested that housing need was subjective:

> Housing condition is an arbitrary way to define need. It is all right in a tight housing market. But many people on the waiting list will only go to certain developments. Need is therefore subjective—a white person in awful housing in South Boston won't go to a project in a nonwhite area.

Although the resolution which originally set up the scoring procedures had suggested that personal problems such as chronic illness and physical disability be weighted, need determination was assessed, for the most part, on more easily measured and verifiable factors, such as housing conditions and excessive rent.[4] One staff member illustrated the deficiency as follows:

> The problem is that there isn't a rational ordering of priorities. Housing condition would only be one of the criteria in an effective system. For example, a person might be living in rather adequate housing, but they live on the third floor and have had a heart attack. For them, housing has an effect on health—they may die if they go up the flight of stairs.

Reflecting on the problems of definition, weighting, inclusiveness, and subjectivity, the Tenant Selection Department staff concluded that the deficiencies of the home visit and scoring system could not be overcome by administrative reforms like inspector training, improved definitions, or scoring weight adjustments. They concluded further that the

> procedure is arbitrary because its philosophical basis, the concept of selection in terms of relative housing need, is too ambitious. Our present system attempts to weigh on an objective and numerical scale a range of housing conditions that are as varied as the needs of the large number of families who apply for public housing. Only the applicant family itself can adequately weigh its needs.[5]

---

[4]Applicant scoring procedure in English council housing also tended to discount personal subjective factors. See R. N. Morris and John Mogey, *The Sociology of Housing* (London: Routledge and Kegan Paul, 1965), p. 13.

[5]BHA, Chief of Tenant Selection, "Proposal to Abolish Scoring," p. 3. Reviews of the point priority system in England have yielded similar criticism. For example, J. B. Cullingworth, *Housing and Local Government*, p. 127.

They therefore recommend that the board of the Boston Housing Authority drop the criterion of relative need based on housing inspections and instead rely on a first come, first serve priority[6] because it applied

> one of the few genuine objective standards to the approval of application for public housing—the date of application. The standard is administratively simple and equitable. Very serious emergencies—families without or about to be without housing, would continue to receive first priority. But the Authority would no longer be attempting the impossible task of distinguishing the extent or severity of need among the needy. All our eligible applicants are in need of housing. We have neither the wisdom nor the capacity to determine among the numbers of applicants what is severe and what is less severe.[7]

Without much debate, the board accepted the recommendations; and what had originated as a progressive and humanitarian concern over allocating a scarce resource on the basis of need was modified under practice to apply only to emergency cases wherein need could be more easily determined.

WORKING CONDITIONS

Statistics indicate that the problems inherent in the tenant selection and assignment process involved more than just the need assessment procedures. As can be seen in Table 1, the vast majority of the 3,280 applicants called up for assignment between September 1969 and June 1970 (while the housing-need criterion was still in effect) were in bad or fair housing. If the housing-need priority was followed, emergency cases (no housing) would be assigned first, followed by displaced-site tenants, and then by applicants according to the severity of their present housing conditions. Table 2, showing the relation of condition of assignee housing to length of time on the waiting list, indicates, however, that need was not strictly followed. For example, under the need priority, emergency and

---

[6]The Philadelphia Housing Authority, coming from the opposite position of the BHA, eliminated priority based solely on the date of application because it discriminated against those most in need. Philadelphia Housing Authority, "Recommended Tenant Selection Policy" (mimeographed, 1970).

[7]BHA, Chief of Tenant Selection, "Proposal to Abolish Scoring," p. 3.

Table 1. Condition of
Assignee Housing

1 Emergency (no housing)[b]	4.3%
2 Displaced from site	11.7
3 Extremely terrible	.7
4 Terrible	2.2
5 Moderately terrible	7.5
6 Bad	33.6
7 Fair	35.6
8 Moderately fair	4.4
Total	100.0%
Total number of cases: 2,898[a]	

[a]The number of cases in this and subsequent tables based on the assignee data falls short of the 3,280 total because staff did not always elicit or record information.

displaced-site tenants should have come before cases in conditions 3 through 8; however, many of those who had been on the waiting list less than a year were assigned before older emergency and site cases.

If, instead of assigning cases according to need, the department operated on the principle of first come, first serve, applicants would be called according to how long they had been on the waiting list, with older cases assigned first. Even though applications were date-stamped and filed

Table 2. Relation of Condition of Assignee Housing to Length of Time on the Waiting List

Length of time on the waiting list	1 + 2 (Emergency, displaced from site)	3 + 4 + 5 (Terrible)	6 (Bad)	7 + 8 (Fair)
Less than 1 year	73.9%	65.0%	65.1%	41.8%
1 year to 23 months	11.8	16.4	14.0	17.8
2 years to 35 months	6.8	9.3	7.3	8.4
3 years to 47 months	2.4	3.1	4.1	6.3
4 years to 59 months	2.0	1.2	2.4	7.9
5 years and over	3.3	5.0	7.2	17.8
Total	100.0%	100.0%	100.0%	100.0%
Number of cases	(459)	(323)	(931)	(1,163)

Table 3. Length of Time on the
Waiting List of Persons Assigned
to Housing

Less than 1 year	57.1%
1 year to 23 months	15.4
2 years to 35 months	7.9
3 years to 47 months	4.6
4 years to 59 months	4.4
5 years and over	10.6
Total	100.0%
Number of cases (2,876)	

chronologically, they were not selected in order. Instead, as Table 3 indicates, most applicants called for assignment were *current* cases: 57.1 percent had waited less than a year. Since the waiting list from previous years totaled over 6,000, it seems likely that the administratively simple priority of date of application suffered a fate similar to that of housing need. Other problems like cumbersome information gathering, poor division of labor, crisis situations, and inadequate vacancy reporting apparently conspired to destroy even the fundamentally easy process of assigning applicants on a first come, first serve basis.

Information Gathering

In part, the destruction of priorities is attributable to the information-gathering requirements of the system introduced by the BHA. The tenant selection process included application, verification, rent computation, home visits, final processing, scoring, and preassignment interviews. The amount of information required and the method of collection created delays and redundancy. The first step, the application interview, focused on information pertinent to eligibility, rent level, and type of unit required. The applicant was asked her name; age; current address and phone number; marital status (single, married, divorced, separated, or widowed); number, names and ages of children; citizenship; whether assets totaled over $6,000; record of employment (including pay scale); sources of income; and veterans' status and military service. After the form was filled out (usually taking about fifteen minutes), the applicant signed it and was given a date-stamped receipt which indicated the file number. Most applicants were told to make sure that they kept the receipt and were told also that the authority would contact them in the near future to obtain further information.

The next stage required the verification of applicant information. The BHA verification system had several operational problems: it failed to inform applicants clearly of what documentation they had to supply, it required documentation that many applicants were reluctant to provide, it called for documentation that was not readily available, and it relied on outside groups to cooperate in providing documentation. Although the federal guidelines suggested that information required of applicants be limited to that necessary for determining eligibility and that applicants be the primary source for verifying statements,[8] local authorities had the power to establish the policies governing the nature and extent of the investigations. According to the BHA procedures, applicants were checked and verified for proof of birthdate; citizenship; income; assets; residency; and, if applicable, marriage, divorce, separation support, eviction, and medical information.[9] Verification was supplied by the applicant, outside agencies, and the BHA itself.

According to one staff member, applicants had little idea of what the application process was or what was required of them:

> The BHA gives out absolutely no written information about anything that goes on here and that is a negative kind of a thing. Unless you are involved with the Housing Authority itself, you don't know what goes on. Applicants were rarely informed either before or during the initial interview of the criteria for eligibility, the purposes of the information required, or the steps in the selection and assignment process.

For example, elderly persons and persons receiving Aid to Families with Dependent Children were required to provide the authority with proof of income by presenting social security, pension, or welfare checks; and since they were not informed of the necessity of income verification in advance of the initial application interview, they had to provide proof at a later time, usually having to make an additional trip to the central office. Moreover, because BHA officials rarely told them that they could send in xerox copies, applicants often brought checks in person on the day they

[8]U.S. Department of Housing and Urban Development, *Manual for Low Rent Housing*, RHM 7465.1.
[9]BHA, "Resolution."

received them—the only day they could produce them. This was not a procedural problem, but it confused and inconvenienced applicants and contributed to feelings of bureaucratic abuse on their part.

Some of the documentation, such as marriage or divorce papers, was of no particular value. The requirement was a holdover from the time when the authority rejected unwed mothers. Continued need for such verification was a great inconvenience for applicants to whom such records were not easily available. Moreover, many Puerto Rican families, whose bonds had been formed in common law marriages, could not obtain either marriage certificates or divorce papers.[10] When faced with providing such information, many applicants were sent to a social worker for a special investigation; others concluded that they would be judged ineligible and simply dropped out. At the very best, applications were held up while information was verified.

Even information collected from the Tenant Selection Department's own files presented problems. For example, each applicant was supposed to be checked for a prior public housing tenancy record to see whether he or she owed the authority back rent or had been evicted as an undesirable tenant.[11] Although such information was supposed to be in the office's central file, frequently the staff had to take the additional step of contacting project managers because managers had not forwarded their records.

The many verifications of information by outside agencies and private concerns caused additional delays. The BHA wrote the Department of Probation for the criminal records of everyone except the elderly; letters from social workers, hospitals, or doctors were often necessary to verify certain health or personal problems that might qualify an applicant for a particular project location; and employers had to supply job records and wage verification. Many of these outsiders had no direct interest in aiding either the applicant or the Housing Authority or had their own

---

[10]A study of client reactions to intake procedures in welfare agencies indicated that clients were bothered most by inquiries which extended to other people with the potential of causing embarrassment or even painful and dangerous experiences. Questions about deserting fathers, which had potential legal implications, were the most bothersome, followed by relatives' support, marriage plans, financial resources, job, and child care. Joel Handler and Ellen Hollingsworth, The "Deserving Poor," pp. 82–85 (Chicago: Markham Publishing, 1971).

[11]Throughout this study applicants are referred to in the feminine because the majority of them were women.

workload problems and were negligent in sending the required information. Thus, long delays in processing and considerable redundancy in correspondence were the costs of not accepting the applicant's statements.

The housing inspection visits by which need was assessed turned out to be even more cumbersome. The department averaged forty applicants a day. However, the two people assigned to carry out home interviews could actually visit only about fifteen persons a day. Moreover, applicants were often absent at the time arranged through a previously mailed notice. Therefore, a second home interview had to be arranged. If the applicant was still away, his or her folder was put in the inactive file. The staff were falling further and further behind in processing cases.

Division of Labor

Errors which grew out of the intricate division of labor also hindered the processing of cases.[12] Different staff members handled each of the steps (application interviews, verification, home interviews, rent computation, final processing, scoring, and assignment). Because no one person was responsible for following through on individual cases, there was an absence of personal responsibility and care. As applications passed through the various steps, files were sometimes completely lost or specific contents within them misplaced. If a piece of information from an outside agency was missing, it had to be secured again, causing additional delays. Without individual responsibility, cases in process were often difficult to locate when inquiries were received. The fine divisions of tasks also produced coordination difficulties.

Crisis Situations

Frequent development of crisis situations, combined with general work overload, often exacerbated problems of adhering to established priorities. Applicant demand was uneven and somewhat unpredictable. On the busiest days as many as one hundred people would travel to the central office to fill out application forms, most of them coming between noon and two o'clock when the department was half-staffed owing to

---

[12]The error problems were documented in a three-month review of administrative procedures. BHA, Director of Management services, "Administrative Reorganization—Tenant Selection" (Boston: BHA, mimeographed, 1972).

lunch breaks. These applicants would crowd into the small waiting room which seated only about twenty people. Many applicants came with their children, who grew very restless. Given this situation, the chief of the Tenant Selection Department had no recourse but to rely on every available person to take applications—clerks, rent computation specialists, preassignment interviewers, and himself. Although such action cut waits to less than two hours, it completely interrupted other processing.

Emergency cases were another unpredictable pressure that interrupted routines. In 1970–1971 emergency status was restricted to applicants who were homeless because of fire or flood or about to be homeless because of eviction due to no fault of their own, and it was given absolute priority for available vacancies. In addition, a person could be admitted to public housing under the emergency classification even if his or her income was too high. Although over-income applicants were supposed to be housed only for a six-month period, they were in fact never evicted. Staff felt that because of the flexibility of the income standards the procedures pertaining to emergency cases introduced much abuse.

With the curtailment of home visits, emergencies became an even more effective means to gain access to housing. Moreover, during 1972, with the concurrence of social agencies, the department chief decided that the emergency categories had been too restrictive and did not reflect the dire conditions in which some people lived. He therefore expanded the category to include overcrowding, the presence of lead paint, and the existence of code violations. The number of emergency cases ballooned to over 350 in eight months. Because of this large increase in emergency cases, another crisis situation engulfed the department. Emergencies began to crowd out people on the waiting list, many of whom were in dire conditions that were not enumerated in the emergency classification.

In the late 1960s, emergencies amounted to only 10 percent of the 2,000 applicants assigned each year. By the early 1970s, however, the proportion of emergency cases had more than doubled. When major fires broke out in Boston (a frequent occurrence in the city's old and dense housing stock) the BHA was often faced with processing and finding housing for a dozen emergency cases in a day. Although a modified application procedure made this task easier (no home visits and only a few verifications), it caused severe interruptions of daily routines.[13]

---

[13]Michael Lipsky has also noted agencies' use of crises as a standard to distribute resources. See Michael Lipsky, *Protest in City Politics* (Chicago: Rand McNally, 1970), pp. 157–158.

Poor Vacancy Reporting

Strict adherence to procedures was often impeded by poor vacancy reporting. In order to match eligible applicants with units, the Tenant Selection Department relied on managers to inform them when vacant units would be ready for occupancy. However, many managers failed to report their vacancies promptly and accurately (the reasons for which are explored in Chapter 6). For example, a study of vacancy reporting by a chief of the Tenant Selection Department indicated that units reported vacant in the department's file were sometimes omitted from the weekly vacancy reports while other units reported vacant on the weekly report were not on file.[14] Some units that had been assigned according to department files were still carried by managers as vacancies. Applicants reportedly assigned to certain units had actually leased others, and other units listed as vacant in the weekly report were actually leased. Finally, managers reported occupancy in cases in which the department either had no record of tenants or listed them as having vacated the apartment. Staff members could never be certain which units were actually available for new applicants.

Although applicant files were to be marked for specific available units, information was so unreliable that the staff tended to over-assign cases in hope that at least some of them would be housed. In emergency situations, however, the staff frantically resorted to calling projects to find out what was available and to convince managers to accept new applicants. Although this procedure usually produced housing, it was terribly time-consuming and inefficient.

Low Morale

Low morale made the BHA staff inflexible and indifferent to its purpose. For example, strict staff adherence to job categories left functional gaps in the process when employees were either out sick or on vacation. Reluctance to do other people's work was partly motivated by the knowledge that one's own responsibility would be piling up in the meantime. Staff members seemed more interested in minimizing their own workloads than in efficiently fulfilling the department's purpose. According to one top staff member, the differential pay scales that grew

[14]BHA Director of Management Services, "Report to the Board—Vacancies" (mimeographed, September 25, 1972).

up over the years reinforced this tendency. Some employees earned lower salaries at jobs with functional responsibilities equal to those of better-paid employees:

> Staff members are constantly looking over each other's backs, formulating opinions about other people: "Why should I, who get paid less than person X, work harder processing more papers?" That situation has led people to seek the lowest common denominator. They can't get fired anyway. But it has led to a lot of resentment and heartache.

According to another staff member, low morale was also caused by applicant anger:

> People coming in are not well versed. I mean that they only see their own problems, not those of the Authority, partly because they have such a desperate need for housing. That creates a lot of pressure and conflict in the department.

Not only was there a greater demand for housing than available vacancies, but most of the projects were in shoddy condition. Moreover, many of the long-term employees blamed the deterioration of housing on the new lower-status clients and were dismayed by the rules that limited applicant screening. Therefore, overall work satisfaction was very low.

Priority Reduction and Abrogation of Power

Owing to the concomitant effects of delays, backlogs, errors, blockages, redundancy, and interruptions, it took the average applicant about six months to get through the eligibility phase. Furthermore, it is important to note that the average hides a rather extreme variation: some applicants were processed immediately (people who were homeless) whereas many others never made it through. Date of application was not a good indicator of when a person might be offered an assignment.

The staff reacted to the work load by eliminating the most taxing parts of the procedures which, in the long run, compounded existing problems.[15] At various periods during 1970–1972 applicants were not

[15]Daniel Katz and Robert Kahn differentiate between adaptive and maladaptive responses to overload situations. Omission and error are dysfunctional, reducing the input is seen as functional. See Daniel Katz and Robert Kahn, *The Social Psychology of Organizations* (New York: John Wiley and Sons, 1966), pp. 231–235.

told what information they had to provide to complete their applications nor were they notified of their eligibility status.[16] Only applicants who pursued their own cases had any chance of getting apartments,[17] and many applicants who might very well have qualified for public housing were simply ignored. One staff member suggested that in the absence of either clear public rules or confidence in the system's fairness, most clients pursued their cases with phone calls and personal visits to the authority. Although this more aggressive behavior may very well have kept their own applications alive, it raised havoc in an already chaotic office. Consequently, cases were frequently being pulled from the files and examined. Since many of these cases were in process, the folders had to be located on another staff member's desk. These search-and-find missions were complicated by the absence of other staff members from their own desks; they, too, were sifting through mountains of files. In the midst of this Kafkaesque confusion, telephone calls were being transferred from one staff member to another. Inevitably, many applicants were disconnected. Some called back or resorted to personal visits. Others, already cynical, became frustrated and gave up. These patterns and other procedural omissions reduced demand, but the actual workload saving is questionable because they gave other applicants an incentive to call or visit the authority. Therefore the BHA staff suffered under a staggering

---

[16]In 1968, 31 applicants brought suit against the New York City Housing Authority claiming that they had not been advised in writing of the disposition of their application to state-aided housing. They also complained that, despite repeated demands, they had not been given regulations and criteria governing admissions. *Holmes* v. *New York Housing Authority*, 398 Federal Register Second Series, 262, (1968) referred to in Charles Ascher, *The Administration of Publicly Aided Housing* (Brussels: International Institute of Administrative Sciences, 1971), p. 39.

[17]Gabriel Almond and Harold Lasswell indicated in a study of recipients of unemployment insurance that aggressive clients compared to nonaggressive clients had been in contact with the agency longer, had more often been government employees, had broken the law more often, came from higher income and education groups, and came more often from occupations which dealt with people. See Gabriel Almond and Harold Lasswell, "Aggressive Behavior by Clients Toward Public Relief Administration," *American Political Science Review*, 28 (1934), 643. Jack Levin and Gerald Taube conclude from a survey of BHA tenants that tenants with lower socioeconomic backgrounds tended to be less knowledgeable about the bureaucracy and less successful in obtaining services than tenants with higher socioeconomic backgrounds. Jack Levin and Gerald Taube, "Bureaucracy and the Socially Handicapped: A Study of Lower Status Tenants in Public Housing," *Sociology and Social Research* 53 (1970), 209–219.

communications overload. On the average day, the department's seventeen members handled approximately 350 calls. According to a HUD report, much of the staff time was "spent answering calls from applicants or interested parties about the status of applications."[18] The chief of the Tenant Selection Department noted that the telephones were constantly ringing, and even the telephone system was inadequate—most callers encountered busy signals. In addition, new applicants, clients with questions about their cases, and clients bringing verification information often crowded the waiting room.

Given the work overload, it is understandable that the department was not able to adhere to the first come, first serve principle, let alone its modification of need and other statutory requirements for assignment. One staff member described the destruction of priorities as follows:

> What you needed to do when you got the vacancy was first of all look at your date of application, secondly to look at your housing need based on the scoring system, and veterans preference and these kinds of things. Then you were to pull the appropriate case for the appropriate unit. But what I am trying to indicate is that in all my years here we have been so caught up in the everyday immediate cases— the emergencies, the ones called on by an applicant during the day, or brought to your attention personally over the telephone by an agency or a hospital—you act on these. The others always get lost. You don't act on those you can't see stuck back in those files.

Letting the daily routine set priority saved the staff the burdensome task of wading through the backing of old files and tracing applicants, many of whom had moved, had died, or would no longer be interested in a unit.[19] In this sense, it was *easier* to handle cases on hand than follow the guidelines. The result, however, was a processing of cases with little regard for date of application or housing need, except in the case of emergencies. The applicants on the waiting list who did not activate their cases had essentially no chance of being housed. As one staff member commented succinctly, "The waiting list is all bottom." Another staff

[18]U.S. Department of Housing and Urban Development, "BHA Audit Report," mimeographed, March 3, 1972.

[19]The behavior of the Tenant Selection staff seems similar to the satisfying approach of finding a course of action that is good enough rather than seeking to maximize goals. See Herbert Simon, *Models of Man* (New York: John Wiley and Sons, 1957), pp. 241–273.

member added: "There is really no list. Everyone talks about it, even I talk about it, and when someone says to me there isn't really a list, I have to return to reality and agree, of course there is no list."

CLIENT REJECTION AND GOAL FAILURE

While housing need and first come, first serve were the priorities to determine the order in which applicants would be called for available units, the 1–2–3 rule was implemented to establish project assignment. The 1–2–3 assignment plan was designed to limit the choice of applicants and the discretion of bureaucrats. The procedure was first to invite an eligible applicant to a preassignment interview at which he or she was offered a unit at the project with the most vacancies. If the first offer was refused, the interviewer offered a unit at the project with the second highest number of vacancies and if that offer was refused, the applicant was offered a unit in the project with the third highest vacancies. If the applicant refused all three offers, he or she was dropped to the bottom of the waiting list. The purpose of this strategy was to provide a straightforward way to determine which choices to present to an applicant and then to assign each applicant in turn on a nondiscriminatory basis. As the original projects began to fill up, applicants would be assigned to other projects where vacancies would have relatively increased. Over time, projects would therefore become integrated and the vacancy rate reduced. However, what appeared to be simple in theory turned out to be unworkable in practice. Of the 3,280 applicants who were offered assignments between June 1969 and September 1970, 724 or 22.1 percent (most of whom were nonwhite) accepted regular assignments consistent with the 1–2–3 rule. Another 926 applicants, or 28.2 percent (most of whom were white), turned down all three assignments, were not given apartments, and went to the bottom of the waiting list. The remaining 1,630, or 49.7 percent of all applicants, obtained housing even though they refused to accept units in projects with the highest number of vacancies. Thus, in almost half of the cases the rules were not followed. To understand the apparent failure of the plan, we will examine the variation in BHA projects which gave rise to applicants' reluctance to accept the 1–2–3 projects, as well as staff views of the plan's legitimacy and the pressures on staff to relax the rules.

Table 4. Selected Population Characteristics, Boston Housing Authority Federal Family Developments, 1970[a]

Characteristics	Average of 15 projects	Range of average of individual projects
Age: Household head over 65 years	32%	8–53%
Dependency: Families on AFDC (as percent of		
nonelderly families	56%	20–72%
Families with no employed member	74%	42–84%
Race: Nonwhite population	52%	2–99%
Transiency: Families with 5 or fewer years of occupancy	56%	39–89%
Turnover: New admissions 1970	15.3%	3–34%

[a]From Maureen Power, 1970 Tenant Status Review of the BHA Population.

Project Variation

A major obstacle encountered by the staff responsible for implementation of the assignment plan was the differences among BHA housing projects. Elderly projects, for example, contained no minors and few workers or nonwhite residents. Compared with family developments, they were relatively new, small-scale projects with low turnover rates and few vacancies. In addition, even family projects varied considerably in physical design, location, and resident composition. Table 4 indicates, for example, the mean and range of key tenant variables among the fifteen federal family developments.

BHA staff had rather clear perceptions of the desirability of projects. In his study of problem tenant identification in BHA projects, Richard Scobie constructed a reputation scale based on the scores that four top ranking BHA officials (including the chief of the Tenant Selection Department) assigned to the physical desirability of BHA family developments.[20] Reputation scores ranged from a high of 1.25 to a low of 6.50 (on a 1–7 scale) with a mean score of 3.7. Scobie found that although several variables such as size of project and racial composition of the tenant population were not associated with reputation, three other variables were statistically significant: child density (as measured by ratios of adult nonelderly men to children, single parent families, percentage of families

[20]Scobie, "Family Interaction," pp. 75–87.

on AFDC, household heads under 30 years old); transiency (as measured by vacated apartments, occupancy of five years or less); and economic dependency (as measured by numbers of households without workers). The BHA officials ranked the 1–2–3 projects, which had the highest vacancy rates, as the worst developments.

Applicant Preferences

The staff's ranking of projects is borne out by applicant preferences. According to one staff member, most applicants were familiar with project conditions and expressed specific preferences at the preassignment interview:

> Most applicants have projects in mind when they come in. They know at least which ones they consider good and which ones they consider bad. And when they really want a project, they usually refuse to take anything else.

Moreover, staff members felt that it was widely known from media reports as well as word of mouth that the 1–2–3 projects were the worst ones. Accordingly, over half of those applicants offered only the 1–2–3 project choice decided to forego project living. As Table 5 indicates, those applicants who refused project assignments expressed a demonstrated knowledge of the projects and a desire to live in particular areas. With the exception of whites in racially changing areas, most applicants wanted to stay in their current neighborhoods. According to one staff member:

> The 1–2–3 projects were always in black areas. While white families definitely didn't want those projects, about 50 percent of black fami-

Table 5. Applicants' Reasons for Refusing Regular (1–2–3) Assignments

Fear	11.3%
Prefer specific area	31.4
Prefer specific project	37.6
Prefer leased housing	9.7
Prefer elderly housing	8.4
Decide at future date	1.4
Total	100.0%
Number of cases (935)	

Table 6. Relation of Race of Assignee to Type
of Assignment

Assignment	Race	
	White	Nonwhite
Regular (1–2–3) assignment	23%	71%
No assignment	77	29
Total	100%	100%
Number of cases	(943)	(698)
gamma[a] = −.76		

[a]Gamma is a measure of association for ordinal data the values for which range from +1 to −1 and will approach +1 when values are concentrated in the extreme cells. High negative relationships appear when data are concentrated in low-high cells. Zero indicates no relationship between the two variables. In the nominal or 2 by 2 cases, gamma equals Yules Q and essentially measures the difference in row percentages. For further details, see James Davis, *Elementary Survey Analysis* (Englewood Cliffs: Prentice-Hall, 1971).

lies didn't want to go either. Therefore, applicants were always refusing them and, as a result, most people went to the bottom of the list.

Although staff felt that most applicants viewed the 1–2–3 projects as undesirable living places, nonwhites were more willing to live in the projects than whites. Of those applicants on whom the rules were imposed, Table 6 confirms that a greater proportion of nonwhites (71 percent) than whites (23 percent) took regular (1–2–3) assignments.

Some staff members suggested that the reluctance of whites to accept assignments at 1–2–3 projects was not based so much on their dislike of the nonwhite areas but on the fact that whites were currently living in better housing than nonwhites and therefore were less willing to accept housing at the projects with the worst physical facilities[21] (see Table 7). For example, according to this data 51 percent of the white applicants

[21]Although staff criticisms of the problems of accurately measuring housing conditions are correct, such measures are still a useful surrogate for need. Although they may do injustice to an individual case, overall many of these problems will average out. The measure is most likely to be accurate when comparing the extreme categories.

Table 7. Relation of Race of Assignee to Condition of
Assignees' Housing

	Race	
Condition of assignee housing	White	Nonwhite
1 + 2 (emergency + displaced site)	13.7%	19.0%
3 + 4 + 5 (terrible)	7.4	17.1
6 (bad)	27.9	39.1
7 + 8 (fair)	51.0	24.8
Total	100.0%	100.0%
Number of cases	(1,718)	(1,164)
gamma = −.37		

resided in fair housing conditions (conditions 7 and 8) compared to only 24.8 percent of the nonwhite applicants. In addition, Table 8 indicates that assignee housing condition was related to whether an applicant received a regular (1–2–3) or no assignment. Over 80 percent of those applicants in conditions 1 and 2 (emergency and displaced site) accepted regular assignments compared with only 16 percent in conditions 7 and 8.

Given that whites were in better housing conditions than nonwhites and that the great majority of assignees in better housing conditions were likely to reject regular (1–2–3) assignments, a question arises as to whether or not race was a factor in explaining the difference between the small percentage of whites (23 percent) accepting regular (1–2–3) assignments and the relatively large percentage of nonwhites (71 percent) accepting regular assignments. If race were not a factor, one would expect

Table 8. Relation of Condition of Assignees' Housing to Whether He or She Received a Regular (1–2–3) Assignment or No Assignment

	Condition of assignees' housing			
Assignment	1 + 2 (Emergency + displaced site)	3 + 4 + 5 (Terrible)	6 (Bad)	7 + 8 (Fair)
Regular (1–2–3) assignment	80.8%	67.9%	54.0%	16.2%
No assignment	19.2	32.1	46.0	83.8
Total	100.0%	100.0%	100.0%	100.0%
Number of cases	(172)	(165)	(509)	(629)
gamma = .70				

Table 9. Relation of Race of Assignees in the Same Housing Condition to Receiving a Regular (1–2–3) Assignment

	Percentage of assignees accepting regular (1–2–3) assignments[a]	
Condition of assignees' housing	White	Nonwhite
1 + 2 (emergency, displaced site)	68%	87%
3 + 4 + 5 (terrible)	49%	75%
6 (bad)	34%	70%
7 + 8 (fair)	10%	48%

[a]Entries in each cell are the percentage of those assignees offered only the choice between regular assignments and no assignments who took regular assignments.

no difference between the percentages of whites and nonwhites in equal housing conditions accepting regular assignments. Table 9 indicates, however, that whites in the same housing condition as nonwhites were less likely to accept regular assignments. For example, only 10 percent of whites in conditions 7 and 8 compared to 48 percent of nonwhites in the same conditions were willing to accept 1–2–3 assignments.

The rejection of the 1–2–3 projects by the elderly compared with the nonelderly is even more striking than the rejection by whites compared with nonwhites. As Table 10 indicates, only a tiny percentage of elderly compared with nonelderly assignees accepted regular assignments. Almost all (94 percent) of the elderly took no assignment rather than accept

Table 10. Relation of Age of Assignee to Whether He or She Received a Regular (1–2–3) Assignment or No Assignment

	Age	
Assignment	Elderly	Nonelderly
Regular (1–2–3) assignment	6.5%	62.1%
No assignment	93.5	37.9
Total	100.0%	100.0%
Number of cases	(539)	(1,107)
gamma = −.92		

Table 11. *Relation of Age of Assignee to Condition of Assignee's Housing*

Condition of assignee's housing	Age	
	Elderly	Nonelderly
1 + 2 (emergency, displaced site)	7.4%	19.7%
3 + 4 + 5 (terrible)	7.1	13.1
6 (bad)	19.3	38.1
7 + 8 (fair)	66.2	29.2
Total	100.0%	100.0%
Number of cases	(875)	(2,015)
gamma = .53		

the 1–2–3 projects. In part, this was because the elderly resided in better housing conditions than nonelderly and were less desperate for public housing units at the worst projects, less likely to desire living in an integrated project or more desirous of living in an age segregated setting rather than a family project (see table 11).

Given that elderly were in better housing conditions than nonelderly and that most assignees in better housing conditions were likely to reject 1–2–3 assignments, is age still a factor in explaining the differences between the small percentage of elderly (6.5 percent) accepting regular assignments and the relatively large percentage of nonelderly (62.1 percent) accepting regular assignments? Just as in the case of race, if age were not a factor, one would expect no difference between the percentages of elderly and nonelderly in equal housing conditions accepting 1–2–3 assignments. Table 12 indicates, however, that elderly in the same

Table 12. *Relation of Age of Assignee in the Same Housing Condition to Receiving a Regular (1–2–3) Assignment*

Condition of assignee's housing	Percentage of assignees accepting regular (1–2–3) assignments[a]	
	Elderly	Nonelderly
1 + 2 (emergency, displaced site)	41%	83%
3 + 4 + 5 (terrible)	35%	72%
6 (bad)	10%	63%
7 + 8 (fair)	3%	37%

[a]Entries in each cell are the percentage of those assignees offered only the choice between regular assignments and no assignments who took regular assignments.

Table 13. Relation of Age and Race of Assignee in the Same Housing
Condition to Receiving a Regular (1–2–3) Assignment

	Percentage of assignees accepting regular (1– 2– 3) assignments[a]	
Condition of assignees' housing[b]	White elderly	Nonwhite elderly
1 + 2 + 3 + 4 + 5 (emergency + displaced site + terrible)	30%	50%
6 + 7 + 8 (bad + fair)	3%	13%

[a]Entries in each cell are the percentage of those assignees offered only the choice between regular assignments and no assignments who took regular assignments.
[b]Categories have been collapsed because of the small numbers of elderly who took regular assignments.

housing conditions as nonelderly were less likely to accept regular assignments. For example, only 3 percent of elderly in conditions 7 and 8 compared to 37 percent of the nonelderly in the same conditions were willing to accept 1–2–3 projects.

Some of the differences between the elderly and nonelderly might be explained by the large proportion of elderly whites. As can be seen in Table 13, elderly whites in the same housing condition as nonwhite elderly were less likely to accept regular assignments. For example, only 3 percent of elderly whites in conditions 6, 7, and 8 compared to 13 percent of nonwhite elderly in the same conditions were willing to accept 1–2–3 assignments.

Shortcomings of the 1–2–3 Rule

Applicant refusal undermined what the staff regarded as the integration and vacancy goals for the assignment plan. Clearly, most whites refused to live in the worst projects in black areas. Since virtually all elderly refused these projects, the number of vacant units remained high, particularly in one- and two-bedroom apartments. Moreover, many of the vacant units were uninhabitable because the authority's severe financial troubles prevented the maintenance crews from preparing them for occupancy. Since all the vacant units (whether habitable or not) were counted in the overall number of vacancies, in the absence of a concentrated rehabilitation effort the same projects continued to be in the top three.

According to a staff member, the resulting consistency of the 1–2–3 projects therefore undermined the waiting list feature of the plan:

> Even if we reached those applicants on the waiting list again, we still had only the same projects to offer. Those three were the projects with the highest number of vacancies the entire time I worked on the 1–2–3. We never did fill them and they were the only projects we had to offer.

Consequently, the plan never progressed to the point at which black applicants were routinely offered assignments at predominantly white projects.

The apparent failure of the plan to achieve its goals was noted at the higher level of the authority. Several times the BHA executive director wrote HUD that the 1–2–3 rule was only increasing the vacancy rate and accelerating segregation (see Chapter 7). Staff members had little faith in the ability of the 1–2–3 plan to achieve its objectives; even for those staff members who believed in integration, the statistics compiled by the administrator indicated that the 1–2–3 rule may have been contributing to increased segregation.

Not only was the plan an apparent failure in terms of its goals, but the implementation of it engendered a great deal of anger on the part of applicants who did not want to go to the 1–2–3 projects. This pressure was directed at the staff members conducting preassignment interviews. One bureaucrat who was often the object of applicant hostility explained his problems:

> The 1–2–3 rule creates a lot of complaints in Tenant Selection. It makes our job that much more difficult. An applicant complains a friend got into Mary Ellen McCormick and why can't she? People tend to look to see who has had less difficulty and then proceed, submitting it as proof that the rule is unnecessary. They throw that at us and put us in an embarrassing situation.

Another staff member echoed the same sentiment:

> The 1–2–3 rule was a nuisance. It was difficult to put up with people's reactions toward being offered these developments. You become an ogre and nobody wanted to be put in that position because you took a lot of flack. If you offered a 1–2–3 project to an applicant and she came away unhappy, you could expect that afternoon or the

next day to hear from this or that important person: "What are you doing? Mrs. Smith has a decent family."

In addition to the pressures from applicants who refused assignments, there were also complaints from those who, either in desperation or ignorance, had accepted placements at the 1–2–3 projects and later regretted their decisions. A central office staff member gave the following description:

> One month after they get sent to an undesirable project they are going to be banging on the manager's door requesting a transfer; then they go before the transfer committee and, if refused, they bang on anyone else's door they can find until they go back before the transfer committee and get approved. They come to Tenant Selection, bang on our door and say, "I've got an approved transfer. Rehouse me immediately."

Along with applicant pressure for assignments at other than 1–2–3 projects came pressures from other parts of the authority. According to the plan, technically, vacant units at these other projects were to be kept unoccupied until the project had risen to the top three. However, the central management staff felt that such a policy would only increase the overall vacancy rate and further jeopardize the authority's solvency. Moreover, project managers wanted to fill these vacancies since they were judged by their superiors in the central office on the basis of rent collected. In addition, present tenants often had friends or relatives who wanted to live in their projects and therefore pressured managers to fill vacant apartments.

Staff Circumvention of the Rule

At one point in 1970, the BHA executive director responded to the problems in the 1–2–3 plan by approving its abandonment and reinstituting the freedom of choice plan. However, when HUD officials learned of his action, they forced the director to rescind his order. Staff members theoretically had to continue offering units at projects with the highest vacancies. Instead, however, they began to expand an informal practice that had grown up as a reaction to applicant pressure: relaxation of the rule by widening the clause that allowed applicants to be exempted from the 1–2–3 projects.

The federal regulations allowed for exceptions from the 1–2–3 rule in two situations: (1) if an applicant was willing to accept the unit offered but was unable to move at the time of the offer or (2) if the applicant presented clear evidence that acceptance of a vacancy would result in undue hardship not related to consideration of race, color, or national origin. Inaccessibility to source of employment and child day care were given as examples of exceptional situations. In such situations, refusal of an offer was not to count as one of the three rejections. The 1,630 applicants mentioned earlier that received housing despite refusal to accept the 1–2–3 projects qualified for those units under the umbrella of exceptional assignments. One staff member commented that the relaxation of the 1–2–3 plan was "like Catch 22. The exception swallowed the rule."

Although the regulations mentioned only two exceptions to the rules, the staff permissively interpreted those conditions so as to increase the number of people affected. Some of the reasons were plausible and others implausible on the basis of the intent of the federal exclusionary clause and the BHA's own regulations. The federal exclusionary clause refers to the applicant's need to live in a specific location. Examples of permissible reasons include the need to be near a health clinic for daily treatment of a medical illness; the need to be near a relative for help with housekeeping, babysitting, or the like; and the need to be close to a job. Since these fall within the spirit of the regulations, we can consider them plausible reasons (see Table 14). BHA regulations gave priority to applicants in certain other conditions as well. For example, veterans or widows of veterans had priority in the state housing program. Moreover, some applicants (that is, single persons under 62) were not eligible for federal projects but were eligible for the state projects. The operation of a large parallel state housing program which did not fall under the federal guidelines greatly expanded the BHA's discretion. In addition, the BHA gave emergency cases and displacees priority over other applicants for any available vacancy, even though they did not necessarily require certain locations. Finally, the leased housing program which had its own separate waiting list did not fall under the 1–2–3 plan and therefore has also been included in the plausible category. The implausible reasons (request of applicant, unit available, or miscellaneous) seem unrelated to either the federal or BHA regulations. Of the 703 cases for whom reasons for exceptional assignments were recorded, 526, or 74.8 percent, were in the realm of plausibility, whereas 177, or 25.2 percent, were not.

The failure of the 1–2–3 rule to achieve its objectives, in addition to

Table 14. Relation of Reasons for Exceptional
Assignment to Whether Reasons are Plausible
or Implausible

Plausible reasons	
Medical	19.0%
Needs to be near relative	5.9
Job	2.3
Speaks language other than English	.6
Qualifies only for state housing	9.7
Veteran	7.4
Emergency housing need	16.2
Displaced from site	36.1
Request of landlord (leased housing)	2.8
Total	100.0%
Number of cases (526)	
Implausible reasons	
Request of applicant	56.5%
Miscellaneous	21.0
Unit available	22.5
Total	100.0%
Number of cases (177)	

the negative feedback and pressure from dissatisfied applicants and other departments of the authority, convinced many Tenant Selection Department staff that the automatic assignment plan was a mistake in principle because it was unresponsive to the needs of the applicants. When asked what he thought was wrong with the 1–2–3 plan, one staff member said:

> A basic problem with the 1–2–3 rule and tenant selection in general is its inhumanity. There is no effort to find out what people's problems are. For example, a woman comes in who lives in Dorchester. Her children use the Harvard Street Clinic there and go to the neighborhood public school. As a family with many problems they are probably doing an adequate job. And we say to them, do you want to go to a 1–2–3 project? We don't try to find out what their background is. And so, by putting them out there, we disrupt their health services, their education, their whole life-style. It makes you wonder.

Other staff members had more specific criticisms. The following is a typical staff response to the question of how the assignment process would work if the 1–2–3 plan was dropped:

Without the 1–2–3 rule you could send cases to any development to fill up your vacancies, giving everyone a fair crack at what they might desire. Wouldn't people ultimately be happier being housed where they would like to live rather than being forced to go to areas they know they won't like? I propose a system by which people are allowed to choose where they want to live. If, for example, a person chooses Mary Ellen McCormick, she could be put on a waiting list there. We could then tell her where she stood in respect to the likelihood that she were to get into Mary Ellen or any other project she might be on the list for. The problem is that HUD calls for a community-wide waiting list with assignments made to the 1–2–3 projects.

Despite disruptions and dissatisfaction, staff members did not completely abandon the 1–2–3 plan. A large number of applicants received 1–2–3 assignments or refused assignments under the procedures. Still, by expanding the exemption clause and allowing almost half of the applicants to be assigned to other projects, the staff undermined the plan's basic operating principle.

CONCLUSION

Although reformers distrusted staff decision making, experience shows that rules cannot be easily substituted for discretion in a bureaucratic organization. The housing-need rule designed to allocate units on the basis of one's housing condition was subjectively applied and arbitrarily weighted. What the reformers thought was a clear rule turned out to be merely a complex and cumbersome way of permitting discretion. Faced with this reality, upper-level staff members formally convinced the governing board to restrict the definition to emergency cases and rely on the priority of first come, first serve. Although date of application was simpler and more objective than housing need, even this criterion encountered logical and practical problems: an increasing number of emergency cases took precedence over older cases; many applicants would only accept units at particular projects; and staff resources were inadequate to maintain a real waiting list. Many of these difficulties were attributable to low staff morale and inefficiency. However, these seemingly neutral bottlenecks set up an applicant self-selection process with strong regressive implications. The aggressive applicant managed to get attention and eventually was housed. Yet, applicants with enough energy to select themselves are rarely the ones with the greatest need or disability.[22] Moreover, other problems were caused by the collection of information intended to keep out "undesirable" applicants. To ignore this data would threaten a large number of staff, managers, and board members. Finally, the 1–2–3 plan failed to integrate projects because white tenants were not sufficiently desperate for housing to be coerced into accepting apartments at the worst black projects. Faced with the infeasibility of the plan and subjected to intense pressure from applicants to go to other projects, staff members relaxed the rules. All of these modifications demonstrate the difficulty of restructuring agencies through rules that are in opposition to established job conceptions, practices, and mores.[23] Rather than enforce outwardly imposed rules, personnel instead attempt to ease work pressures, satisfy applicant demands, and follow their own sense of justice.

[22]See Almond and Lasswell, "Aggressive Behavior," and Levin and Taube, "Bureaucracy."

[23]Similar findings were documented in Blau's study of an employment office. See Peter Blau, *Dynamics of Bureaucracy* (Chicago: University of Chicago Press, 1963), especially pp. 19–35.

CHAPTER FOUR

Discretion, Staff Norms, and Outcomes

As discussed in Chapter 3, the rules imposed by the Boston Housing Authority did not place effective limits on decision making and therefore the staff had considerable freedom to choose among possible courses of action in aiding individual applicants. This chapter describes the discretion available to staff members, develops a bureaucrat typology to predict how various staff members are likely to use discretion, and examines the outcomes of discretionary decision making for several broad categories of applicants. Because the typology could not be tested directly against the outcomes, the analysis does not empirically verify the causal links between different sorts of bureaucrats and the results of their decisions for applicants. Nevertheless, the separate pieces take us a long way in understanding how discretion is used and provide a good picture of the outcomes.

STAFF DISCRETION

In the absence of clear rules, the staff had great latitude in providing information, assessing need, and becoming advocates for applicants. Most applicants had little knowledge of either the formal or informal departmental procedures. One staff member who did preassignment interviews observed:

> Very few people are familiar with any regulations, period. There has never been a handbook of regulations distributed to the public on

what they can have, the income limits, the procedures, or anything.
You have to explain to them what the regulations are.

Therefore, individual bureaucrats had control over information, a vital
resource in this context. As explained by another staff person:

> Then whoever was doing the interview could inform her what she
> could do to get an exceptional assignment. If there were others that
> he didn't want to tell, he didn't. He had a lot of control over that.

Not only did staff control information, they decided which applicants
had priority and the projects to which they were sent. Although need had
been formally dropped as a priority criterion, staff members still used it as
a justification for giving some applicants preference over others:[1]

> When calls come in, I go and look up a case to figure out where the
> case is and what the chances are for getting in. But because there are
> no longer any real priorities, except for emergencies, the status is
> always unclear and the call can have an effect on whether the person
> gets in. We do, for instance, still respond to need. If the person is in
> very bad housing, she may need an immediate assignment. Or a
> person in bad health may need a particular location—to be near a
> doctor, or relatives. The process becomes individual decisions by the
> staff.

Even in emergencies, when the need priority had been retained, discretion was used since the rules did not seem to apply equitably to all
situations:

> The trouble with making rules and the reason the whole thing is so
> hard is that you want to set down priorities and there are always
> things that don't fit. It is fine to say that these are our priorities. You

---

[1]A study of an English housing council found that although the council gave no
points for need, it attempted to take need into account in making decisions. The
authors felt that such a scheme was highly susceptible to bias and could degener-
ate into a random process. See Morris and Mogey, *The Sociology of Housing*, p.
19. Another study found that small authorities use a merit system whereby each
applicant's needs are assessed individually. Disgruntled applicants, however,
often appealed to elected councillors. Such procedures therefore avoided the
rigidities of point systems but they presented their own problems of consistency
and impartiality. See Charles Ascher, *The Administration of Publicly Aided
Housing*, p. 33.

should have lists, but you also have to make exceptions. For example, we set up a rule that eviction qualifies a person for an emergency priority, but eviction for nonpayment of rent is not an emergency because technically it is the fault of the tenant. But what if a person is in an apartment in which the rent has risen from $100 to $200 a month? It isn't fair to say that he is just some slob who doesn't pay his rent, because there is no way in God's earth that he could pay it.

In addition, the staff exercised considerable discretion in assigning cases to projects. Technically, emergency applicants were offered only one assignment at the project with the highest vacancy. If they refused to accept that offering, they were then dropped to the bottom of the waiting list. However, as one staff member described, there was still latitude for responsiveness and many people with emergency cases were offered apartments at other projects:

> When you stop and think about it, you can take the attitude that if you are an emergency and refuse to go to the worst project, then you are not an emergency, and I guess pragmatically that is all you can do. On the other hand, you just can't help understanding why an applicant may not be able to deal with the situation there. You stop and think, well, what would you do? How would you feel?

In dealing with exceptional assignments to projects other than those with the highest vacancies, the rules were even more vague and discretion was even wider. As the chief of the Tenant Selection Department pointed out, applicants came in with a variety of reasons for obtaining assignments to particular projects:

> Applicants brought doctors' letters stating that they had to be in East Boston to be near the water; they suffer from dizziness and need to be near their mother who must come down every day to do their shopping; they have a mother who is partially bedridden and have to be close to take care of the house for her; they have to be near a specific clinic to go in two or three times a week for emergency treatment. Decisions about these cases are hard ones.

The chief further explained that although he questioned the validity of some applicants' reasons for exceptional assignments, he could do little to verify the information:

> Medical letters would come in, and who am I to judge? If a doctor wrote a letter, I didn't question it. Unfortunately doctors would

sometimes go along with applicants, figuring that they can help them get an apartment. But there is no way to dispute a doctor. There is no way to have a hearing with a doctor present. You accept it on face value. But doctors' letters were coming in a dime a dozen.

More importantly, the breakdown of the rules opened the floodgate of need. Not every applicant had information about doctors' letters or access to a sympathetic physician; nonetheless, the Tenant Selection Department was deluged with thousands of letters documenting need, thus making it difficult to distinguish among cases. As one staff member observed, advocacy was an indispensable ingredient for success under these conditions:

> Need is fine; it is good to have the need, but need was not always the basis. There is no continuous system for checking letters to see who is really needy and who is not. The need priority never worked as well as it should have. On the surface, we collected the information. But it daily became so much more of an advocacy process. A person who had no advocate whatsoever, from any source, just went past the boards regardless of need.

Given staff discretion in supplying information, determining need, and providing advocacy, a client's success depended on the attitudes of the personnel with whom he or she came in contact.

BUREAUCRATIC TYPES AND THE USE OF DISCRETION

In 1970 the Tenant Selection Department employed 17 white-collar workers (11 white women, 1 black woman, 2 white men, and 3 black men). Their main duties focused on either record keeping or interaction with applicants. Men occupied the two top positions and the field work jobs. As can be seen in Table 15, staff occupied a range of positions and their salaries differed with the amount of responsibility involved in their jobs, at least on paper.

Personnel came to the department through a number of different channels. Most had fallen into jobs at the authority and had not actually sought careers in public housing. Many of those who had worked for the authority the longest (about one-third had been there over ten years) had obtained their jobs through politicians, relatives, or friends. Several of

Table 15. *Tenant Selection Department*
Staff Positions and Salaries, 1970

Upper level	
Chief	$14,394
Preassignment interviewer	12,922
Tenant relations aid	9,707
Middle level	
Record clerk	8,023
Final review clerk (2)	7,292
Secretary	7,292
Interviewer (2)	7,292
Field worker (2)	7,292
Lower level	
Clerk typist (5)	6,627
Receptionist	6,627

the more recently hired staff had started in training programs (e.g., Neighborhood Youth Corps.).

Job mobility within the department was somewhat limited. Lower-level staff were promoted to middle-level positions, but the chief usually came from outside the department. Given the limited range of positions and the slow turnover of staff, promotions came infrequently and resulted in only slight salary increases.

According to one staff member, the department's personnel formed into "cliques that made moral judgments about who should and should not be housed." Basically, their attitudes toward clients separated the staff into four groups: traditionalists, reformers, survivalists, and avoiders.[2] These four groups differed widely with respect to the providing of

[2]The typology employed bears some resemblance to that put forth by Anthony Downs. Downs attempts to predict bureaucratic behavior through an economic model based on goal maximization. Bureaucratic goals include power, money income, prestige, convenience, security, personal loyalty, and the public interest. He then posits five ideal bureaucratic types which exhibit various goal combinations: climbers, conservors, zealots, advocates, and statesmen. Anthony Downs, *Inside Bureaucracy* (Boston: Little, Brown and Co., 1966), especially pp. 79–111.

James Q. Wilson has criticized Downs's model on the grounds that predictions that result are hard to operationalize, tests are difficult to conceive, and, if tests were used, it is hard to imagine what we could have learned, for behavior seemingly produced by one kind of motive could have been produced by another or some combination of several motives. James Q. Wilson, *Political Organizations* (New York: Basic Books, 1973), p. 25.

information, priority, or advocacy and to the kinds of clients to whom they responded.

Traditionalists

Traditionalists wanted to preserve and enhance working-class values. They favored intact families whose behavior they considered conventional. Most traditionalists were long-term BHA personnel and had obtained their jobs through political support. They usually had high school or college diplomas.

The BHA had been an integral part of most traditionalists' lives. According to one observer, they were immersed in its mechanisms and depended on their involvement for status, social support, and psychological well-being.[3] Traditionalists therefore longed for the "happy years" when clients were working-class and middle-class and projects were attractive and easy to maintain. They viewed public housing as a real estate operation without the profit motive rather than as a social welfare institution.

Traditionalists resisted the client shifts which began in the early 1960s and criticized the reformers for their permissive attitudes. Moreover, traditionalists supported a return to extensive screening as one way to restore status, prestige, order, and financial solvency to the authority. One traditionalist in the Tenant Selection Department said,

> A project is a place now that a family with decent standards just doesn't want to live in. And this is really because of the type of families they have put in the projects. No question about it, I can understand that these families need to have a home, but you can't expect to fill up a project with them and make it a decent place. This

---

Although the typology employed in this chapter may have some of the same problems that Wilson ascribes to Downs's ideal types, its formation was based not on motives but on staff members' primary orientation toward applicants. From observations and interviews it appeared clear that staff had two basic views of which clients the bureaucracy should serve and could be divided into two types: traditionalists and reformers. But a significant number of staff members did not seem to operate on their beliefs. Their behavior seemed to be best explained by their positions in the department. The avoider and survivalist types were created out of that understanding. Since applicants could encounter any of the types, staff orientations had important impact on the disposition of cases.
[3]Lewis Popper, "The Boston Housing Authority," p. 85.

blanket tenant selection I just can't go along with. I can understand the purpose of it, but I think that it is going to ruin the Housing Authority.

While traditionalists did not have the power to change eligibility requirements, they nevertheless continued to act on their values when the situation permitted. One reform staff member cited the following case as an example:

> A lady with two kids who had separated from her husband came in looking for housing. One staff member wouldn't house her because her separation was not official. She just couldn't live with her husband anymore but he didn't want to encourage that sort of thing.

Other traditionalists continued to screen out applicants with minor criminal records, even when there had been no conviction, and illegitimate children. As noted in Chapter 3, all such cases were then subject to review by a social worker with a reformer's orientation, who usually ruled them acceptable.

Although traditionalists could not directly exclude many people, they could do a great deal for applicants they favored. When asked whether certain types of people received preferential treatment, one staff member responded:

> People feel badly for the elderly. Also middle-class families and whole families, if it is a really nice family and they strike you as just really good people, but they are just in a bad situation, for example, because they lost their home in a fire. Staff react to doing something for a good family. It is not that they don't care about somebody else who is badly off, but they give preferential treatment to good families.

In particular, many emergency cases were looked on by traditionalists as victims of misfortune rather than as persons with moral failings. One of the primary ways discretion was used was to send "good" families to prime projects. According to a reformer, traditionalists accomplished this by taking advantage of the exceptions to the 1–2–3 rule:

> A black person would come in, it might even be a middle-class person, and a [traditionalist] staff member would say 1–2–3. A white person would come in and he would try to make a special exception.

> And there were ways to make exceptions, that is what I found out.
> You could discuss with people all the projects, tell them how to get
> around the rule by getting a letter saying they had to be treated at a
> certain clinic. But you didn't feel an obligation to tell everyone about
> exemptions, only those people with whom you felt sympathy.

By the late 1960s, however, traditionalists had lost much of their
power. Even though the breakdown of the rules allowed for considerable
discretion, traditionalists had to compete with reformers for assignments.
In addition, the shift from white working-class to welfare minority applicants left the traditionalists with a limited clientele, primarily the elderly.
Finally, the traditionalists lost their leader: when the reform board took
over in 1969, the chief of the department, who had been flamboyant,
outspoken, and not afraid to support "good" families, was transferred to a
position in which he had little interaction with clients and no control over
their destiny. His replacement was the black reform-oriented assistant
chief who for many years had been a manager. With the traditionalist
chief's departure, the traditionalists became less active.

Reformers

Reformers operated on an explicit theory of choice based on a principle of need. They primarily aided nonwhite applicants in desperate housing conditions. In 1970, the department had four identifiable reformers at
middle- and upper-level positions. In addition, the chief of the department had the assistance of two reform-oriented aides who were assigned
to help him on a part-time basis. The placement of these reformers in the
Tenant Selection Department reflected the new concern over equity.

In contrast to traditionalists, reformers were committed to housing
applicants most in need, even if such a policy resulted in public housing
becoming the last resort for poor families. For this reason, one reformer
expressed her displeasure that many high-income tenants continued to
receive favorable assignments and reside in projects:

> I get mad about it personally because I have to deal with the very
> poor every day. When you see them trying to make it out there in the
> private rental market, it is just humanly impossible.

Reformers also felt that "problem" families should not be barred from
public housing but instead supplied with helpful services. One champion

of the social service cause felt that social workers should conduct first interviews in order to take the family's history and to identify needed services. A family's history would include their experience with employment, health care, child care, and social agencies. Such information could be used to help identify families needing specialized social services and to allow staff to assign them to projects where such services were available.

Reform staff were resentful of the way other staff members handled applicants. Applicants often became upset because they did not feel they were being fairly treated.[4] Reformers felt that other staff types were unresponsive to applicants feelings and were particularly inept at handling applicant anger. One reformer characterized the situation as follows:

> If a belligerent applicant comes in swearing and screaming, many staff members get scared or angry and say they won't deal with the person. Well, I have found it to be true that something must be truly bothering the applicant. Often they have really been through the mill and are taking it out on you because otherwise whom are they going to take it out on? If I can defuse her somehow, I can find out whether she is just obnoxious, which is sometimes true, or whether she has had it up to here and ends up swearing. Applicants often just come in and need to talk with someone who is sympathetic.

When this same reformer was asked what she felt were the qualities of a good interviewer in addition to being able to handle anger, she described desirable behavior:

> You could just take an application, get down all the information and say, "OK, we will notify you." There are people who do that. Then there are those who take it all down and if the person says, "I want to go to Mary Ellen McCormick," the interviewer responds, "Well, quite honestly you might have to wait twenty years to get into that project." There are a couple who will tell them the truth. Finally, the interviewer may think that the applicant has a real problem or is desperate and that something should be done. They will bring the

---

[4]R. D. Cramond has noted a similar problem in Scottish public housing: "Many schemes . . . do not enjoy public confidence because allocations are not seen to be made in accordance with definite known rules." Quoted in D. V. Donnison, *The Government of Housing* (Harmondsworth, Middlesex, England: Penguin Books, 1967), p. 292.

case to the preassignment interviewer or the chief and say, "Look, you have to help this lady, I feel so badly for her."

Following a case through the process was considered particularly important. One of the reform aides to the chief described what this meant:

> Tenant Selection would respond to me only because I would hand-deliver the case and say a particular person had to be taken care of. I had to become their advocate. I learned how you got the vacate notices and where you went and all that sort of business. In emergency transfers, for example, when someone who lived in a project had been throttled or the ceiling had caved in because of water leaks, we had the responsibility as landlords to get them the hell out of there. I would go upstairs, get the vacate notices and pull them out, see what they had, attach them to the case folder, and tell the chief, "I think you had better sign these and get them out right away." But if someone would call and say, "What can I do?" I would be at a loss to explain it. I knew if I got to the right person at the right time I could do something but I couldn't tell the applicant how to do it. And that was because there wasn't any system.

The role of advocate put reformers in a very difficult personal situation because they were essentially competing with other staff members and outsiders for assignments. In addition, according to one reformer, filling this role necessitated working outside the system, which was very complex and time-consuming. Only a limited number of clients could be served in this way. Not only did reformers experience futility in helping a small number of desperate people through the process, but they faced antagonism from the rest of the staff.

> There is nothing worse than to be enthusiastic and try to do something and see people looking at you as if you were a nut. You take a lot of grief from the rest of the staff because you have expressed a special interest and because you may work a minute past five or because you may come in at eight-thirty in the morning instead of nine.

And reportedly even greater resentment occurred when reformers sent nonwhite families to predominantly white projects. Many of the other staff lived in these areas and feared the influx of black lower-class families.

In response to the problems that they found with the tenant selection process, several reformers began to formulate the framework for a better system. The reformers put together a tenant selection and assignment plan to insure the staff informed applicants of the priority and preference regulations, the full range of BHA housing, and the waiting list for each project. They submitted the detailed proposal to the BHA board and HUD but received little support.

In the absence of a new system, reformers found themselves trapped by the same conditions that affected the behavior of other staff. For example, reformers criticized other staff for not telling applicants when they might expect to get assigned, but as long as staff responded to need, and not just the date of application, it was difficult to predict with much accuracy when an applicant would get an apartment. It was always possible that the next person in line would have greater need than the person being served. Moreover, because the department no longer used a scoring system and operated primarily on a case-by-case basis, reformers could not dispel applicants' impressions that political favoritism was more important than need in determining prime assignments.[5] In addition, reformers acknowledged that they were rarely able to help applicants choose the project best suited to them because there was an inherent conflict between the best-suited project and project availability. Applicants in great need of housing often had to make the expedient decision to take any available unit. Moreover, time constraints often kept reformers from calling applicants to tell them when a unit was available. Therefore, as one reformer indicated, even reformers tended to respond to those applicants who acted as their own advocates:

> They call all the time and finally their name is in your head all the time and an apartment comes up and you automatically say, "Mrs. Smith" because she has called. You deal with so many people and so many names and so many phone calls every day, that the one that sticks out is bound to come out on top.

In addition, the case-by-case process left the door open to personal interpretations of need, and even reformers had their own prejudices. One reformer acknowledged, for example, that she tended to favor the upwardly mobile:

> Tenant assignment is personal. I have a prejudice too. If a married man comes in—and usually if he is young he tends to be black,

---

[5]A similar predicament exists in English council housing. See Morris and Mogey, *The Sociology of Housing*, p. 21.

although race doesn't matter—I feel there are not that many whole
families, and this guy might have just lost a job, and the whole world
is against him, and he may need one break. I will bust my back to
give him that one break. Even if he is a brand new applicant I will
give him an apartment. And that is a prejudice. I just feel they
deserve it. So prejudices have a lot to do with it. You do react to
personalities. Someone might know how to talk to you better.

Finally, faced with the lack of structural change and eroding support
from above, reformers began to leave the authority in 1971. Commenting
on the reformers' departure, one staff member said:

The bureaucrats are the ones who win out in the end. They are the
ones who come here for life, bide their time, and stay. The reformers
came in like a charging herd of bulls, and not one of them is left. But
it is natural, if you are young and intelligent and want to do things,
you wouldn't stick around a place like this.

Reformers' career ladders led them elsewhere and left the department in
the hands of the survivalists.

Survivalists

Survivalists were most concerned with the preservation and enhancement of their jobs. Although they generally shared the traditionalists' view of good tenants, survivalists were willing to accommodate
to pressure, even if it contradicted their beliefs, because they were interested in maintaining their positions no matter who was in power.
Financial concerns seemed to be their original reason, but according to
one staff member, when they had finally risen to mid-level positions,
their anxiety shifted to protecting the nature of their jobs. According to
another staff member, survivors, who occupied about half the middle-
and upper-level jobs, followed a typical *modus operandi:*

The way to survive is not to make decisions. That is why Mr. P. is still
here. How many political things has he lived through? Just bend with
the wind, don't make yourself too available, don't ever make decisions. You can get away with such behavior in a place like this. The
BHA fosters the attitude that you shouldn't step out on a limb.

"Not stepping out on a limb" included avoidance of initiative in informing
applicants of the formal and informal procedures, projects, waiting times,

and the like. Bending with the wind, however, indicated survivalists' accession to pressure, whether or not it was in line with their values. A staff member described such behavior as follows:

> Mr. P. is a status quo person. He sees colleagues as coming and going. He doesn't have to please colleagues to keep his job. He responds more to outside pressure such as state representatives. State reps can hurt you, although they may not help you. People tend to call Mr. P. from political positions. He opened the door in the first place and people remember. People like Mr. P. mitigate against reform, are less able to recognize human feelings and less flexible.

Survivalists' resistance to change was not so great as traditionalists' because the former responded to pressure from reformers. A reformer indicated that she was able to force Mr. P. to act by pushing him into a corner:

> He can't deal with any kind of pressure. I mean, I can pressure him to give priority to an applicant. I don't have the same influence over him that a politician has, but I can back him into a corner.

The reformers often accused survivalists of racism in assigning applicants to projects. However, although these charges may have been correct, in that whites got better assignments than blacks, the reasons are more closely related to survivalists' acceding to influence than to their own racist attitudes; as one reformer himself noted, white applicants created the most pressure:

> Who got exceptional assignments to the better projects? Mostly white people in South Boston and Charlestown. For one thing they knew how to deal with the political system, whereas low-income blacks and Puerto Ricans thought they were at the mercy of the system and never bothered to try to manipulate it. Also blacks and Puerto Ricans came more or less hat in hand. They would usually come in and say they were looking for any kind of housing, whereas whites would come in and say they only wanted to be housed in Mary Ellen McCormick or Old Colony, and they would be told the way to be housed there was to get an exceptional assignment.

A survivalist pointed out the pressure on staff was often very specific:

> It was so much more easily acceptable to tell a black family that they had to go to a 1–2–3 project than to have to face a nice white family

across from you and tell them I can only offer you the 1–2–3 projects. The family might then tell you that they know of a vacancy at Mary Ellen McCormick. And some of these people would come not only with the information but the keys to the apartment right in their hand. In addition, they would say, "Obviously you are one of those reform people. If I was black and on welfare, I could get what I want."

Although survivalists often acceded to pressure initially, they were cautious and did not do any more than was necessary. One survivalist, for example, described the following example as typical: "An applicant would ask angrily, 'Well, how can I get in this place?' We didn't tell them about doctors' letters, but we would say there must be an exceptional reason." In addition, survivalists often did not follow through with their promises, apparently hoping that the pressure might subside or disappear over time. For example, a number of times survivalists told applicants that they did not have units at particular projects at the moment but would call the applicant when something opened up. When asked whether in fact the applicants were called, a staff member commented:

> Those people rarely ever get called. They would leave the desk having refused the 1–2–3 projects and their folders would be put back in the file. These staff will promise people the moon to get them off their backs. What they do is the thing that is quickest and easiest to get rid of the person. Nobody tells applicants the truth.[6]

In the case of emergencies, one survivalist noted that it was important to document refusals to protect oneself from politicians who might call to find out what happened. Although he often told people that he would call back and then usually did not, the staff member felt that unless people took the initiative to contact him, they must have found housing elsewhere and were not such an emergency.

Avoiders

Avoiders sought the most limited role in relation to applicants and neither acted on their own nor responded to pressures. Most avoiders

---

[6]A study of social welfare agencies points out that caseworkers seek to avoid confrontation, minimize their administrative decision making, and deliver virtually no services. See Joel Handler and Ellen Jane Hollingsworth, *The "Deserving Poor,"* p. xi.

were clerical workers with little hope for advancement and little incentive to do anything except to follow the rules strictly and do only as much as their job required. According to a staff member, a lingering fear about insecurity was one of the motivating forces of their behavior:

> There is an economic fear among the women who work in Tenant Selection. While those women aren't earning very much, they are supporting themselves and their families. They are afraid to join the union or to sign any kind of petition because they might lose their jobs. If they really thought about it, they couldn't lose their jobs unless they did something terribly wrong.

Low-level skills and the sense that few other job options existed led most avoiders to view procedural changes apprehensively:

> There is a certain group of employees that feel that anything new is a complete threat to their jobs. They feel you come to work and this is your job and this is the way you always did it. You always had to do step A before step B. Also you had to have permission from on high before anybody would act. Everything is slow and methodical, and the whole emphasis is on housing, and housing is not tenants.

The behavior of avoiders toward applicants is best explained by the strict way in which they defined their roles as clerks. For example, when asked what upset clerks, one staff member commented:

> Being put on the spot. Having to answer to applicants. The staff has lived in an atmosphere where it didn't really want to talk to people beyond a simple, "What is your name, what is your age." This approach is easier. The tone of Tenant Selection has been to be very happy doing the paper work but not having to face confrontation with a human being.

Therefore, although avoiders made judgments about applicants, they seldom became advocates even for those they favored. One avoider said that at first he tried to help needy applicants get decent assignments but he soon discovered that less needy people were going to projects. When he complained to the chief, he was told to mind his own business. He concluded that he didn't "get paid enough to do otherwise" and therefore ceased to be an advocate. This is an example of how avoiders sought a limited role partly because they felt that they could do very little and because there were few incentives, and possible disincentives to get involved.

Clerks sought to limit their involvement with applicants not only because of their role definition, but also to avoid unpleasant client conflicts. Applicants were often refused what they wanted, and they blamed any staff member they had dealt with. Although most clerks had little face-to-face interaction with applicants, they answered many of the phone calls:

> The telephone is the source of an enormous pressure. A lot of questions, a lot of anger, a lot of obscenities, and a lot of blame goes on over that telephone. Ordinary staff don't want to have to deal with it because they are placed in a position where they don't feel they have any authority or power to do anything. All they want is to get people off their backs.

Avoiders, therefore, transferred most of the calls to upper-level staff whose job definitions made them *responsible* for handling applicant problems. Upper-level staff complained that avoiders' unwillingness even to answer applicants' simple questions only increased their already heavy workload. However, as the following exchange indicates, avoiders sensed that upper-level staff might also be able to help applicants in a way they could not:

> (*To applicant*) I am only a clerk. Don't try to pin me down. I'm sure that if you come into the office, the chief or his assistant will see you. (*To another clerk*) The lady said she has tried for weeks to call the chief. She seems to think she may do better if she sees him in person. In fact she may do better. I sympathize with her. This is a public agency, I told her.

The avoidance of personal conflict extended to the point of anonymity. According to a staff member, if an applicant asked a clerk her name the clerk "got scared because she didn't want to be involved in anything. She closed up like a clam." Applicants encountering avoiders were therefore unlikely to get much assistance. The best that might happen is that an applicant would be passed to another staff member more willing to take responsibility.

OUTCOMES

An ideal empirical test of the effect of outcomes would relate the assignment of applicants to desirable or undesirable projects to the deci-

Table 16. Relation of Race to Whether
Assignee Received a Regular (1–2–3),
Exceptional or No Assignment

	Race	
Assignment	White	Nonwhite
Regular (1–2–3)	11.2%	38.1%
Exceptional	51.6%	46.6%
No assignment	37.2%	15.3%
Total	100.0%	100.0%
Number of cases	(1,950)	(1,307)
gamma = −.55		

sions of different bureaucratic types. However, because no one person was responsible for individual cases, that test would be difficult. In addition, as has been discussed, a number of cases did not follow the normal processing. In recognition of these problems, the empirical findings are therefore limited to an examination of the distribution of exceptional assignments to other than 1–2–3 projects.

Three-quarters of the staff members in the department were white, and many seemed to have attitudes that favored whites over nonwhites. In addition, a number of staff noted that whites tended to act more aggressively and have the political support necessary to get into better projects. One might, therefore, expect that a greater percentage of whites compared to nonwhites would receive exceptional assignments, especially since whites often were not willing to go to the 1–2–3 projects. However, Table 16 indicates that out of all assignments (including regular, exceptional, and no assignment), 51.6 percent of whites received exceptional assignments as compared to 46.2 percent of nonwhites, a difference that is not significant. This outcome suggests, however, not the absence of bias, but a balance between the two primary client orientations of the traditionalists and the reformers. Moreover, one cannot completely discount the hypothesis that discretion favored whites over nonwhites. For example, as Table 17 indicates, whites received a larger proportion of implausible exceptional assignments (28.5 percent) than nonwhites (17.7 percent).

Even among applicants receiving plausible exceptional assignments, there appear to be differences between whites and nonwhites. For example, Table 18 indicates that a greater proportion of whites (34.7 percent)

*Table 17. Relation of Race to Whether Assignee Received
a Plausible or Implausible Exceptional Assignment*

	Race	
Assignment	White	Nonwhite
Plausible exceptional assignment	71.5%	82.3%
Implausible exceptional assignment	28.5%	17.7%
Total	100.0%	100.0%
Number of cases	(410)	(270)
gamma = −.18		

than nonwhites (18.9 percent) received exceptional assignments for reasons related to the federal regulations. These decisions should be considered highly discretionary since the acceptability of such reasons was based on an explanation from a staff member or an outside third party and since these reasons required special verification (e.g., a letter from a doctor indicating health problems). On the other hand, a lower proportion of whites (65.3 percent) compared to nonwhites (81.1 percent) received exceptional assignments for reasons related to BHA rules. Unlike the need exemptions of the federal regulations, the BHA-related exceptions were automatically asked of each applicant and the answers re-

*Table 18. Relation of Race to Whether
Assignee Received a Plausible Exception to
the (1–2–3) Rule Based on Federal
Regulations (High Discretion) or BHA
Regulations (Low Discretion)*

Plausible exceptional assignment	Race	
	White	Nonwhite
Federal regulations (high discretion)	34.7%	18.9%
BHA regulations (low discretion)	65.3%	81.1%
Total	100.0%	100.0%
Number of cases	(303)	(222)
gamma = .35		

corded on the application form (e.g., do you have veteran status?) and therefore can be considered of a low discretionary nature.

Even if one acknowledges that whites received more implausible and exceptional assignments, one is still struck by the original finding that whites did not receive a significantly greater percentage of overall exceptional assignments than nonwhites. It appears that several organizational constraints may have controlled bureaucratic discretion. For example, 50 percent of nonwhites compared to 30 percent of whites were assigned units in leased housing and in a new project for the elderly that opened up in a black area of the city. Staff members had a strong incentive to use these new units because of their desirability. Moreover, the small number of vacancies in desirable white projects limited the number of exceptional assignments that could be granted to whites. Finally, over 50 percent of nonwhites, compared to less than 20 percent of whites, received exceptional assignments because they were displaced by public action. In order to proceed with urban renewal and highway construction projects, there was a need to house such applicants.

Most staff members were sympathetic with the plight of the elderly: the aged caused relatively few serious problems for managers and were considered the "deserving poor." One might therefore expect that exceptional assignments would be more readily granted to the elderly than the nonelderly. However, Table 19 indicates that out of all assignments (including regular, exceptional, and no assignment) only 44 percent of the elderly as compared to 52 percent of the nonelderly received exceptional assignments.

Table 19. Relation of Age to Whether Assignee Received a Regular (1–2–3), Exceptional, or No Assignment

	Age	
Assignment	Elderly	Nonelderly
Regular (1–2–3)	3.7%	29.8%
Exceptional	44.0%	52.0%
No assignment	52.3%	18.2%
	100.0%	100.0%
Number of cases	(963)	(2,308)
gamma = −.68		

Table 20. Relation of Age to Whether Assignee
Received a Plausible or Implausible
Exceptional Assignment

	Age	
Assignment	Elderly	Nonelderly
Plausible exceptional assignment	71.4%	75.6%
Implausible exceptional assignment	28.6%	24.4%
Total	100.0%	100.0%
Number of cases	(140)	(562)
gamma = −.11		

Although Table 20 indicates that the elderly received proportionally more (28.6 percent) implausible exceptional assignments than the nonelderly (24.4 percent), the difference is not very striking. Moreover, although Table 21 indicates that a greater proportion of the elderly (33 percent) than the nonelderly (26.8 percent) received exceptional assignments for reasons related to the federal regulations (high discretion), the difference is not large.

One major organizational constraint limited the number of exceptional assignments given to the elderly: very few vacancies occurred in the projects that most elderly wanted. For example, of the applicants who

Table 21. Relation of Age to Whether Assignee
Received a Plausible Exception to the (1–2–3) Rule
Based on Federal Regulations (High Discretion) or
BHA Regulations (Low Discretion)

Plausible exceptional assignment	Age	
	Elderly	Nonelderly
Federal regulations (high discretion)	33.0%	26.8%
BHA regulations (low discretion)	67.0%	73.2%
Total	100.0%	100.0%
Number of cases	(100)	(425)
gamma = .10		

rejected the 1–2–3 projects and were offered nothing else, a higher proportion of the elderly (64 percent) as compared to the nonelderly (36 percent) listed particular projects they wanted. The desires of the elderly were also more concentrated than the nonelderly: 68 percent of the elderly requested one of five projects whereas only 42 percent of others' demands were similarly concentrated. Moreover, the five projects singled out by the elderly were all small projects with very low turnover. Although there were approximately 2,500 elderly on the waiting list, only 72 vacancies per year occurred in elderly projects.

CONCLUSION

The breakdown of the rules left decisions about applicant priority and assignment open to staff discretion. The staff was split into four groups that had very different orientations towards clients. Traditionalists wanted to preserve and enhance working-class values: they supported intact families whose behavior they considered conventional. Reformers operated on an explicit theory of choice based on a principle of need. Survivalists, the largest group in the department, were most concerned with the preservation and enhancement of their jobs; rather than operating on beliefs, survivalists responded to pressure. Finally, avoiders sought a very limited role in relation to applicants and neither acted on their beliefs nor responded to pressure.

An applicant's chance of securing housing depended on the attitude of the staff member who dealt with her. If a staff member became interested in a case, he could have a big impact on what happened. Some cases would be processed and the applicant offered 1–2–3 projects and nothing else, whereas other applicants would be encouraged to claim exceptions and be assigned to better projects. Given the predominance of traditionalists, survivalists, and avoiders, it would be expected that white and elderly applicants would receive more exceptional assignments than nonwhites and nonelderly. Although whites did get more exceptional assignments for implausible and highly discretionary reasons than nonwhites, the overall outcomes did not favor whites or the elderly: organizational constraints controlled the number of exceptional assignments passed out to favored groups. For example, although most staff had sympathy for the elderly, bureaucratic discretion was limited by the few vacancies that were available in projects the elderly desired.

The inability of rules to control discretion and the existence of bureaucrats with different client orientations suggest that change could be brought about by replacing recalcitrant staff with new people. For example, if the authority wanted to operate strictly on the basis of need, more reformers would have to be recruited. It is important, however, to recognize the limits of such a strategy. Without overall support at the top, reformers were not willing to stay at the BHA. Moreover, reformers, as did other staff members, responded to the conditions in which they were placed. In an overloaded system, reformers could not deal well with client needs and tended to respond to the most active or vocal clients. And, as we will see in the next chapter, reformers as well as other staff members were somewhat subject to the influence of outside third-party sponsors.

CHAPTER FIVE

The Influence of Third-Party Sponsors

Third-party sponsors played key roles in affecting how Tenant Selection Department staff used discretion and thus influenced which applicants were admitted into projects. Although many third-party sponsors intervened between clients and the Boston Housing Authority, three types were the most active: social agencies, politicians, and board members. Social agencies included the Red Cross, little city halls (neighborhood-based offices of the mayor), community organizations, and local welfare offices. Politicians included city councilmen, state representatives and senators, congressmen, and United States senators. These third-party sponsors provided referrals, information, access, and services that influenced the type of client that the authority attracted, the demands made by applicants on the system, and the speed with which applications were processed. They also intervened directly as advocates on behalf of individual applicants or groups of applicants. In this mode, third-party sponsors' ability to aid clients depended on the resources they had to exchange with staff.[1] These exchanges could be either of a personal nature or related directly to the survival of the organization. The next two cases illustrate the difference third party intervention could make in the outcome for an applicant:

1. Mrs. S. was white, forty years old, and had a 14-year-old daughter. She had been in psychiatric treatment for several years because of depression and anxiety related to her

---

[1]For a discussion of the concept of exchange, see Sol Levine and Paul White, "Exchange as a Conceptual Framework for the Study of Interorganizational Relationships," in *A Sociological Reader on Complex Organizations*, Amitai Etzioni, ed., 2nd ed. (New York: Holt, Rinehart and Winston, 1969), pp. 117–132.

problem-ridden marriage. In early 1972 she left Boston with her husband and daughter for North Carolina to try to get a fresh start but in the spring found it necessary to leave her husband and return to Boston where she and her daughter took up residence with Mrs. S.'s mother.

With the breakup of her marriage, Mrs. S. was even more depressed. Her situation was aggravated by having to live with her mother, a chronic psychotic, who was also in treatment. Mrs. S. cried frequently, had trouble sleeping, and had lost considerable weight. Her psychiatrist suggested that Mrs. S. would do much better if she and her daughter lived by themselves. Her neighborhood community health center recommended that she apply to the BHA for housing. Armed with letters from her doctors emphasizing her problems and indicating that the recovery of her emotional and physical health depended on rapid and early placement, Mrs. S. filed an application in July 1972.

By September of 1972, Mrs. S.'s application was approved. When she was offered available vacancies at Columbia Point, however, she refused, indicating that she wanted to live at Orient Heights near her mother. Her refusal of available vacancies declassified her as an emergency, and her case was put back on the waiting list. Mrs. S. then called a board member whom she knew, and with his support her case was reactivated. In January 1973, six months after she had applied, Mrs. S. moved into a unit at Orient Heights.

2. Mrs. F. was a 47-year-old white woman who lived in a BHA project with her five children. She was separated from her husband and on welfare.[2] Mrs. F. suffered from blood clots in her legs and could barely walk at times. Therefore she could rarely get downstairs to watch her children play. Moreover, the crowded conditions in her apartment only added to her problems; she constantly bruised herself trying to squeeze through the one-foot space that separated the twin beds in her room.

When her leg disease was diagnosed in June 1972, Mrs. F.'s social worker recommended that she apply for a transfer to a more spacious first-floor apartment. In July, the BHA transfer committee gave Mrs. F. a number one priority to move into a larger apartment. However, emergency cases were given a zero priority and had precedence over Mrs. F. Given the large number of zero priority cases and new applicants, Mrs. F. was far down the line on the waiting list.

Mrs. F. could have appealed her case, but neither she nor the social worker who was assisting her knew about that right. When the social worker called the BHA to find out what could be done to expedite Mrs. F.'s transfer, she was switched from one department to another. Each department claimed that it had nothing to do with medical transfers. When the social worker finally contacted the Tenant Selection Department staff member with whom she had originally talked, she was told that the person who could really help was not in and would call her back. No one called back. Subsequent calls only evoked the response that there was nothing the authority could do at the moment and that someone would get back to her. A doctor's letter detailing Mrs. F.'s medical history and indicating the perils of her climbing stairs did not produce any change in the status of her case and Mrs. F. still had not been transferred in July 1973, one year after her request had been approved.

In late October, Mrs. F. spotted a first-floor vacancy in her present project and told the BHA of her willingness to transfer there. Although the BHA agreed to the transfer, one week before Mrs. F. was to move, she died. Although many factors were involved in Mrs. F.'s death, her social worker felt that a major one was inadequate housing.

---

[2]This story is drawn from Tom Sheehan, "D Street Death: The Only Transfer," *The Boston Phoenix*, November 20, 1973, pp. A20–21. It is typical of many cases I followed.

REFERRALS

Referral of constituents and clients to the Boston Housing Authority was the most common role played by third-party sponsors. Both social agencies and local and state politicians in Boston acted as service institutions, and those who represented working-class and lower-class population were constantly beseiged by citizens seeking help with housing problems ranging from eviction and code violations to high rents and disputes with neighbors.[3] According to politicians and social agency workers, citizens were referred to the Housing Authority in one of two circumstances: (1) when housing problems were of an emergency nature such as homelessness due to fire, flood, or eviction or (2) when clients were very poor or had an unusually large number of children.[4] In these two situations, clients were often judged "BHA material." Families in less desperate situations were sent to the appropriate agency (e.g., housing code inspection, rent control) or, if the third party specialized in housing, assisted in finding dwelling units in the private market.

According to BHA staff, as clients shifted from working class to lower class, third-party referrals came more from social agencies than from politicians. Social agencies served poorer citizens who had fewer options for decent housing and were more willing to take almost anything offered them. Although some social agencies did refer their clients to private housing, the majority found it easier to deal with the Housing Authority because it was a centralized landlord operating thousands of units. Social

---

[3]Martin Shefter points out that state representatives in Boston spend most of their time responding to their constituents' requests for services in order to get reelected and because they feel it is a useful and praiseworthy function. Martin Shefter, "City Hall and State House: State Legislative Involvement in the Politics of New York and Boston," Diss., Harvard University, 1970, especially pp. 41–49.

[4]Some of the material on the role of politicians and agencies draws on interviews conducted for a Ford Foundation study of city services. The project was organized by Ralph Jones and the interviews carried out by students with state representatives and little city hall staff. For an analysis of the little city hall program see Eric Nordlinger, *Decentralizing the City: A Study of Boston's Little City Halls* (Boston: The Urban Observatory, 1972). One study estimates that the monthly consumption benefit or subsidy for public housing tenants occupying a two-bedroom apartment in Boston is $98, based on a real market rent of $167 minus tenant monthly rent of $69. See Arthur Solomon, *Housing the Urban Poor* (Cambridge: MIT Press, 1974), p. 69.

agencies therefore performed the classic broker role described by Wilensky and Lebeaux as devotion: "putting people in touch with community resources they need but can hardly name let alone locate."[5]

Politicians were the other primary group to make referrals. Their constituents were more likely to be working-class or elderly citizens who had established contacts with city agencies. These constituents were rather sophisticated about how to use available services and sought out politicians not so much for referrals as for direct advocacy. Because their current housing conditions were generally not as severe as those of applicants who came through social agencies, they were apt to be more discriminating about the type of unit they would accept. They turned to politicians when unhappy with the treatment they received from the Housing Authority. As will be seen later, the fact that social agencies and politicians tended to serve different classes of clients had important implications for their interaction with the authority.

INFORMATION

Third-party sponsors not only referred applicants to the authority; they furnished them with information about how the system worked. As was noted in Chapter 3, very few applicants were familiar with the rules and procedures of the department or the housing alternatives available to them at the BHA. Staff members usually exerted little effort to bridge the information gap and often exaggerated or hedged on the chances of obtaining a desirable apartment to avoid angering or disappointing applicants. This problem, however, was not one of simply misleading an applicant: a great deal of uncertainty surrounded available vacancies and the priority of one applicant over another. In response to this situation, applicants often turned to third parties to obtain accurate information. Third parties therefore often called the department simply to check on the status of an applicant's case. One city councillor said:

> You see I have had many people calling my office saying, "I have been number one on a list," and yet I can't find what list they are talking about. They have been evidently given to understand that they have been on the list for so long that the next apartment will be theirs and it isn't true.

---

[5]Harold Wilensky and Charles Lebeaux, *Industrial Society and Social Welfare* (New York: Russell Sage Foundation, 1958), p. 286.

Social agencies and politicians in frequent contact with authority staff were more likely than applicants to be knowledgeable about the current rules and procedures as well as the informal workings of the department. This knowledge could aid clients in obtaining high priority through being classified as an emergency or an exceptional assignment.

The ability to inform clients about the BHA was an important resource to third parties. Detailed knowledge, however, was limited to a few agencies in the inner-city core that specialized in housing—little city halls, private fair housing groups, and neighborhood community organizations. These agencies were up-to-date on BHA rules and procedures, kept in constant contact in regard to vacancies and therefore were in a good position to pass information to their clients, who tended to be the most disadvantaged and had the most difficulty in procuring such information when in contact with the authority. Most other agencies as well as most politicians, however, were poorly informed. One staff member of the BHA felt that there was a tremendous amount of ignorance about the operations of the Housing Authority among welfare departments and politicians because housing was not viewed as a major concern. Moreover, it was difficult for outsiders to keep up with the changes in rules and procedures. Many third-party sponsors therefore relied on personal contacts rather than procedural information to aid their clients.

ACCESS

Adequate information, by itself, was not sufficient to obtain for an applicant a rapid and agreeable placement. Since applications were dealt with on a case-by-case basis with a great deal of discretion available to bureaucrats, it made a great deal of difference whom the applicant had contact with in the department. Third parties could therefore provide access to potentially sympathetic members of the department who might otherwise remain unknown.

In the past, access had been the special province of the politician. In the 1960s, as discussed in Chapter 2, reformers sought to reduce this influence and assign vacancies on an equitable basis. One strategy used by reformers was to place reform-oriented staff in the central office of the Tenant Selection Department. The effect of this action was to open up access to both poorer tenants and their third-party supporters. For example, when a social worker was hired by the authority to handle "problem families," for the first time social agencies had the name of someone sympathetic in the department to whom they could send clients. If the client went in on his or her own without the name of such a person, the client was more likely to be seen by unsympathetic staff and experience long delays or be automatically sent to an undesirable project. A reform staff member was more likely to carry through for this type of client. While there were no secrets in the department about the sympathies of various staff members, they were not well known to all agencies. Little city halls institutionalized their access by having direct contact with certain departmental members. Since workers in social agencies often had short careers,[6] the lack of institutionalized contact worked to the disadvantage of many poor clients, and those social agency workers who had personal contacts appeared to guard them jealously.

SERVICE

As was noted earlier, the Tenant Selection Department operated under overloaded work conditions that resulted in great inefficiency and certain inequities. One approach to solving this problem was to allow other agencies to perform some of the normal duties of the department. For example, at one time applicants were filled out only at the central office or at the projects but reforms during the 1960s made applications more widely available by placing them at city departments, local welfare offices, little city halls, and community organizations. A number of agencies took advantage of these changes in order to speed up the application process for their clients and to aid those who might either hesitate to apply or be easily discouraged. According to social agency workers, this service was particularly valuable to elderly and Puerto Rican families who either lacked mobility or operated under language handicaps. Several agency workers suggested that Puerto Rican families in particular did not feel as "put-out or embarrassed" in explaining such matters as common law marriages to people that they knew. These services, which included pulling together the necessary documents for verification, were provided by a small number of intermediary social agencies. Politicians rarely performed this function because they either lacked the resources or did not see it as part of their role.

[6]Caseworker turnover is documented in Sharon Galm, "Welfare," pp. 32–33, and Handler and Hollingsworth, *The "Deserving Poor,"* pp. 202–203.

A consequence of delegating responsibility to outside agencies was that discretion also passed to them. In the early 1960s, for example, when emergency status was restricted to applicants who were homeless because of fire, flood, or eviction, verification was performed by the Housing Authority. In the middle 1960s, owing to a shortage of staff, the Housing Authority allowed verification of emergency conditions to be done by the Red Cross, the Boston Redevelopment Authority Relocation Division, the Housing Inspection Department, and the courts. Staff members felt that third-party advocates often took advantage of this delegation of responsibility to verify emergency status[7] and often withheld any information that would lower their client's priority.

> Agencies would call and say, "Mrs. Smith is out in the street" and would give a whole spiel. But they would never say that the reason that she was out in the street was because she didn't pay her rent. And they would play the whole thing and bring in a letter showing the person was being evicted. And welfare workers were great ones for doing something quick because it was a problem to them until they had someone housed.

When emergency cases were expanded to include overcrowding, the presence of lead paint, and the existence of code violations, the department allowed social agencies such as welfare offices, little city halls, antipoverty agencies, and hospitals to document these conditions. The number of emergency cases more than doubled, with most of the increase found in the new categories and documented by the social agencies. Burnouts and freezeouts held constant, while evictions, code violations, medical concerns, and overcrowded conditions accounted for the majority of the new emergency cases. Traditionalists sensed that the expansion of categories meant a further lessening of the standards. They saw the new policy as another reformist attempt to place discretion in the hands of outside social agencies bent on increasing the number of undesirable tenants:

---

[7]Michael Lipsky, in his study of code enforcement and protest groups in New York, notes that when protest leaders began to report not only crisis cases but also buildings requiring less attention, they violated the norms for protest group leaders who participate in "crisis" administrative relationships. Lipsky, *Protest in City Politics*, p. 159.

It got out of hand because people were abusing it. People began calling most everything an emergency. It was particularly abused by the agencies who used it to increase the number of people they could get in. Agencies, social workers, hospitals and even individual tenants responded quickly—the word spread fast that you could get in if you were an emergency. People were determining themselves an emergency.

The new policy also became objectionable to some reformers in the department who felt that the expansion of the emergency categories absolved other agencies of their responsibility to deal with poor housing conditions. For example, instead of applicants and agency workers pressuring the Housing Inspection Department and the courts to force landlords to fix up buildings and eliminate such problems as lead paint, cases were being automatically sent to the Housing Authority. The balance swung back again when a new chief of tenant selection took over (the other had left for another job) and set the creation of a rational ordering of priorities as his main task. He designed a program to categorize people in such a way that they would be competing only with people in similar conditions. He felt that such a system would cut down on the pressures in the department. His first concrete action was to revert to the old system of emergency classification with strict controls over documentation.

ADVOCACY

Although social agencies and politicians aided a large number of applicants through referrals, information, access, and direct service, these modest expenditures of influence were often not sufficient to get a person into any project quickly, let alone a specific project. Third parties therefore often assumed the role of advocate and directly intervened on behalf of their clients. Bureaucrats often responded to such cases for the same reasons they responded to aggressive applicants: these cases increased the workload and became "troublesome." However, advocacy by third parties differed from problems caused by aggressive applicants because of the resource exchanges that took place between third parties and staff. The staff provided higher priorities and more desirable assignments to "sponsored" applicants in exchange for a variety of incentives offered by third-party advocates. These included a reduction in the overall work pressure on the bureaucrat; the absorption of strong personal pressures from some applicants; the ability to deal with bureaucrats as status equals or superiors; influence in obtaining jobs, promotions, demotions, and firings for staff members; and the mobilization of political resources that the authority needed in order to survive. As will be explored later, these exchanges varied according to the powers of the third parties, the type of client they represented, their interest in the client, and the merits of the applicant's case.

Social Agencies

The decentralized nature of the system provided no routine channels of contact between the welfare department and the BHA. Most agencies simply referred clients to the authority. However, a small number of welfare workers from the inner city, where housing conditions were the worst, played more active roles. These welfare workers developed their own contacts within the BHA and regularly put pressure on the authority to house their clients. Although the little city halls had more formalized procedures for contact (each had a list of contact people at various city agencies), the most active ones still tended to be in the city core.

Active social agencies concentrated most of their work on documenting the merits of a client's case and convincing the bureaucracy that the applicant should be given a priority or an exception. Pressure to house applicants occurred through a number of channels—letters, phone calls, and personal visits. According to a BHA staff member, each of these approaches was likely to have a different effect on bureaucratic behavior:

> The welfare worker usually calls in on the phone or sends a letter. She rarely comes in because of the time constraints on her. A personal appearance, however, has the largest effect—you don't forget. A phone call you can just forget about until they call again.

Staff members therefore assessed an agency worker's interest in an applicant by the amount of effort that he or she expended. While letters were necessary to document the merits of a case and to legitimize giving an applicant a higher priority than another, they usually did not put any real pressure on the authority. Staff spent a certain amount of time reading, filing, and sometimes answering letters. However, literally thousands of cases on the waiting list had supporting letters from social workers, hospitals, and even politicians telling about the applicant's great need for an apartment. Although the letters were necessary to validate need, they were usually not sufficient to obtain a higher priority. More effective pressure occurred through personal transactions in which third parties and staff members could negotiate exchanges and gauge each other's stake in a case.

The most effective agency workers, described by staff as being "just fantastic for applicants" would call the first thing in the morning after a case was sent in and inquire as to whether anything had occurred. The following scenario, described by a staff member of the Housing Authority, recounts a series of telephone calls between such an agency type and a Tenant Selection Department staff member concerning the transfer of a tenant from one project to another:

> Usually the first call that would come in would say: "My client was beaten up last week and you haven't done anything about it. I think that you have some responsibility." You say, "Well, we are going to meet on it next week," and they say, "Can we call to find out?" and you say, "Sure." They would call and want to know whether it was approved and you say, "Yeah," and they say, "When can they move—next week?" You would say, "No," and you would go that whole route.

Several strategies underlay this agency worker's approach. First, he took the initiative, exerted continual pressure on the authority, and was willing to pursue the case. In this way, the staff member knew that he had a high level of interest in the applicant. Second, he pinned responsibility for following through on a particular staff member with whom he had rapport, even though the department did not formally operate in this manner. In fact, as we discussed earlier, many staff members eschewed such responsibility because of the tensions that it created. Third, he appealed to the merits of his client's case. He therefore operated on the principle that need was a sufficient cause for getting his client's request met and that his counterpart in the agency shared the same view.

If the above strategy proved ineffective, the agency worker adopted an even more active stance by "bugging all the levels." He stayed in touch not only with the intermediate level staff but also with project managers and the departmental chief concerning the status of the case, potential vacancies, and prospects for action. In some situations, when it was known that a certain family was going to be evicted, such an agency worker did all the necessary work in advance by filling out the application forms, obtaining the necessary verification, and informing the department in sufficient time to get the client an apartment when necessary.

The activity of social agencies put constant pressure on the department. This pressure created some antagonism on the part of staff members who resented housing AFDC families and longed for the old days of the working-class tenants. However, most department staff members readily acknowledged that advocacy by agency workers was a tremendous help in getting clients housed. Therefore, an applicant with an active agency worker often had a better chance of being housed than an applicant without such support. One survivalist staff member, when asked about his relationship with social agencies, commented:

> We have no trouble with social agencies. They are trained with some degree of education. They are doing the same thing: meeting people, trying to serve them, compromising. Sometimes they get you to understand the situation of their client, the applicant. They also get the client to understand the situation at the BHA. They can take off some of the pressure of the angry applicant.

Many staff members viewed agency workers as a closer reference group than clients. This identification is explained partly by similarity of tasks. As with the staff itself, the really effective facilitators were those agency workers able to move papers. These workers were respected in the department for their good performance in filling out the necessary forms and obtaining accurate documentation. Upper-level staff had confidence in the detail and reliability of their work. As was stressed earlier, the efforts of these outside groups could save the department staff considerable time.

In addition to task similarities, staff identification with social agency workers is explained by similarity in backgrounds—both were white-collar working class or lower middle class, whereas most applicants were considered lower class. Staff members often felt they could talk more easily with social agency workers than with clients. Moreover, they had dealt with the same agency people over a period of time. In contrast, several different staff members might have seen any one applicant about different transactions, none often enough for anything other than a superficial relationship to develop. Relationships with social agencies were therefore more long-lasting, trusting, and collegial than relationships with applicants; these relationships operated according to rules and within certain norms of interpersonal behavior.

There are lots of people I deal with whose judgment I really trust. They are not going to call me about everybody who walks in their office. If I say I can't do anything they are going to understand, they don't get hysterical. They might even say: "I have to make this phone call but don't break your back," or "Someone really has to help this person," and they really know a lot about them. These are the ones whose judgment you trust. There are other social workers who are new on the job and don't know anything and they just think that the person is desperate and I just say, "Sure, sure, sure," and hang up. In other words you expect an advocate for an applicant to come on in a certain way.

As the preceding interview indicates, staff members could negotiate with workers concerning the relative merits of cases. Moreover, agency workers often played a mediator role, translating the worlds of the client and the department in terms that made them understandable to each, and therefore facilitating compromises. Agency workers often tried, for example, to convince an applicant that he or she must follow the departmental procedures and wait for an apartment. In such cases the agency worker acted as a buffer protecting staff members from the angry applicant and holding the interaction within the norms of pleasantry. On the other hand, agency workers would constantly pressure staff members about the particular circumstances of a case about which they felt strongly. Although social agencies provided clients with information and documentation to help place them in specific projects, most of the intervention of the active agency workers was aimed at getting their clients into public housing faster than the clients would be able to without help. One might assume that agency workers would consider locational placement an integral part of their professional responsibility. Social workers, for example, are normally expected to know their clients in depth and to deal with their interrelated problems on a comprehensive social service basis. In public agencies, however, social workers often dealt separately with facets of a person's life. This behavior is partly explained by the conditions under which agency workers, and particularly social case workers, operated: large caseloads precluded detailed knowledge of clients and emergency housing situations necessitated the rapid placement of a client into any available unit.[8] Because the agency worker did not usually try to get

---

[8]Caseworkers with a large number of clients do not have time to perform routine income maintenance and service functions properly. See Sharon Galm, "Welfare," pp. 26–34.

his client into the best housing, his advocacy was not too threatening to traditionalist staff members. Moreover, for many social workers, established contacts and general knowledge about the Boston Housing Authority operations were limited because of inadequate training and the short time that most social workers remained on the job. Finally, the placement of a client into a prime project was an enterprise that often took more effort and, as will be discussed, necessitated more influence than was generally available even to the active social agency worker.

Social agencies, while often interceding to help individual clients, also intervened on behalf of classes or groups of clients. For example, when a new elderly project opened, social agencies were often concerned about the policies that would determine who had priority for admission. They usually acted on behalf of a group of applicants—urban renewal dislocatees, new groups within the community such as the Spanish-speaking, or applicants who had been on the waiting list for long periods of time. This type of activity often involved conflicts between agencies that served different clientele. The reformers within the department were particularly attuned to these types of pressure because they often anticipated crises. Also, reformers viewed these actions by agencies as closely allied with the purposes of a public agency—to establish policies so that each client would be treated fairly according to an explicit objective policy.

Politicians

Advocacy by politicians generally occurred on behalf of a clientele different from that served by social agencies, usually white working class or elderly persons rather than AFDC families. According to an upper-level BHA official:

> There was an aura of politics around the BHA. Applicants thought that you needed to know someone in order to get into a project. In the past, political leverage was needed, but this has decreased in each successive administration. It was probably at its height during the first years. But as the demand for public housing by the working class and middle class declined, the political importance of it did also.

In spite of this, many working-class and elderly families still sought political assistance to get into prime family projects or small elderly projects. Those elderly citizens who had worked for the city seemed to feel they had a right to public housing and that it was owed to them as a reward for their service. According to one staff member:

> As opposed to low-income blacks and Puerto Ricans who generally acted as if they were at the mercy of the system and rarely tried to manipulate it, low-income whites think that they know how to deal with the political system. Instead of coming "hat in hand," a white woman comes and knows her sister-in-law got in through politics, and she comes the same route.[9]

The political route, however, was no longer smooth. An applicant would often try to invoke the name of a politician, as if the mere mention of it would get immediate and desired placement. However, that was usually sufficient only if the applicant would have qualified anyway, or if the politician had taken other steps to insure success. Another common approach was for the applicant to come into the Housing Authority with a note from a politician stating that he or she hoped that the authority would "take a particular interest" in that case. Although these letters were very common, staff members did not tend to pay particular attention to them; for the most part they subjected such sponsored cases to the normal processing. There were literally hundreds of cases on the waiting list with such notes attached to them.

Letters were ineffective because they involved no direct exchange between the bureaucrat and the politician. If the applicant did get in, the staff member had difficulty in obtaining any political credit for the success. Moreover, individual staff members could not gauge the interest of the politician by the presence of a letter. Therefore, staff viewed letters as rather low-level investments. On the other hand, if the applicant was successful, the politician would get credit even if he or she did not deserve it.

Another low level tactic employed by politicians was to make an

---

[9]Gideon Sjoberg *et al.* point out that the lower-class person lacks knowledge of the rules of the game. Lower-class people frequently stand in awe of bureaucratic regulations. On the other hand, middle-class people learn how to manipulate bureaucratic rules to their advantage and even to acquire special treatment by working through the "private" or "backstage" (as opposed to the "public") sector of the bureaucracy. Gideon Sjoberg, Richard Brymenr, and Buford Farris, "Bureaucracy and the Lower Class," *Sociology and Social Research*, 49 (1966), 325–337.

appointment for a constituent with the chief of tenant selection, a staff member who had definite decision-making power. Although this strategy produced beneficial effects for some applicants, staff members felt it was often a ploy "to get the constituent off the politician's back." In a similar approach, the politician might call the chief of tenant selection and ask about the procedures and their bearing on his constituent's case. The chief typically responded that the politician already knew the answer because, in fact, he had called up about a similar case earlier in the week. The chief sensed that the politician was only calling because the constituent who was in his office would not be satisfied with just a letter or an appointment with the chief (who may have already turned down the case). In this situation a type of ritualized game occurred between the politician and the bureaucrat, usually unbeknownst to the applicant.[10] The politician rarely learned anything that he did not already know and the call had little bearing on the outcome of the case. Still, in the context of this pretense, the politician was able to demonstrate to his constituent that he had connections among high-level staff members and that he had tried to do something. The blame was therefore transferred to the bureaucracy for not responding to the case. The bureaucracy in turn fell back on the rules and procedures as the rationale for not taking the actions that the client desired.

If a politician was authentically interested in aiding an applicant he made his intentions known by creating a strong argument on behalf of his client and stating it directly to a staff member with whom he had an established relationship. The staff member might then respond by taking

---

[10]For a discussion of the ritual drama of mutual pretense in hospitals, see Barney Glaser and Anselm Strauss, *Awareness of Dying* (Chicago: Aldine, 1965), pp. 64–78. Charles Ascher, formerly the executive director of the New York Housing Authority, has similarly noted: "The role of the political personality may not be to obtain a dwelling for his constituents. He has fulfilled his political role by making a plea to the administrator. If the administrator fails to exercise discretion in favor of the constituent, it may be because the constituent presents a less meritorious case than other applicants or because the administrator assesses the political weight of the intervenors unfavorably—or has already received too many intercessions from the same politician. The political personality can always blame that 'damned bureaucrat' and absolve himself before his constituent." Charles Ascher, *The Administration of Publicly-Aided Housing* (Brussels: International Institute of Administrative Sciences) p. 14.

personal responsibility for the case. Departmental staff acceded to this type of pressure for some of the same reasons they yielded to pressure from social agencies: work substitution, shared goals, and the reduction of unpleasant client pressures. However, because the clients generally differed from those represented by social agencies, the importance of these factors varied and had different consequences. Moreover, politicians had other resources to influence staff behavior: status, power over jobs, and resources that affected organizational survival.

Politicians were less likely than agency workers to spend the time necessary to prepare a constituent's application and file. The constituency that they represented was usually better educated, more mobile, and able to pursue those aspects of their own cases. Moreover, most local politicians did not have the staff to undertake this function and most national politicians did not see it as their role. The exchange value of this function for most politicians was therefore rather low.

Political advocacy usually occurred for working-class white families or the elderly. These applicants conformed to what traditionalists considered desirable and worthy applicants. They also were the type of constituent that politicians were most likely to support actively: political campaign contributors, relatives, or friends—in short, they were considered "good solid citizens."[11] Thus, there was a commonality of interest concerning the appropriate target populations that led staff traditionalists to do the politicians' bidding—staff members who still wished to preserve the remaining vestiges of a once-attractive program and politicians seeking rewards to pass out to their loyal constituents.

Politicians could also defuse the temper of angry applicants by confirming that certain procedures had to be followed. Many applicants who invoked the name of a politician, for example, became hostile when told they had to obtain documentation in order to be designated an exceptional assignment or that openings existed only in certain developments. According to one staff member:

> People would flip out and give instances of friends or relatives who got in because of certain politicians. Their sister-in-law got in without a doctor's letter—why do they have to go through that inconvenience?

---

[11]Because voters help advance politicians' careers, they feel they have a right to expect that politicians will reciprocate when they need help. See Martin Shefter, "City Hall and State House," p. 47.

A politician, who might be viewed as a more reliable source of authority than the staff member, could confirm that it was indeed necessary to go through the procedures. Moreover, as one staff member suggested, politicians often played the same mediator role as social agencies:

> If I said that the only place that I could send her was Columbia Point and she refused it, the politician would say she never told him that. He would call back and say, "She is now willing to take Columbia Point." He never argued about the system but usually wanted to know why we hadn't housed an applicant. In some cases we would be able to document that we had offered applicants a number of choices and they had refused them, and the politician wasn't aware of it and he would go back and say, "Now look, if you really want housing they have housing here for you."

In addition to workload substitutes, shared values, and mediation, politicians had other sources of influence relatively unavailable to a social agency. For example, politicians had sometimes been influential in obtaining jobs for staff members with the expectation that something would be provided in return. Although this debt might be paid by campaign contributions, it could be directly discharged by aiding sponsored applicants in getting prime assignments. An added incentive for heeding political advocacy was the persistent view among many staff that continued survival at the Housing Authority depended partly on the action of politicians who could be influential in promotions, demotions, firings, or even job assignments.[12] When departmental problems occurred for those staff members who had obtained their jobs through political influence, they sometimes threatened to seek the protection of their original sponsor. However, there was a high probability that their original sponsor was no longer in office or that his influence had declined in the authority. In order to protect oneself against this occurrence, the staff member had an incentive to broaden his support by acceding to the requests of a number of politicians. At this point, some staff took on the politicians as their reference group. This type of activity, however, placed them in a double bind. If a staff member aided one politician and not other, he was subject to the negative efforts of the unaided ones who might try to get him transferred or fired. However, if he became a propolitical advocate, he

[12]Martin Shefter also found that city employees, even though protected by the civil service, believed that politicians could advance their careers. See Martin Shefter, "City Hall and State House," p. 50.

was subject to the resentment of those staff members who disliked political interference. For all of the talk about political influence in the department, politicians rarely came to the aid of a middle-level or lower-level
staff member. However, many middle-aged traditionalists or survivalists
had developed skills that were not easily transferable and had fears based
on earlier experiences of losing their jobs. They continued to believe in
political protection, even though it was somewhat of a myth. In city
council hearings politicians had made it difficult for reformers by giving
them adverse publicity; and many employees, sensing the dangers in the
shifts of politics, sought to secure their jobs by joining the union.

Political reference groups also served another purpose for some employees. Most staff had low-level jobs that paid very little. In addition,
staff were susceptible to abuse about which they could do little or nothing. In some occupations, professional norms protect workers by imbuing
them with a sense of mission and status.[13] Most departmental employees,
however, had had no professional training, and any sense of mission had
been negated by the problems of public housing. At the same time,
accordance of a certain status was no longer available from clients or even
from fellow staff members. One way that some staff held on to the power
and status that remained available was through exchanges with politicians.

Although survivalists and traditionalists had a number of incentives
to do a politician's bidding, the channels for politicians began to dry up.
One state representative, for example, commented that although he received many requests for help in getting BHA housing, he was unable to
fulfill most of them. He blamed this situation on the basic shortage of
units and "an unresponsive attitude on the part of recent BHA management."[14] During this period, the new board majority had split from the
mayor and adopted its own independent stance. One result was a lessening of political patronage appointees. For example, the chief of tenant
selection was able to hire several of his own staff, and personnel were

[13] A comprehensive discussion of the implications of professionalism is found in
Wilbert Moore, *The Professions: Roles and Rules* (New York: Russell Sage
Foundation, 1970).

[14] Martin Shefter found that city departmental officials responded to state representatives out of a sense of propriety: a legislator's function was to seek redress
for his constituent's grievance. Martin Shefter, "City Hall and State House," p.
49. In contrast, many BHA reformers characterized such requests as illegitimate
and referred to them as pressure.

being promoted through a non–civil service merit system. The new staff, primarily clerical workers, were generally angered by political intervention.

Even traditionalists and survivalists limited the extent of their involvement for politically sponsored cases. Staff members were usually unwilling to push cases that did not meet the basic legal requirements of the program since HUD rather carefully scrutinized applicant income limits and reported any violations to the administrator. If a politician wanted to get an overincome applicant in, he was therefore likely to approach the administrator or a board member. In addition, the degree of freedom for political advocacy was related to the views of the chief of the department, who not only set policy but also had the power to review all cases. Strong reformer chiefs often turned down a number of cases presented by middle-level staff which they felt were motivated solely by political considerations and did not deserve any particular priority. When the department was run by such a chief, however, the politicians relied even more heavily on mid-level staff or board members, thereby increasing the pressure.

Reformers in upper-level positions were also susceptible to political influence. Although these staff members were generally not as open to personal exchanges with politicians as traditionalists or survivalists, they sometimes did favors for those politicians willing to help the BHA. As was described earlier, the Housing Authority was in a serious financial plight; it needed "friends in high places" just to survive and therefore depended on politicians for a number of resources. First, the authority ran a large state housing program which relied on the state government to provide subsidies. Since the state program was not so deeply subsidized as the federal program, housing authorities lobbied for bills to increase the state payment of the debt. One staff member commented that

> state representatives who call to get people in have to be paid attention to—housing needs allies, and when there is key legislation before the House, it is important that these people be listened to and taken care of. Their influence pertains to the state program, but also they use their influence to get applicants into federally sponsored projects.

Second, the Housing Authority was seeking additional subsidies from the federal government to remain solvent and repair projects. Over and above the normal payments for the debt service, the federal government had begun to pay some of the operating subsidies. Under the Brooke Amendment, special grants were available to reduce rents to 25 percent of tenants' income.[15] In addition, there were special modernization grants to upgrade the management and physical aspects of projects. Both of these programs depended on annual appropriations from the federal government and therefore on the support of congressmen, senators, the executive branch, and HUD. Third, the Housing Authority depended on the city to provide a number of services such as garbage collection and police protection. As the projects deteriorated and the clientele shifted, the authority relied more and more on police to keep the peace, reduce vandalism, and protect residents. Since the authority itself had few resources to hire private security guards, it was constantly attempting to increase special city policy detachments. Fourth, the authority needed political support to build new housing projects. Even though much of this housing was elderly rather than family housing, neighborhood groups often opposed it. Their opposition was related to the intrusion of large, modern buildings into traditional neighborhoods and fear about people from outside the neighborhood, particularly blacks, coming into white areas. As a result, the Housing Authority relied on city councillors and state representatives close to neighborhood groups to attend meetings and speak in support of building the new developments.

Although the authority had many potential resources to exchange for political support (contracts, jobs, legal fees), reformers recognized that assignment to projects was still an important bargaining tool. Questions remained, however, concerning to what extent, to whom, and under what conditions favors would be granted. One chief of the department, a reformer, stated that politics "has an undue effect when it exhibits itself above and beyond other considerations." In other words, politics should be allowed to have an effect only if the applicant is both qualified in terms of the requirements of the program and "needy." Politics should not prevail to the point, as in the past, when overincome people were accepted or low-priority applicants were assigned to prime projects. In addition, he argued that politics "should affect decisions only when doing a favor for a politician has some immediate beneficial impact on the agency as a

[15]For a discussion of the Brooke amendment, see Mary Nenno, "Housing and Urban Development Act of 1969," *Journal of Housing*, 27 (1970), 14–17; Mary Nenno, "Housing and Urban Development Legislation of 1970," *Journal of Housing*, 28 (1971), 17–18; and George Genung, Jr., "Where Have We Come with the Brooke Amendment?" *Journal of Housing*, 27 (1970), 232–235.

whole and is not for one's personal gain." In the past, political favors had involved whole blocks of apartments in new developments. The reformer felt, however, that it would be dangerous, and no longer a favor, "if a politician were given a block of apartments, that might leak into the papers and be too flagrant. Favoritism can operate only when it is behind the scenes and doesn't get out."

The question of *whom* to give favors to was also a difficult problem.[16] One staff member suggested that favors be granted to elective officials who weighed the relative importance of bills to the Housing Authority. However, to suggest that the criterion was the voting behavior of individual politicians is an oversimplification. The criterion was not only the way a politician voted, but how he used his influence to affect how others voted. In other words, the authority had to weigh the relative importance of politicians. Rather than granting large favors to a variety of politicians, the authority would provide small favors to those who were powerful. However, another high-level staff member complained:

> One of the problems about politics is that the board was not open about it. There was never a clear policy or strategy of which ones should be cultivated and which ones shouldn't. However, to assist one politician and not another is the worst possible kind of situation. Word gets around quickly that you helped one person and not the other. The board majority should have provided leadership and some policy.

Thus, although high-level reform staff members acknowledged that politics necessarily played a role, they were often unclear as to how to respond. One approach was to resist political favoritism in the department itself and instead to let it operate directly through members of the board.

Board Members and the Administrator

When the new tenant-oriented majority gained power on the board in 1969 they pledged that they would not interfere with tenant selection and assignment. Staff members felt that several board members, includ-

---

[16]See quotation from Charles Ascher in note 10 of this chapter. Charles Ascher, *The Administration of Publicly-Aided Housing,* p. 14.

ing two of the three recent appointees, had lists of people they wanted to get in. But the reform-oriented tenant selection chief sensed that

> the board is not as vigorous in terms of political support as it used to be. They still pursue some patronage but it is minimal and generally conscientious. They are not simply doing someone a favor but because they feel the applicant really needs it. Usually when a board member intercedes for someone, however, it is a personal friend or pressure has been brought on him by politicians.

During the course of their tenure, however, the new majority did become involved in advocacy for applicants, although still at a much reduced level relative to the old board.

The board and the administrator were the most successful third-party sponsors in terms of the proportion of their requests met by the staff. Their success depended primarily on the power they wielded over employees: board members could directly influence transfers and promotions and, for upper-level or new employees not protected by union status, could also potentially affect firings. Although staff were often unhappy about the pressure from the board members and the administrator, they generally acquiesced to it. For example, the chief of tenant selection said:

> There is a certain amount of politics you must play; there is no question about it. But when anybody asks me to deviate from my regular procedures I always object and others do too. But there is always someone who is your boss and then he says, "Look, I understand this all right, but I want it done."

These directives from board members and the administrator were known among staff members as "mandates."[17] A staff member acknowledged that when a board member or the administrator sent up a secretary with

---

[17]John Mollenkopf points out that bargaining involves the discovery of a mutually satisfactory rate of exchange among various goods, whereas coercion or struggle involves applying force to compel a behavior change. See John Mollenkopf, "Community Organization and City Politics," Diss., Harvard University, 1973. Mandates appear to be coercive and are explained not so much by bargaining between people in relatively homogeneous relations but by the rules and position of the social system. Thus the political economy analysis seems more explanatory than exchange theory. See Mayer Zald, *Organizational Change: The Political Economy of the YMCA*. (Chicago: University of Chicago Press, 1970).

the mandate to make sure an applicant was housed, that person would be housed automatically.

CONCLUSION

Applicants' chances for good assignments depended not only on their own behavior and contact with staff but also on the actions of third-party sponsors interested in helping them obtain public housing. Social workers and politicians, for example, often provided their clients and constituents with information, access, and services that influenced the demands made upon the Tenant Selection Department and the speed with which cases were processed. These third party-sponsors also intervened directly as advocates on behalf of individual applicants or groups of applicants. In this mode, third-party influence on bureaucratic behavior depended on resources generally unavailable to individual applicants. Social workers, for example, relied on their ability to reduce the overall work pressure, absorb personal pressure from applicants, and deal with bureaucrats as status equals. Since they usually represented lower-status clients interested in any available project, social workers made relatively low demands on staff. Politicians, on the other hand, relied more on their ability to affect promotions, demotions, and firings. Although their ability to influence job mobility began to wane, politicians also affected overall resource mobilization and were considered by many staff as superiors. Moreover, because politicians usually represented desirable clients interested in the better projects, traditionalists and survivalists were often willing to help them. Finally, the most powerful third-party sponsors were board members and the administrator. Their interactions with staff were characterized by coercion rather than exchange because they could directly affect job mobility. Although politicians were much less active than social agency staff, they tended to use their influence to help constituents get into the better projects.

Boston Housing Authority Archives

Mary Ellen McCormick project, early 1940s.

Boston Housing Authority Archives

Mary Ellen McCormick project, one of the best maintained developments with a low turnover rate, had changed very little in outward appearance after 40 years of occupancy, 1980.

Columbia Point project under construction, 1954.

By the 1980s much of the Columbia Point project had been boarded up, leaving only this section still occupied by tenants.

Charlestown Public Housing construction site, 1940.

Charlestown project and adjoining neighborhood before occupancy, 1940.

Boston Globe Photo

Charlestown project illustrating dilapidated conditions and racial problems at the time the court appointed a special master, 1976.

Boston Globe Photo

Antipoverty workers helping revitalize the tenant-managed Bromley-Heath project, 1979.

Goody, Clancy and Associates, Inc.

West Broadway project before modernization, early 1980s.

Cymie Payne

West Broadway project, modernized under the Court receivership, 1986.

CHAPTER SIX

Project-Level Discretion

Rule implementation encountered difficulties at the project level as well as at the central office. According to the procedures, project managers were required to accept all applicants sent to them by the Tenant Selection Department. However, unlike central office staff, managers were in a position that called for sustained interaction with the same tenants, and therefore they resisted central office policies that negated their power personally to select applicants whom they considered "good" tenants.

Although status and tenant relations were primary forces motivating managers' desire for control, situational constraints (such as project turnover rates) affected the amount of discretion available to individual managers. Moreover, a manager's orientation toward clients affected which applicants he viewed as desirable and undesirable. Traditionalist managers tended to favor working-class tenants whose behavior they considered conventional. Although reform managers believed in housing those applicants with the greatest need, they were faced with a dilemma: to maximize the benefits of current tenants by restricting the number and type of new tenants, or to maximize the benefits of the needy by accepting all applicants sent from the central office waiting list.

MANAGERIAL PRACTICES FOR CONTROLLING ADMISSIONS AT THE PROJECTS

Background of Managers and Nature of the Job

In 1970, thirteen project managers had responsibility for the 36 BHA projects. According to a study, the composite manager was white, male,

52 years of age, and of Irish descent.[1] He managed three projects with a total of approximately 1,200 families and 4,200 people. He was assisted by 42 employees including an assistant manager, cashier, four clerical workers, and 36 part-time and full-time maintenance workers. He was a long-time BHA employee and had advanced from cashier to assistant manager to manager. Several managers had been with the BHA over 30 years; none was a recent employee.

Until the 1960s managers had wide discretion in both selection and assignment of tenants.[2] According to one manager:

> In the early days we were very selective. The income levels were low, people were not earning very much money, and you could really pick the best families. If we didn't like a family we could refuse them and send them back to the central office. We would get a record from the board of probation and talk with the applicant. Usually if the family was troublesome they had a record. And, of course, families and mothers with illegitimate children were considered bad in those days. They were unacceptable and we limited them.

By the middle 1960s, however, central office reformers had curtailed formal applicant screening. Since applicants could no longer be excluded on such criteria as having illegitimate children or having minor criminal records, a large number of formerly unacceptable applicants became eligible for public housing.

Managers opposed the procedural changes that would send them random assignees from the waiting list because low-status tenants threatened their job concept, their own status, their relations with current tenants, and their political importance. In 1970, managers were formally responsible for collecting rents, supervising maintenance, and transferring and evicting tenants. Informally, managers acted as father confessors, arbiters of family fights, and focal points for complaints. The nature of the tenant composition was clearly the most important determinant of the difficulty of their job; therefore, managers wanted tenants who paid rent on time, got along with neighbors, and took care of the physical

---

[1]Hipshman, *Public Housing*, pp. 21–24. For a national survey of public housing managers, see Chester Hartman and Margaret Levi, "Public Housing Managers: An Appraisal," *Journal of the American Institute of Planners*, 39 (1973), 125–137.

[2]For a lively account of the experience of a manager of an early model tenement, see Abraham Goldfeld, *The Diary of a Housing Manager* (Chicago: National Association of Housing Officials, 1938).

premises. Moreover, given their class backgrounds and their lack of training in interpersonal relationships, managers best understood the lives of tenants who were like themselves: white working-class or lower-middle-class families whose behavior they considered conventional. Managers wanted to keep out tenants who might cause them problems at all costs.

Managers felt that the recently employed reformers did not understand the daily problems of running a project. In contrast to the reformers' concern over equity, managers worried that the admission of lower-class clients would create conflict with existing working-class tenants, require additional services that were generally unavailable, and put a drain on scarce maintenance resources. Managers also desired "good" clients as a reflection of their own status; they sensed that as projects shifted from working class to lower class, their own community standing dropped. In addition, lower-status clients threatened to diminish a manager's political worth. According to a central office staff member, managers had operated through their own political networks:

> Managers themselves have been very much ingrained in the political system and have their own political ties; and a politician might, because of his inroads with managers, know about a vacancy becoming available at a project before Tenant Selection staff even knew.

With a different clientele, politicians would not be as interested in apartments for their constituents. Lacking formal powers, managers created three informal mechanisms to circumvent central office procedures and insure desirable tenants: concealment of information, expansion of choices, and substitution of tenants.

Project-Level Control Mechanisms

Concealment of Information. In 1970, managers were required to inform the central office when a tenant moved out and again after the maintenance crew had renovated the apartment and it was ready for occupancy. In theory, the staff of the Tenant Selection Department could then send an appropriate family from the waiting list to view the apartment and, if they liked it, to sign a lease. Managers subverted these procedures by concealing vacancy information. According to central office staff, managers only periodically reported vacancies, never doing it consistently. Tenant Selection Department staff even felt that managers' semi-annual reports were suspect. One staff member said, "All they would do was take what they had the last time and add or subtract a few vacancies."

Managers claimed that the vacancy reporting problems were not caused by their intentional withholding of information but by the uncertainty connected with move-outs and apartment rehabilitation. They pointed out, for example, that a large number of tenants vacated their apartments without informing the manager to avoid paying back rent. One central office reformer, investigating the vacancy problem, agreed:

> We tried to look around and see what ways we could update and make the place a little more efficient. The first thing we realized after not being there too long was that information was so poor. We didn't really know how many vacancies we had. We knew that there were more than a thousand, but we didn't know how many. One project was so bad that we went over there and we took the rent cards and found that some of the back rents were in arrears four and five hundred dollars. We asked the manager, "How do you know that they are still there?" and he didn't know. So we took a master key and went door by door and found that there were people who had moved out, had never been reported, and there was no rent card on them.

Even when they knew of vacancies, managers reported that they could not accurately predict when apartments would be ready for occupancy because rehabilitation depended on obtaining maintenance personnel, supplies, and equipment, often in short supply. Moreover, during the period between move-out and rehabilitation, apartments were sometimes vandalized and therefore in need of even more repairs. If they were not quickly occupied after rehabilitation, apartments could be vandalized again.

In projects where unreported move-outs and rehabilitation problems were minimal, managers also failed to report vacancy information. Central office staff alleged that in such situations managers concealed vacancy information to avoid accepting random case assignees from the waiting list.

Expansion of Choices. Managers acquired discretion over assignments by accumulating cases on hand, commonly referred to as *pool cases.* Even though case files were technically supposed to be marked for available units, Tenant Selection Department staff sent out excess cases to projects. Central office bureaucrats supported this practice because they preferred to transfer applicant pressure to managers rather than bear it themselves. One tenant selection staff member felt that this action actually won her the applicants' gratitude (even if it was short-lived):

> Sending pool cases, yeah, why not? Someone calls and says, I want East Boston. You had a two-bedroom unit, you didn't know when it was going to be ready, but you plucked the vacate notice on the file and shipped it out. And there you have satisfied the applicant or caller. You say, "I just sent your case," and the applicant says, "Oh, aren't you a wonderful person."

Although the project-level accumulation of files made managers the object of considerable applicant abuse, staff members felt that the resulting discretion provided full compensation:

> It gave the managers a beautiful opportunity to shuffle. If they got pressure from someone to go ahead and house a person, they could ignore the dates of application—ignore anything. They were given free responsibility. Once a case got to them, they could shuffle about and choose their own tenants. Nobody knew the difference.

As time went on, pool cases became increasingly frustrating to those central office staff who believed applicants should be housed on the basis of need and first come, first serve. One annoyed staff member described typical interactions with managers as follows:

> I would call up a manager and say, "Hey, I understand that you have a vacant apartment," and he would say, "Oh, no, we filled it with a case on hand."
> Or, if a manager moved someone from one unit into another unit, Tenant Selection was always supposed to be notified if there was a vacancy. There was a great discrepancy in the whole vacancy scene. We thought we had an apartment vacant and would call up for it to find that the manager would say, "I just moved such and such a family into it." Well, where did he get the family? From his file drawer of pool cases. Who knows about the family except for him?

Managers especially resorted to pool cases in order to avoid accepting emergency cases, which had a high concentration of unscreened welfare and minority persons.

According to one reformer, the most disturbing aspect of the pool case system was the injustice suffered by unhoused assignees whose files accumulated at the projects:

> If anyone said that they wanted to go to a certain development, the case was just automatically sent there whether or not a unit was available. So at many developments cases were stacked from floor to ceiling. I came across one case that had lain at a project for three years. If it hadn't been called back to Tenant Selection, it would have lain there for the next nine years.

Substitution. The primary purpose of transferring a tenant from one apartment to another was adjustment of a family's housing changes in location of employment, physical health, transportation needs, child care, and family size. In the 1960s, managers had complete discretion in granting transfers. Central office staff felt that managers used their power in the interests of favoritism and patronage rather than basing their decisions on need; good tenants were rewarded by transfers to desirable apartments and tenants in disfavor were punished by being forced to remain in their present units. In addition, as a central office staff member pointed out, managers also transfered tenants to avoid housing new assignees:

> We realized that we had all those vacancies. We would send the painters in and paint the place, get it ready for occupancy. But the manager would transfer a family from another apartment into the freshly painted and fixed-up unit. So when the assignee came from Tenant Selection, the old apartment was, of course, a dump, and they would refuse it. So we had a hell of a time trying to lease new housing.

Centralization and the Reduction of Managerial Discretion. In early 1970, the new administrator of the BHA hired several new reform-oriented staff members and charged them with evaluating current practices. The evaluation team, composed of two city planners, an ex-priest, and two law school students, quickly discovered that critical vacancy and arrears problems were combining with decreasing rents and rising maintenance costs to create severe financial difficulties. In addition, the team received complaints from applicants, some staff members, and the third parties about the insensitive and unfair treatment reported by applicants and assignees. The reformers concluded that the problems of inefficiency and inequity emanated largely from a decentralized organization composed of staff responsive to the wrong values. The team singled out the project managers, whom they suspected of running independent fiefdoms, for special attention.

With the backing of the administrator, the reformers began a crusade to change managers' attitudes and to shake up the old power structure. Their tactics included T-groups, the recruitment of new managers, and the transfer of managers from one project to another. The movement of some managers to less desirable projects (referred to by staff members as musical managers) was carried out with the intent of forcing the worst managers to resign.[3] These strategies, however, proved ineffective. One manager quit because of ill health, but no managers resigned and most continued to carry out their old practices; only two of the thirteen managers appeared sympathetic to the new equity principles. According to one evaluation team member, the reformers abandoned their attempts to change managers' attitudes and reluctantly attempted to strip away their powers:

> If the manager gets enough assignees he can select the ones he wants. In some respects it is to his advantage to have the cases out there. It makes you really haggle over centralization because with a really good manager you want to trust his judgment. He would be able to deal with these people—put them together in ways that could work. But the managers are such a liability now, we just can't risk it. I change my mind every day.

Another reformer was more emphatic:

> We became aware that the decentralized system had broken down any kind of responsibility. It was just a kind of dying organization that had to be brought into a very tight organization. There was very little hope of getting eleven new managers and making them all efficient. What was needed was a tight central administration that could control things. Caught up as the authority is with tenure and union, you could not fire managers and therefore you weren't going to have fresh vacancies for a while.

---

[3]See description of MacDonnell, "Process of Change," p. 83.

The reformers decided to eliminate some managerial functions and to centralize others, with the goal of reducing managerial discretion.[4]

To improve vacancy reporting, the reformers devised a new system of written records which would require project managers to send an updated weekly report to the central office indicating the condition of each vacant apartment. Through the new systems, reformers in the Tenant Selection Department hoped to send an applicant to a specific available unit with some certainty that the apartment would be leased to the assignee if it suited him or her. As a complement to the reporting system, the reformers began to centralize rent collections and to computerize the data accounting system so that staff could discuss rent arrears with tenants before back payments became so large that clients resorted to clandestine move-outs. Reformers also sought to make apartment rehabilitation more efficient by centralizing maintenance and sending special crews to projects with high vacancy rates.

Because of their belief in assignment based on need and date of application, reformers had a strong impetus to eliminate pool cases. In 1971, supported by HUD officials who found that the pool case system violated the assignment plan, the Tenant Selection Department recalled applicant case files from project offices. As a result, central office desks became piled with folders, and the Tenant Selection Department staff began the task of sorting through the assignees to determine which ones still wanted housing.

The evaluation team also recommended that a central committee make the decision about transfers. BHA staff and tenants appointed by the Tenants Policy Committee were equally represented.[5] Transfer requests were forwarded from the projects to the Transfer Committee, where explicit criteria governed decisions. Once approved, transferees were given a priority number indicating the order in which they would be

---

[4]Michael Scholnick notes that in 1969 the administrator made three minor changes in the weekly routine of project managers: the filling out of report sheets on their activities and problems, holding staff meetings every week, and observing maintenance men as they checked in each morning. Scholnick commented that managers did not like these changes. See Michael Scholnick, "Organizational Change at the Boston Housing Authority," unpublished master's thesis, Harvard Graduate School of Design, 1970, pp. 22–23.

[5]Boston Housing Authority, "Tenant Transfer Review Policy and Procedure," (n.p., mimeographed, n.d.).

placed in units relative to assignees from the waiting list. For example, if a transferee had a score of two, he or she was in line for an apartment after two new applicants had been assigned to available units. Since case folders were under control of the Tenant Selection Department staff, managers could no longer substitute transferees to avoid new cases.

Managerial Resistance to Reform. Within a year, the reformers had tightened up vacancy reporting, eliminated pool cases, and shifted transfers to the central office. According to a tenant selection staff member, the loss of discretion was a major setback for managers:

> Up until fairly recently the managers have had tremendous power in determining who will move within their development, either from the outside or within its own bounds. This is all being taken away from them. And it's not easy for them to accept.

Managers demonstrated their displeasure by actively resisting the reforms. Although written vacancy reports had become mandatory, managers still did not cooperate in filling them out. As a result, the reformers required the managers to telephone the Tenant Selection Department daily and report the condition of vacant units. When managers did not call, tenant selection staff resorted to phoning projects, especially when emergency housing was needed. These efforts were enormously time-consuming and inefficient. The reformers therefore switched to a strategy involving area supervisors, who had been hired to oversee the operations of several projects and to provide a closer link between the projects and the central administration. According to a proponent of that strategy, area supervisors were expected to be more responsive than managers:

> What we tried to do was to have the area supervisors responsible for vacancy reporting. They would call in a couple of times a week to let us know what was available. Because the area supervisors were usually concerned about filling the vacancies and since they didn't have to live with the people, they weren't as particular as some of the managers about seeing the case. The area supervisors were vying with each other to show the greatest progress in their area.

The reformer glumly admitted, however, that the supervisors were often unsuccessful in obtaining the vacancy information:

> A manager would still say, "No, I don't have anything." You can get a
> supervisor saying, "I have five vacancies in South Boston," and get
> the manager saying, "Those five vacancies are already taken."

Finally, when maintenance had been separated from project management, the reformers ordered the maintenance department to inform Tenant Selection Department staff as well as managers when an apartment
was ready for occupancy. The unit's description was then posted on a
large board in the Tenant Selection Department so that all staff members
had access to it.

Managers found it increasingly necessary to turn to non-reform central office staff and politicians to obtain desirable tenants once the separate reporting procedure had eliminated much of their discretion. For
example, when a vacancy was ready, managers would get in touch with a
sympathetic tenant selection staff member to avoid advertising the vacant
apartment to the entire department. One staff member commented:

> A manager would call up and say: "I want such and such a case for this
> vacancy." Now you don't know why the manager wants that case. It
> could be any number of reasons such as monetary, but I think that it
> was often for social reasons—the manager or a tenant had a friend
> that wanted to live in the project.

According to the same staff member, managers operated through their
own networks in the Tenant Selection Department. Traditionalists and
survivalists would cooperate partly out of a mutual interest in retaining
higher-status clients. According to one staff member, managers also
opened up the possibilities for exchange:

> Managers would call up willing to make trades with you—sort of you
> scratch my back and I will scratch yours. If you accept his case, which
> he says he has verified as an emergency by going to the applicant's
> house himself, then he will take yours.

In addition, managers had relationships with politicians that allowed
them to get better assignees. They let politicians know of a vacancy before
it had been renovated, and the politicians could then attempt to use their
influence at various levels of authority.

Finally, managers resorted to more subtle means to control transfers
as well. Decisions about transfers had been shifted to the central level,
but application forms were still filled out at the projects and managers

were allowed to comment on the merits of the case. However, managers seldom gave tenants bad reports; since reasons for refusal of transfer were noted in rejection letters sent to the tenants, managers usually wanted to avoid straining client relationships. Moreover, a tenant could appeal the decision, thereby drawing the manager into a direct confrontation. According to a member of the Transfer Committee, managers would instead informally discourage people they did not like:

> Someone would go in and ask for a transfer and a manager would say something like, "You are in arrears; you can't make it out." The manager didn't have the right to make that judgment; that was the province of the Committee on Transfers. Or a manager would say: "I don't have any forms; why don't you come back some other time."

On the other hand, the same committee member reported that managers could be very supportive to tenants they liked:
To people they wanted to transfer they would give a strong recommendation: "Excellent tenant, good rent payer," or suggest that the tenant get a letter from a doctor to insure a high priority.
Thus, although reformers had greatly restricted managers' control over assignment and even intraproject transfers, managers still maintained a certain degree of discretion.

SITUATION AS A DETERMINANT OF DISCRETION

In spite of the reforms limiting managerial discretion in selecting and assigning eligible applicants, better-off assignees still got into high-reputation projects whereas worse-off assignees were sent to the projects with poor reputations. The influence of third-party sponsors and decisions at the central office contributed to these results, as shown in earlier chapters. Such outcomes can also be affected by project variables such as size of units, waiting period for admittance, nature of the present project residents, and the assignment rules that determine the distribution of applicants.[6] The situational constraints affected overall tenant composi-

[6]Kurt Lewin observed that forces at work that affect admissions vary not only with who the gatekeeper is, but also in terms of situational factors. Kurt Lewin, "Frontiers in Group Dynamics: II. Channels of Group Life: Social Planning and Action Research," *Human Relations I* (1947), referred to in Irwin Deutscher, "The Gatekeeper." Deutscher draws on Lewin's analysis to suggest that vacancy rates affect whether the gatekeeper can keep out "Undesirables." See pp. 46–47.

Table 22. *Comparison Profiles of Two Projects*[a]

	Columbia Point	Mary Ellen McCormick
Number of units	1,444	1,018
Scobie Reputation Score[b]	5.3 (low)	2.0 (high)
Assignment rule	Regular 1–2–3	Exception to 1–2–3
Manager style	Reform	Reform
AFDC	66%	20%
Household head over 65	30%	40%
No employed household member	67%	42%
Child:Adult male ratio[c]	1:10.5	1:4.6
5 years or less occupancy	53%	39%
Vacancy rate as of	166 units =	11 units =
31 December 1971	12%	1%
Percentage nonwhite	75%	2%
Move-ins (1970)	185 = 18%	30 = 3%

[a]From Maureen Power, Tenant Status Review of the BHA Population, 1970 and 1971.

[b]Richard Scobie, "Family Interaction as a Factor in Problem-Tenant Identification in Public Housing" (unpublished Ph.D. dissertation, Florence Heller School, Brandeis University, Waltham Mass., 1972), p. 89.

[c]Richard Scobie, 1969 Tenant Status Review of the BHA population.

tion in the short run and allowed some managers to retain more control over assignments than others.

Project Profiles

In order to study the effect of situation on the amount of discretion available to managers, two projects were chosen for this study from among the fifteen federal family developments. These projects, Mary Ellen McCormick and Columbia Point, were selected to emphasize differences in key project variables and the phenomenon of reputation referred to earlier. Moreover, Columbia Point was among the 1–2–3 projects and Mary Ellen McCormick was not. Table 22 gives some of the major comparisons between the two projects.

Mary Ellen McCormick. Although identifiable as a project by brick structures, box-like architecture, and large number of units, Mary Ellen McCormick earned its high reputation on the basis of such design features as balconies, large penthouse apartments, and abundant landscaping.[7] It was the oldest project managed by the BHA but continued to be considered the best because its three-story walk-up buildings were clean, well maintained, quiet, and safe. Although the manager reported "old-fashioned" but persistent problems with alcoholism, he found only traces of the vandalism, drug use, and muggings that characterized some other projects. Since BHA rents were determined only by apartment size and family income, tenants viewed Mary Ellen McCormick as a bargain relative to other developments with fewer amenities and in worse condition. As a result, applicant and third-party pressure for admittance to the project was enormous. Politicians long considered McCormick apartments as plums for their constituents.

Mary Ellen McCormick's high standing was also attributable to the nature of its residents. Predominantly white, Roman Catholic, and Irish, the tenants more closely resembled the middle class than the residents of any other large project. Although family incomes were low (54 percent less than $3,000), most of those with the smallest incomes were elderly people rather than families with children. Persons over 65 years of age represented 40 percent of household heads. These elderly were considered the deserving poor and presented few problems for the manager. Because the project contained no apartments with more than three bedrooms, the manager did not have to contend with the large number of children that lived in other projects.

Many residents affectionately referred to the project as "Mary Ellen" and considered it their home. As of 1969, 10 percent of the residents had lived there for over thirty years, and 21 percent for over twenty years.[8] The stability of the project was reflected both in low vacancies (1 percent in December 1971) and small turnover (3 percent per year); accordingly, few apartments per year were available relative to applicant demand, and assignees had to receive exceptions to the 1–2–3 rule.

Although Eddie Powers, the manager at Mary Ellen, had worked for the authority over ten years, he was the only "old-timer" considered to be a progressive. The reformers transferred him to the project in 1970, with the expectation that he would resist political interference. Concerned with tenant relations, he supported the assignment of a private agency social worker to handle the problem of alcoholism.

---

[7]Project descriptions draw heavily from Scobie, "Family Interaction," pp. 64–96.
[8]Scobie, "Family Interaction," p. 90.

Columbia Point. With its 1,400 units divided into identical seven-story brick elevator buildings, the mere mention of Columbia Point evoked the negative images associated with public housing: institutionalization, vandalism, and dependency.[9] Built in the 1950s on a spit of land near the city sewage plant, the project was characterized by broken windows, filthy stairwells, asphalt playgrounds, and inoperable elevators. Reports of muggings and robberies abounded. Understandably, the project had a low score of 5.3 on Scobie's reputation scale and was referred to, even by its residents, as "the Point."

The problems of Columbia Point were exacerbated by its residents' poverty. Columbia Point families had slightly higher average family incomes than residents of Mary Ellen McCormick, but the families at the Point were larger (owing to the availability of units containing more than three bedrooms) and hence per capita income was lower. Persons over 65 represented only 30 percent of household heads.

In spite of its poor reputation, Columbia Point housed a large number of residents who had lived there for a long period of time: 47 percent of its families had been there over five years. Nevertheless, Columbia Point's turnover rate of 18 percent was substantial. It received regular assignments under the 1–2–3 rule because of its high vacancy rate of 12 percent.

Although a large percentage of whites still lived in this project in 1970, they were predominantly elderly persons living in one corner of the development. The majority of the remaining tenants were nonwhite families with female heads. Of the nonelderly families, 66.4 percent received AFDC and 67 percent had no employed member.

Bill Tucker, the acting manager of Columbia Point at the time of the study, was the only new person that the reformers had been able to place in such a responsible position. He, along with Eddie Powers at Mary Ellen, was considered a reformer sympathetic to the issues of equity and fairness.

The Influence of Situation at Mary Ellen McCormick[10]

Eddie Powers asserted that situational factors such as unit size protected the nature of his assignees and made discriminatory behavior at his

[9]For a description of the negative image of public housing see Richard Coleman, "Exploration," and Chester Hartman, "Social Values."

[10]The participant observation studies for this section were conducted at Mary Ellen McCormick and Columbia Point following the reforms that tightened up

Table 23. *Bedroom Size of Occupied Units*
by Project, 1970[a]

Number of bedrooms	Mary Ellen McCormick	Columbia Point
1	420 (42.5%)	148 (14.2%)
2	445 (44.9%)	330 (32.2%)
3	125 (12.6%)	350 (34.1%)
4		150 (14.6%)
5		40 (3.9%)
breakthrough		10 (1.0%)
Total[b]	990 100.0%	1028 100.0%

[a]From Maureen Power, Tenant Status Review of the BHA Population, 1971.
[b]Totals differ from those in Table 22 because of vacancies and units converted to nonresidential uses (e.g., community rooms).

project and the central office unnecessary. He pointed out, for example, that the distribution of *apartment sizes* varied greatly among developments; Mary Ellen McCormick had a large proportion of one-bedroom units and no units above three bedrooms, whereas Columbia Point had a wider range of apartments including a number of large units. Based on his assumption that welfare assignees (which included minority families) tended to have many children and therefore needed more than three bedrooms, Powers concluded that they could not be housed at his project but instead were sent to projects such as Columbia Point (see Tables 23 and 24). Furthermore, he indicated that the elderly (overwhelmingly white in most projects) occupied most one-bedroom apartments. Although it is correct that unit size constrained individual project composition, Powers' physical determinism argument does not explain the project differences among small families occupying two- and three-bedroom apartments. Among families with four members, a larger percentage of higher-income tenants resided in Mary Ellen McCormick than in Columbia Point (see Table 25). Families with incomes exceeding BHA limitations comprised 13 percent of Mary Ellen's population but only 4 percent of Columbia Point's tenants.

vacancy reporting, eliminated pool cases, and centralized transfers. Jeffrey Prottas, a graduate student in political science at MIT, carried out much of the field work at the two projects. His findings are summarized in *People Processing* (Lexington, Mass.: Lexington Press, 1979).

Table 24. Number of Minors in Family for
Tenants Who Moved in During 1969[a]

Number of minors	Mary Ellen McCormick	Columbia Point
1	7 (43.9%)	22 (18.8%)
2	1 (6.2%)	23 (19.7%)
3	4 (25.0%)	16 (13.7%)
4	1 (6.2%)	18 (15.3%)
5	2 (12.5%)	12 (10.3%)
6		14 (11.9%)
7	1 (6.2%)	4 (3.4%)
8		4 (3.4%)
9		1 (0.9%)
10		3 (2.6%)
Total	16 100.0%	117 100.3%

[a]From Maureen Power, Tenant Status Review of the
BHA Population, 1970.

Powers identified *waiting period* as another situational variable explaining the superiority of Mary Ellen over other projects. Since the
turnover at his project was very low, he contended that only those applicants who could afford to wait for an available unit would be housed. A
central office staff member supported this assumption, pointing out that
knowledge about projects and procedures was also an important factor.

Table 25. Income Distribution for a Family
of Four by Project, 1970[a]

Income	Mary Ellen McCormick	Columbia Point
Less than $1000		
$1000–$1999		
$2000–$2999	5 (12.5%)	30 (20.8%)
$3000–$3999	15 (37.5%)	65 (44.8%)
$4000–$4999		20 (13.8%)
$5000–$5999		10 (6.9%)
$6000–$6999	5 (12.5%)	5 (3.4%)
$7000–$7999	5 (12.5%)	10 (6.9%)
$8000–$8999		
$9000–$9999	5 (12.5%)	
over $9999	5 (12.5%)	5 (3.4%)
Total	40 100.0%	145 100.0%

[a]From Maureen Power, Tenant Status Review of the
BHA Population, 1970.

A great deal of patience, however, was also necessary to obtain an apartment at Columbia Point; in 1970, for example, an applicant had to wait an average of 12 months for an assignment to Columbia Point compared to 17 months for assignment to Mary Ellen; the difference of 5 months does not seem significant. In addition, assignment, as was noted earlier in the discussion of pool cases, does not necessarily result in tenancy. Therefore, in addition to needing patience, an applicant awaiting assignment to Mary Ellen also needed to do her homework. As a first step, he or she would have to obtain the customary letters from doctors and hospitals documenting the need for an exceptional assignment, a basic requirement for admission to other than a 1–2–3 project. The applicant would then have to secure the active support of a well-entrenched politician or a board member. Although one might conclude from this evidence that waiting period and vacancies played somewhat minor roles in the admission of individual applicants to Mary Ellen, it would be a mistake to overlook their broader effects: because only a few two- and three-bedroom units opened up each year at Mary Ellen, a small amount of focused political interference was sufficient to insure that they would be filled by desirable tenants.

Eddie Powers had no inclinations to resist the procedural changes instituted by his colleagues at the central level. He actually found that strict adherence to the new vacancy system helped guarantee good tenants. When a vacancy occurred, Powers sent the Tenant Selection Department a notice indicating that an apartment would be ready for occupancy in approximately a month. Although some apartments were vacated because of unexpected deaths, very few tenants left unannounced to avoid paying back rent, so Powers could even send in such an early notice. Tenant Selection Department staff, in turn, sent him the file of an applicant willing to wait a month for the apartment. Thus, he avoided serious emergency cases which, as has been pointed out, were often unscreened and the focus of advocacy by social agencies. If he found the assignee acceptable on the basis of information contained in the applicant's file and gleaned through his personal network, Powers immediately brought the applicant in and signed a lease. Since his next vacancy report indicated that the apartment was "vacant but leased," he avoided housing emergencies that might bump his assignee in the interim between notice of the original vacancy and occupancy of the new tenant. If staff from the Tenant Selection Department called about the availability of the unit, Powers would report that it was already leased to an assignee.

In addition to providing protection, the new procedures also reduced the stress associated with the position of manager at Mary Ellen McCormick. Since the manager no longer directly controlled assignments, applicant and third-party pressure for admittance to the project was transferred to the central office staff. Applicants and third parties still kept in touch with him about vacancies (doing one's homework included finding out about potential vacancies), but the intensity of the interaction was much lower than it had been when the manager had had decision-making power. Nevertheless, the project still did not receive random assignees; even though Eddie Powers was uninvolved in politics himself, he received the cream of the applicants.

Although almost all of the assignees he received were acceptable, Powers was occasionally sent an objectionable family whom he would formally reject. When applicant screening was reduced and pool cases were eliminated, the manager's increasing use of the veto led reformers to insist that managers invoke it infrequently and detail in writing the reasons for rejection. Reformers would no longer accept explanations—such as "I just couldn't handle it," "There are already too many cases," or "I already have too many children in the building"—that managers had always used to avoid undesirable tenants. Powers, however, was conscientious and tended to reject only applicants who had been evicted for interfering with the rights of others or negligence or had been convicted of such crimes as assault with a deadly weapon or prostitution. Because he was rarely sent such an undesirable tenant, when one slipped through his veto was highly effective.

In a few instances, Powers received an applicant he did not want but whom he could not reject within the guidelines. For instance, sometimes he was sent an assignee with severe emotional problems with which he felt he could not cope. Because reformers were unlikely to sustain his veto, Powers turned to the technique of inaction. After the central office judged an applicant eligible on such occasions, he or she was assigned to a development and the file was forwarded to the project manager who was responsible for arranging an interview. At that time, the assignee was supposed to view the apartment and, if it was suitable, sign a lease. In a small number of cases, however, Powers did not inform assignees of the interview or took advantage of their inability to meet him at the specific time. According to a central office staff member, this strategy was widespread among other managers:

> Managers would pretend to have called someone in. This would account for the many refusals we got saying, "I was never offered this

apartment, I never refused this apartment, I never even got a letter." Or an elderly lady who got a letter happened to be in the hospital and called the manager and told him, "I'm in the hospital, I can't come now." So as quickly as he could, upon hanging up the phone, he would write, "Not interested" on the file and ship it back. The next thing, the poor lady would get a refusal letter.

Although the manager at Mary Ellen seldom used this tactic, it contributed to his fail-safe system. In spite of the reforms, his project continued to house better-off tenants.

The Influence of Situation at Columbia Point

The situation at Columbia Point offered the manager little protection from low-status clients. With its 12 percent vacancy rate, Columbia Point was a mainstay of the 1–2–3 projects, thus serving as a refuge for applicants with few contacts, a majority of whom were nonwhites. Even though an average week found 70 percent of its 166 vacancies uninhabitable, a large number of units were still available for occupancy; hence, Columbia Point received many emergency cases and the manager, Bill Tucker, could not employ the "vacant but leased" strategy. Since it was one of the few projects with units having more than three bedrooms, Columbia Point housed a number of large families. The project was also known as a "dumping ground" for tenants; assignees were often sent there when other managers had refused to accept them.

Virtually all white applicants and most black applicants in decent housing who were offered Columbia Point refused to go there and instead remained in their present housing, sought private housing, or used pressure and contacts to obtain assignments to better public housing projects. Rejection of the project even extended to many homeless whites who chose to remain in Chardon Street, a residential missionary facility, rather than accept emergency housing at Columbia Point. Moreover, many tenants already residing in the project sought transfers to other places such as Mary Ellen, thereby raising the vacancy rate at Columbia Point.

In order to keep these problems under control and to form a stable community with the opportunity to develop, Tucker tried to influence the flood of applicants assigned to his project. The only formal procedural tool at his disposal was the right to veto undesirable assignees. Since he received a greater percentage of such assignees than the manager of Mary

Ellen, the central office staff was likely to uphold his veto, especially when he had hard data to support his contentions. According to a central office staff member, such information was sometimes available in the applicant files sent to the project:

> A manager would examine a case primarily by looking at two things: (1) former tenancy record, if that person had been a former tenant and had left owing money or had been checked off as undesirable; and (2) the probation record: prostitution, drug addiction, assault, anything of that nature. These two things were the determining factors in a case history. And he would often refuse them on those grounds.

In order to avoid unpleasant client contact, Tucker often used the veto without seeing the applicant in person. His veto power was limited, however, by the frequency with which he used it. Since he housed a greater number of new families than the manager of Mary Ellen (185 versus 30 in 1970) and received a disproportionate number of undesirable tenants, his ability to reject 10 percent, for example, left many of his problems unsolved. Moreover, because the veto was based only on the information that appeared in the skimpy BHA applicant files, criminals without records, female heads of households unable to manage their large families, and tenants who posed problems in tenant relations often slipped through. Although effective in the most extreme cases, the formal veto eliminated only a small number of identifiably troublesome tenants.

Given the limits of outright rejection, Tucker was forced to resort to more informal techniques in order to influence admissions. One strategy involved discouraging assignees during the project interview. Tucker would emphasize the high crime level at the project or offer applicants apartments only partially renovated, situated in run-down buildings, or located on the first floor where they could easily be broken into. Tucker had this flexibility because his project contained a large number of vacant units in various states of repair and desirability. On the other hand, dissuasion was not a viable strategy for the manager of Mary Ellen because, with a small number of vacancies, he had no latitude in assigning apartments; applicants were automatically slotted for specific units. Moreover, he could not otherwise dissuade applicants because of the high reputation and superior facilities of the project. However, Tucker also discovered that dissuasion was a poor strategy to control admissions; some potentially troublesome applicants still insisted on taking apartments at

Columbia Point; and although dissuasion might be employed more often than refusal, if Tucker used it too frequently or too forcefully, central office reformers would even assign applicants to specific units at his project.

Since he could not rely on refusal and dissuasion, Tucker resorted to the simpler although more uncertain policy of *inaction* to influence assignments: he did not arrange interviews. Whereas Powers used this strategy sparingly to avoid particular assignees. Tucker employed inaction as his major mechanism for influencing assignments. The staff at the project office did not send letters or phone applicants to arrange interviews. Instead, the only non-emergency cases they housed were assignees who contacted the project themselves.

Tucker's official rationale coincided with the Tenant Selection Department staff's explanation for housing current applicants rather than those on the waiting list: both claimed inadequate resources to send out notices. The manager felt, of course, that his reliance on applicant initiative had distinct payoffs beyond the conservation of scarce staff time and resources.

Tucker assumed that following the laissez-faire assignment system rather than the official procedures produced two benefits: better tenants and fewer occupants.[11] He felt that the aggressiveness and awareness of self-motivated assignees would reflect in their care for the project and participation in community life. Some of these assignees, for example, wanted to live in the project because friends or relatives lived there; these tenants helped create a more closely knit neighborhood. Fewer entrants led to a smaller population; therefore, individual tenants would receive more of such scarce resources as paint, doors, and refrigerators. In addition, Tucker was free to pay closer attention to tenants' problems. With fewer new tenants, a sense of community also had a better opportunity to develop.

Tucker's approach created inequities because it favored aggressive assignees. Assignees aware of the informal procedures but hesitant to pursue their cases, or ignorant of the informal procedures and reluctant to act, were not housed.[12] Other assignees, unfamiliar with the informal

---

[11]Tucker's approach is similar to that described by Michael Lipsky as simplifying. Lipsky, *Street-Level Bureaucracy*, pp. 83–86.

[12]For a conceptual discussion of awareness contexts, see Glaser and Strauss, *Awareness of Dying*.

procedures but persistent enough to call the office, might arrange an interview. Only assignees who foresaw the pitfalls in awaiting the manager's call and who strongly advocated their cases were relatively certain of obtaining an apartment. Although the most needy are often the least aggressive, the reform manager nonetheless held out the unrealistic expectation that aware, aggressive assignees included a majority of the most needy, a point on which he had no data to make such a judgment.[13] Tucker was willing to trade the equity of new applicants for project benefits such as better tenants and more resources per tenant. Still, regardless of his attempts, some aggressive, aware assignees turned out to be problem tenants; others had not taken the initiative on their own but were actually supported by aggressive, aware social workers. Moreover, the decreasing population led the central office staff to reduce some resources.

In addition to its unpredictability in securing desirable tenants, Tucker's strategy was inadequate in treating situational problems. Inaction did not reduce the large number of emergency cases the project received because these assignees were sent directly from the central office. In fact, since his slowdown resulted in a higher overall vacancy rate, he was likely to get more emergency cases. Given the project's stock of three-, four-, and five-bedroom apartments, Tucker continued to receive large families. Moreover, desirable elderly families refused to take assignments. Nevertheless, he persisted for lack of any better strategy.

Tucker had considered selecting among the applicants sent to him the ones he wanted. In employing his tactics of rejection and dissuasion, Tucker did weed out the most undesirable applicants. But he had little basis on whether to differentiate among others from the remaining pool. Given the large number of assignees that he received, he had inadequate resources to inquire deeply into applicants' backgrounds. Lacking adequate information, he therefore adhered to simplified assumptions. He operated on these assumptions without empirical validation, depending instead on his own intuition.

PERSONAL STYLE AS A DETERMINANT OF OUTCOME

Although situation was important in determining the degree of discretion available to individual managers, reformers felt that new manag-

---

[13]See Almond and Lasswell, "Aggressive Behavior."

ers would behave differently, even in the same situation. At the central staff level, for example, traditionalists resisted welfare clients and sought conventional working-class families, whereas reformers sought to house applicants in the greatest need. The effect of managerial style will be examined by observing the behavior of two different types of managers who, one after the other, supervised Columbia Point.[14]

Traditional Style

Jimmy Sullivan, an Irishman in his late fifties, obtained his first Housing Authority job through the efforts of a World War II friend who became a city councillor. Over the years, Sullivan moved up the ladder of positions at the authority and in the early 1960s became manager of one of the better projects. His later promotions were based primarily on his seniority, rent collection record, and help from his political friends.

During the major period of Sullivan's career, the central management office viewed public housing essentially as a real estate operation without profit.[15] They made it clear that managers would be judged on their ability to collect rents and keep order. Accordingly, if a tenant was guilty of tardy rent payment, breach of the peace, or drunkenness, Sullivan warned him several times; if the tenant persisted in his behavior, Sullivan evicted him. In order to avoid such undesirable tenants (among whom he included unwed mothers and families on welfare) in the first place, Sullivan relied on formal and informal tactics (concealment of vacancies, pool cases, transfers, rejections, and the like). He depended on political sponsorship and personal networks to obtain only working-class and elderly whites, many of the latter being retired city employees.

Sullivan felt that tenant counseling services were not the province of the Housing Authority and would only increase managerial problems. When a social service aide was assigned to his project, Sullivan limited his activities to inspecting buildings and showing apartments. Upon discovering that the aide was soliciting the services of social agencies for tenants, Sullivan insisted that the aide be transferred to another project. His view was not motivated so much by a lack of compassion for his tenants as by a belief that the proper order could not result from the "coddling" and "permissiveness" in which social agencies indulged.

[14]For a discussion of police styles, see Wilson, *Varieties of Police Behavior.*
[15]For a description of management views, see Popper, *The Boston Housing Authority,* pp. 27–28.

With the advent of the reform regime in 1969, Sullivan himself was transferred or, as he put it, "exiled" to Columbia Point, a place that he felt was beyond reclamation. Accordingly, he demonstrated little empathy for the problems of tenants except elderly whites, who, like himself, seemed to be trapped at the project. Instead of finagling assignments to obtain better tenants, Sullivan acquiesced to reforms that he interpreted to mean "house anyone." He simply accepted all applicants central office sent to the project and restricted his role to collecting rents.

Reform Style

After two years, Sullivan became seriously ill and Bill Tucker, an assistant manager appointed by the new administrator in 1969, took over as acting manager. Tucker, a black, was young (in his mid-thirties), college-educated, and experienced in social service work. He was the only high-ranking BHA managerial official who had grown up in public housing. He had two qualities that critics of public housing have proposed as necessary for better project management: professional training and a background closely paralleling those of the project tenants.[16]

As assistant manager, Tucker had stressed social services and rapport with tenants. On assuming the position of acting project manager, he continued to support social service programs and encouraged tenant organizations to pressure the Housing Authority for improvements. Tucker also accepted integration as a goal and in the few instances wherein white families accepted a new assignment to Columbia Point, he gave them preference.

Other managers felt that Tucker was a member of the central office reform conspiracy because he did not oppose welfare families and supported integration. For this reason, they prevented him from becoming a permanent manager by threatening to call an authority-wide strike. While Tucker's reference group was initially the central office reform group, many of whom were his personal friends, his loyalties began to have a project orientation when he found that only the most desperate families were sent to his project. According to a central office reformer, Tucker then became more discriminating about assignments and opposed the distribution of applicants:

[16]Hartman and Levi, "Public Housing Managers," p. 136.

When the new administrator took office in 1969, he was able to bring in a new assistant manager, Bill Tucker. Tucker became more discretionary than Sullivan had been about the kinds of cases that he wanted to accept. He didn't want to accept every case that was shipped out to Columbia Point because he felt that he got the riff-raff.

To improve his project, Tucker turned to the strategies of rejection, dissuasion, and inaction. As a result, an apparent paradox developed: the behavior of initially reform-oriented managers was the reverse of what the reformers had expected. Jimmy Sullivan, the traditionalist manager, did not counteract the selection reforms because he was unconcerned with the welfare of his tenants. On the other hand, Tucker, who supported the underlying principles of equity, opposed the reforms in order to decrease his project's burden and increase the resources available to residents. By taking this stand, however, Tucker sacrificed the interests of many low-status applicants, an outcome unforeseen by the reformers.

CONCLUSION

It has been the theme of this chapter that project managers seek to protect their jobs and to minimize the strains of managing clients. When threatened with a shift in clientele, traditionalist managers attempted to avoid getting undesirable tenants. Central office reformers, committed to equity, countered this avoidance by reducing managers' ability to discriminate among applicants and placing two reform-oriented people in managerial positions. The response of the two reform-oriented managers varied with the situations in their projects. Bill Tucker, the manager of Columbia Point, a project with a high vacancy rate and a large number of minority welfare assignees, counteracted the new policies by resorting to highly simplified and uncertain techniques, typical of street-level bureaucrats, to influence the composition of his project. On the other hand, Eddie Powers, the manager of Mary Ellen McCormick, a project with a high reputation and a low vacancy rate, had to use the same techniques, only sparingly, to insure good assignees. His procurement of desirable tenants was enhanced, however, by the actions at the central level. As noted in Chapter 5, even reformers deferred to political influence concerning prime projects to secure more resources for the authority.

In addition to situation, a manager's style also affected his response to the reforms. Jimmy Sullivan, a traditionalist alienated from lower-status tenants, abstained from efforts to influence assignments while manager at Columbia Point. On the other hand, Tucker, the recently recruited reform manager who succeeded Sullivan, attempted to manipulate assignments to improve the project. As a result, reforms which were adopted to increase accountability and equity actually generated antithetical behavior from the reform manager at the low-reputation project.

Tucker's efforts to maximize the welfare of a smaller number of tenants were at the expense of a large number of incoming assignees. Therefore, not only were opportunities for admission to high-reputation projects (such as Mary Ellen McCormick) still restricted to those participants with political connections, but a large number of assignees shunted to low-reputation projects (such as Columbia Point) were otherwise stranded without housing. Although the reformers had replaced two recalcitrant managers with liberals, they had overlooked the implications of both their failure to distribute assignees equitably at the central level and their inability to equalize project situations. The better-off assignees were still sent to Mary Ellen McCormick and the families with problems concentrated at Columbia Point. Tucker was therefore faced with the dilemma of helping to maximize the interests of all potential applicants or the interests of those tenants already at the project. In the absence of additional resources to improve conditions and cope with the problems of his tenants, Tucker chose not to impoverish Columbia Point tenants for the benefit of those applicants on the waiting list.

CHAPTER SEVEN

Federal Intervention
HUD Monitoring, Feedback, and Evaluation

The tenant selection and assignment rules were designed by the federal government to limit bureaucratic discretion and to achieve the reformers' version of equity. Previous chapters have demonstrated that such factors as work conditions, client rejection, bureaucratic norms, third-party influence, and lower-level resistance undermined the implementation of the rules. As is evident in the following discussion of the feedback and control mechanisms which operated in the late 1960s and early 1970s, the strength of the enforcement powers of the Department of Housing and Urban Development over the Boston Housing Authority were never fully defined or tested. Significant but often officially unacknowledged compromises apparently developed as a direct result of the unwillingness of either party to provoke an outright showdown.

Although HUD was responsible for insuring that local agencies carried out the rules, successful enforcement was contingent on HUD's knowledge of BHA activities, its evaluation of any noncompliance that it found, and its powers to alter behavior deemed unacceptable. The dynamics of these three factors are examined in this chapter.

MONITORING THE BHA

HUD's knowledge of BHA activities came through both planned administrative channels and fortuitous feedback.[1] Among the planned

[1]Herbert Kaufman, *Administrative Feedback: Monitoring Subordinates' Behavior* (Washington, D.C.: Brookings Institution, 1973).

methods were written reports, regular audits, and special audits. The fortuitous channels included unsolicited feedback from both the public and the BHA. The feedback process will be examined chronologically.

Written Reports

HUD's most frequent monitoring of tenant selection and assignment occurred through written records submitted quarterly to the HUD regional office. On official forms, the BHA recorded the assignee's name, race, income, source of income, rent, number of bedrooms, and project in which housed. These records were used primarily to check that new tenants met the income limits and were charged the correct rent. From these reports, HUD could also periodically assess the changing racial composition of projects.

In March 1970, the HUD regional office requested that the BHA compile statistical data which would document its experience under the 1–2–3 assignment rule. The BHA, drawing on its quarterly reports, submitted a table comparing project racial composition and vacancy rates in 1963 (when the NAACP–CORE agreement took effect), 1968 (when the HUD 1–2–3 rule was adopted), and 1969 (after one year's experience with the 1–2–3 rule).[2] The report accompanying the table pointed out that although three times as many applicants were offered housing in 1969 compared to previous years, vacancies and segregation had both increased. The predominant concentration of vacancies (75 percent of the total) continued to be found at the three projects offered to applicants who did not qualify for other locations under the HUD plan. The authority claimed that, on the basis of data requested by HUD, these three locations were regarded as the least desirable by the majority of applicants: two-thirds of all applicants offered the 1–2–3 projects rejected them. The report concluded:

> There are increasing signs that the community at large and low-income housing applicants in particular regard the HUD Tenant Assignment Plan to result inevitably in accelerating segregated housing patterns in all locations. There is evidence of an accelerated move-out rate among white tenants in developments with heavy concentrations of nonwhite tenants. When the Authority was required to abandon its

---

[2]Daniel Finn, Administrator of the BHA, letter to Herman Hillman, Assistant Regional Administrator for Housing Assistance, March 16, 1970.

integration objectives, the community at large, applicants, and tenants have reacted by concluding that segregation, both for white and black, was the only pattern that could emerge.[3]

Regular Audits

Although the BHA report indicated that the 1–2–3 rule was not achieving its objectives, HUD could not tell whether the authority was correctly implementing the plan from the data presented. HUD obtained more detailed firsthand information on BHA operations through on-site occupancy audits. Before the adoption of the HUD assignment plan, these audits concentrated on efficiency criteria such as the identification of over-income tenants and incorrect rent charges. After the adoption of the priority and assignment rules, however, the audit was expanded to cover procedures.

Occupancy audits were traditionally conducted by staff sent from the New York regional office. In November 1970, however, consistent with the Nixon administration policy of *new federalism*, supervision for the BHA was transferred to a new regional office in Boston.[4] According to one HUD official, instead of having infrequent contact with the BHA, the regional staff could now almost literally "run across the street." One of the first tasks that befell Boston's new regional staff was to investigate the BHA tenant selection and assignment operations which were reportedly in "bad shape." The new HUD staff also wanted to assess the current status of the BHA.

The HUD occupancy audit was conducted over a six-month period from December 1970 to June 1971. The assigned auditor spent ten working days in the central Tenant Selection Department and forty-one days at projects. Although the auditor's mandate was wide—"to go over the

---

[3]*Ibid.*

[4]For a discussion of the rationale of the reorganization plan, see Report of the Regional Realignment Working Group (Washington, D.C.: n.p., 1970); Richard Van Dusen, "New Federalism," *Journal of Housing* 26 (1969), 581–583.

For a discussion of the tensions between the regional and Washington HUD offices, see Richard LeGates, *Can the Federal Welfare Bureaucracies Control Their Programs: The Case of HUD and Urban Renewal. Working Paper No. 176.* (Berkeley: Institute of Urban and Regional Development, University of California, 1972), pp. 5–9.

entire tenant selection operation"—his techniques were specific.[5] He first went through the latest BHA guidelines and regulations, submitted and accepted by HUD, to see if they differed from the ones the BHA actually used. The auditor found that the existing departmental regulations were often not up to date with HUD revisions.[6] Moreover, department regulations still said that the authority housed people according to need, even though it did not follow that policy and it was no longer required by law. The auditor was next supposed to investigate BHA compliance with the priority and assignment rules. However, given the time limits, the auditor felt it was impossible to reconstruct the waiting list, a task he estimated would take two or three people over a month.[7] Moreover, monitoring the first come, first serve priority system was especially difficult given the BHA's method of record keeping: instead of actually keeping a list of eligible applicants by date, the Tenant Selection Department kept applicant records on cards and in files by name, status, unit size required, and date of application. The auditor felt the BHA's system was easy to abuse and hard to check: it was easy to pull files out of order but difficult to manipulate a list even by erasures.

After his ten days in the central office, the auditor went out to the projects and examined tenant files through a ten percent sample. He discovered that over 10 percent of the tenants exceeded the income limits and that many tenants lived in units that were either too large or too small relative to family size. His major finding in relation to the priority and assignment rules was that the authority violated them by allowing managers to use considerable discretion in selecting applicants. While examining tenant files at one of the projects, the auditor heard an assistant manager telling one applicant that she could be housed and telling someone else that she could not. When asked how he made these decisions,

[5]HUD auditors have written instructions and procedures that guide them in their work. U.S. Department of Housing and Urban Development, "Check List of Activities Involved in Conducting Occupancy Audits of Local Housing and Urban Development." (Washington D.C., 1967).

[6]HUD findings and recommendations are drawn from interviews and HUD, Boston Area Office, Housing Services and Property Management Division, "Occupancy Audit Report of the Boston Housing Authority" (Boston: n.p., mimeographed, December 8, 1970, to June 8, 1971).

[7]A study of HUD's monitoring of urban renewal activities similarly found that HUD's staff is inadequate to understand and control the program they are mandated to administer. Richard LeGates, *Can the Bureaucracies Control Programs*, pp. 9–16.

the manager indicated that he had a file of applicants from which he could select those he wanted. When the auditor examined the folders, he realized that some applicants had been waiting over three years. These were the "pool cases"—groups of eligible applicants sent to a local project office to be housed at the convenience of that office. According to the 1–2–3 rule, the files of those who had turned down apartments or had been rejected by the manager were supposed to be returned to the central office to be offered another choice. Moreover, tenants were supposed to be selected on a first come, first serve basis and only sent to projects when there were actual available vacancies.

The auditor's findings and recommendations were contained in a report to the BHA executive director. The report requested the BHA to update its regulations and to send over-income tenants notices to look for private housing. If the tenants were unable to find accommodations, they were to document their search. The report also requested that the BHA transfer tenants so that their living quarters matched family size and withdraw all the pool cases from projects and place them on the central community-wide waiting list according to date of application.

It took the BHA one year to respond formally to the HUD audit. The eight-page memo from the executive director suggested in general and vague terms that the authority would provide better records of activities such as notifying over-income tenants to seek private housing and documenting their inability to find it.[8] In reference to pool cases, the BHA memo said, "The practice of holding pool cases at the various developments has been discontinued and the recall of cases to the tenant office completed." The new policy was to retain only one or two cases for each size of unit to assure early occupancy of available units. Since the reformers wanted to reduce the discretion of managers, they were quite willing to adopt this policy.

Unsolicited BHA Feedback

HUD received additional feedback through the initiative of the BHA itself. For example, in 1971, reformers at the Housing Authority, dissatisfied with the priority and assignment procedures, carried out their own evaluation and formulated alternative policies which they felt would be

[8]Herman Hemingway, letter to Irving Solomon, HUD Boston Area Office, March 2, 1972.

more equitable.[9] The reformers presented their recommendations to the HUD regional staff in July 1971.

The reformers claimed that the 1–2–3 rule, which they interpreted as intending to reduce segregation and vacancies, was only aggravating the situation. They pointed out, for example, that the percentage of blacks in 1–2–3 developments and other predominantly nonwhite developments had not been reduced, nor had the racial balance at predominantly white developments been improved. In addition, the BHA claimed that the 1–2–3 rule was not successful in reducing vacancies or channeling applicants into high-vacancy areas. They reported that at the end of 1969, the first year of the 1–2–3 rule's enforcement at the BHA, both system-wide and 1–2–3 project vacancy rates were higher than ever. As an explanation of the plan's failure, the reformers noted that white applicants and many nonwhite applicants chose no housing rather than take assignments to the projects with the highest vacancy rates. In addition, for a variety of financial, social, and political reasons, the authority filled vacancies in other than 1–2–3 projects through the use of exceptional assignments. The reformers claimed that a disproportionate amount of the exceptional assignments went to whites because they knew how to bypass the 1–2–3 rules and were more familiar with the range and characteristics of the developments.

The reformers proposed that the HUD 1–2–3 plan be replaced with one that left the choice of development up to the applicant with the BHA staff providing counsel and advice. Their revised plan was based on the belief that:

> tenant selection, the point of entry into the housing system, can be a unique opportunity to learn more about prospective tenants so that we can assist them in making a sound housing choice, in assuming the responsibilities of tenancy, and in adjusting to life in public housing.[10]

The vital core of the proposed change was an in-depth social interview designed to identify high-risk families and needed social supports, provide pre-occupancy training, and assist applicants in making sound and realistic housing choices. Among the factors to be taken into consideration

[9]BHA proposals and notes on the meeting with HUD are found in a memorandum from Phil MacDonnell to Those Concerned at the Central Office, July 29, 1971.
[10]U.S. HUD chief of tenant selection, memorandum to the administrator of the BHA, 29 July 1971.

were family mobility, enrollment of school-age children, employment, health care, use of social agencies, and the willingness of families to live in an integrated setting.

Unlike the existing system in which applicants were given little information about developments and the selection process, the revised plan was designed to acquaint them with the full range of housing opportunities, the turnover rates related to specific developments, and priority regulations. Based on that knowledge and their needs, applicants could then choose a project. At the close of the interview, applicants would be given a form letter indicating housing choice, potential waiting period, and whom to call for follow-up or changes in their choice or family status. Applicants would then be placed on a list and prioritized, in chronological order (first come, first serve) by the number of bedrooms required. Displaced persons, veterans, and families willing to live in integrated settings were considered exceptions and would get highest priority. Staff would contact applicants when an appropriate vacancy became available.

The reformers also called for the creation of two new Tenant Selection Department positions: housing specialist and rental agent. The housing specialist, a case worker with knowledge of the welfare system and experience with low-income clients, would conduct the social interview in which the applicants determined their housing choices. Although the housing specialist would therefore have considerable discretion, the reformers felt that he or she would use it in a professional manner, equitably and sensitively. The qualifications for the rental agent were knowledge of the possible socioeconomic problems of low-income families and familiarity with the public housing program and city neighborhoods. His or her function would be to meet with eligible applicants at various developments, to arrange meetings between applicants and managers to sign leases, and to return case files to the Tenant Selection Department in instances of rejection. In effect, the rental agent would take over several of the functions which the reformers believed managers had abused in their efforts to maintain control.

Although HUD staff felt that the reformers' revised plan had many merits, they pointed out that it did not qualify as a replacement for the 1–2–3 plan because the BHA could not prove its superiority in achieving integration or reducing vacancies. They acknowledged that other northern cities had also found problems with the 1–2–3 rule but because of its apparent effectiveness in the South, Washington officials insisted that it be retained. HUD staff suggested that the BHA inform all applicants of the availability of exceptional assignments to insure nondiscrimination. In addition, HUD staff believed that the BHA could incorporate many of the revised plan objectives into the existing framework of the 1–2–3 rule. The BHA staff interpreted HUD's response to mean that although they could not formally drop the 1–2–3 rule, HUD would not rigidly enforce it. According to one BHA staff member who attended the meeting, several HUD staff members even suggested ways to get around the rule.

Public Channels

HUD received feedback not only from the BHA but also through such public channels as the Boston City Council. On October 6, 1970, the council first passed a resolution asking the BHA to rescind the 1–2–3 rule and then, having been informed that it was a federal regulation, decided to hold a public hearing to investigate BHA tenant selection and assignment practices.[11] At the hearing, city councillors questioned upper-level BHA officials about both the 1–2–3 assignment rule and the first come, first serve priority rule.[12]

City councillors were unanimous in their opposition to the 1–2–3 rule. They agreed with the BHA executive director that the rule contributed to vacancy problems and racial segregation and found the 1–2–3 rule particularly repugnant because their constituents could not easily choose where they wanted to live. Although city councillors were familiar with exceptional assignments to other than 1–2–3 projects, they often received calls from angry constituents and had to spend time helping people document special needs. One city councillor complained:

> Housing and trying to place applicants into housing has been the most frustrating experience in my entire career. I think that we could get somebody into the White House eaiser than to get them into the public housing units. I have had many applicants for public housing who have run into this rule of three refusals and have gone to the bottom of the list.

---

[11]*Boston Globe*, October 6, 1971.

[12]I attended the city council hearing and also had the transcript of the meeting typed. Boston City Council, Committee on Public Services, "Excerpt of Testimony from Public Hearing: Public Housing in the City of Boston," October 7, 1970.

Although it did not have the legal power to change the regulations, the city council suggested that the BHA use congressional influence to force HUD to abandon the rule. In the meantime, one city councillor urged the BHA to disregard the rule. When the BHA executive director pointed out that HUD threatened to withhold funds if his staff did not implement the rule, the councillor answered that at such a point, the state's two United States senators could be called upon to exert pressure to release the money.

Several city councillors advocated that the authority adhere to the first come, first serve rule. Although the chief of the Tenant Selection Department claimed that his staff selected applicants on the basis of date of application, under questioning he admitted that no written rules were passed out to applicants explaining the procedures, nor was there an open list on which applicants could check their standing. One city councillor, supporting such an open list, said:

> What has become the problem in the city is the fact that many people, and I don't know whether it is justified or not, but many people feel that with political pressure they can get into elderly housing projects. Now that is why I want established a list according to the markings that you put on applications. As I understand it, when an applicant comes to you he gets a number. If this is so, then we can check and find out why number 25 was taken ahead of number 1. I only want a plan that is judicious for all of the people and I don't want to hear that so and so's mother was put into a senior citizen's housing project just because some pressure was brought to bear upon your office.

To insure that the department followed the first come, first serve principle, several other councillors suggested that it stop taking new applications until the older cases were housed. One council member, noting that the executive director had indicated that 2,500 elderly applicants were waiting for the 72 vacant units that opened up each year, said:

> In the interest of human consideration and the taxpayer you should close the list for a year. Don't you think people have feelings? Don't you think it would be better to tell the people the boat is never going to come from Portugal, instead of having them wait and pray each night they are on the list?

Special Audits

HUD's most accurate and thorough knowledge of BHA tenant selection and assignment procedures came through a special audit. In late
1972, the secretary of HUD ordered an on-site examination of the twenty-
five largest housing authorities in financial trouble. This special management audit was much more intensive and probing than the regular occupancy audit. Teams of HUD officials from all over the country were
involved. Approximately forty people, including high-level HUD staff not
often in the field, spent three weeks at the BHA in a *blitzkrieg* operation.
These HUD officials solicited information directly from tenants and
lower-level staff as well as from top-level personnel in an effort to get a
balanced and overall view of the problems. The auditors also looked
carefully at interdepartmental relations.

HUD found that the waiting list (the core of the priority system)
stood at about 6,100.[13] In many cases no action had been taken in two
years and some applications dated back more than ten years. The existence of these cases clearly indicated that the BHA was not following the
first come, first serve principle. Moreover, because of the workload, staff
had stopped sending applicants notification of their eligibility. Failure to
issue such notices was a violation of HUD regulations.

HUD also discovered that the BHA was improperly implementing
the 1–2–3 tenant assignment rule. BHA policy was unclear with respect
to how vacancies in leased housing were filled, which families were referred to state-aided housing, and the priority that transferees had in
relation to applicants on the waiting list. In addition, HUD auditors found
that the BHA was housing most families on an emergency or exceptional
basis without formally defining these special circumstances or informing
all applicants of their availability. Moreover, the BHA failed to document
many of its emergency and exceptional cases thoroughly in order to justify
their special circumstances. Furthermore, HUD officials found abuses
even in those cases which were documented. They noticed, for example,
that one doctor wrote over thirty letters to help applicants obtain exceptional assignments. Observing that the doctor wrote virtually the same
letter for each applicant, one official commented that "maybe two of them
were legitimate." Another official stated that the BHA's placement of

[13]HUD findings and recommendations are drawn from interviews and from
HUD, Boston Area Office, "Occupancy Audit," March 31, 1972.

emergencies or exceptions was "the politician's way of working pull into the system."

In addressing the problems of priority and assignment, HUD auditors found that the vacancy report system was still inadequate. A HUD sample of vacancies indicated that some units listed as vacant were occupied whereas other units listed as vacant were not in good enough condition to be occupied. This led one HUD official to state angrily, "The HUD occupancy auditor is never able to determine correctly the number of vacancies at a given time because of the BHA's outright lies and subtle omissions." Moreover, managers still failed to return the folders of assignees who had refused housing to the central office, thus preventing those applicants from being offered second and third offers in accord with the 1–2–3 rule.

In its report to the authority, HUD recommended a number of changes that ranged from structural reforms to tighter definition of terms. The report began by pointing out, "The Tenant Selection Department at the BHA is in need of restructure on all levels of its operations."[14] It specifically mentioned inefficient overlapping of functions and unclear perceptions of precise job responsibilities. In order to overcome problems of this nature, they recommended the preparation of a departmental handbook clearly describing the steps taken in processing an application: assignment, rejection, or any of the temporary degrees of status along the way. In addition, the handbook was "to define for each employee his unique contribution to the process."

Although greater efficiency was useful, one HUD auditor suggested that still further basic personnel changes were necessary.

> The Tenant Selection Department is blatantly in need of revamping.
> It will take 3 to 5 years because attitudinal changes are necessary.

Lack of funds and the seniority of many staff made the recruitment of new people a long-term project. In the meantime, the report suggested the next best alternative:

> A comprehensive "in-house" training program should be instituted to increase individual competence in specific job assignments, and very

---

[14]*Ibid.*

importantly to demonstrate emphatically to the staff the fundamental
and critical nature of the department's job. [15]

In relation to implementation of policy, HUD called for strict adherence to the first come, first serve principle. To help insure that the staff
would house people from the waiting list rather than recent applicants,
HUD suggested that the department update the waiting list by sending
applicants letters inquiring whether or not they still desired BHA housing.
To make this possible in terms of workload, HUD would allow the Tenant
Selection Department to forego full processing of new applicants and
instead simply register their requests. In addition, HUD wanted the BHA
to establish a reassignment transfer policy as well as to institute a better
control system for obtaining project vacancy information.

In relation to the 1–2–3 rule, HUD asked that the BHA amend its
tenant selection and assignment plan to specify the order of assignment
for leased and state-aided housing relative to conventional public housing. HUD also wanted the BHA to define what constituted an *emergency*
or *exception* and to make their availability known both during applicant
interviews and in public notices.

EVALUATION

All of HUD's feedback mechanisms strongly indicated that the BHA
was not following the priority and assignment plan. Although its audits
only scratched the surface, HUD clearly perceived that its rules were not
effective in limiting discretion. HUD suggested ways in which the BHA
could more easily adhere to the first come, first serve rule which HUD
continued to uphold as an important principle. However, HUD did not
insist on compliance with the 1–2–3 rule, which the BHA claimed was
unworkable, even though, as one HUD auditor indicated, the BHA had
never given the 1–2–3 rule a chance:

> The BHA's view of the 1–2–3 rule is that it was rammed down their
> throats by HUD. That is in fact true. However, it was never really
> used by them. The BHA subverted the 1–2–3 plan by making the
> exception the rule. They put central emphasis in their tenant selec-

---

[15]*Ibid.*

tion practices on what was peripherally detailed in the formal tenant selection policy.

By requiring only clear definition of terms and public assignment rules, rather than strict compliance with the regulations, HUD staff seemed to concur that the 1–2–3 plan was not feasible. For example, one HUD official noted that the plan could not bring about integration in many cities because the applicant waiting lists were either all white or all nonwhite. Although Boston was one of the major cities where a large number of whites were still eager for public housing (many of them being elderly), this HUD official felt that the designation of an apartment in a predominantly black family project as suitable was unfair:

> One of the issues in the 1–2–3 rule is what is a suitable apartment. For example, an apartment in Mission Hill may not be "suitable" for an 80 year old woman—it is unsafe. A suitable apartment should be one into which a tenant can move and not be afraid.

Another HUD staff person who upheld the automatic assignment principle of the 1–2–3 felt that the plan was unworkable because projects were unequal: "It is not the purpose of public housing to satisfy the desires of applicants but the needs. But to implement the laws, the projects should be equal. Projects, however, differ in physical conditions and safety."

At the national level where it had originated, HUD officials corroborated the regional staff's lack of enthusiasm for the 1–2–3 rule. One official commented: "We sought compliance for something we didn't believe in." For example, a HUD group responsible for reviewing the priority and assignment plan pointed out that applicants for low-rent housing legitimately complained that they had no real housing choice under the 1–2–3 rule and were usually offered the least desirable housing.[16] The group cited the Kaiser Committee Report which broadly argued that recipients of housing assistance should be given more choice in their assignments, pointing out that HUD was promoting new housing programs to bring this about. They therefore recommended the adoption of an alternative which they called an *assignment choice* plan. Under their proposed plan, when an applicant's name appeared at the top of the community-wide waiting list, he or she would be offered a unit in any

[16]HUD's evaluation is drawn from Dorothy Willis, "Briefing Paper."

location in which a suitable vacancy existed. If the offer was refused, project choice would be recorded and the application moved to the bottom of the waiting list. When the application again reached the top, it would remain there until a unit of suitable size became available in the project of the applicant's choice. In essence, this plan was a reversion to the applicant preference plan with the added stipulation that people be housed on a first come, first serve basis.

National HUD officials also found fault with the 1–2–3 rule because it was unclear whether it was meant to reduce vacancies, to promote integration, or to maintain racial balance. If the objective was to reduce vacancies, HUD officials felt that giving operating subsidies to improve projects was a much better strategy. If the objective was to promote integration, they suggested that the pioneer family approach originated by the BHA (see Chapter 2) was more likely to succeed. If the objective was racial balance, a quota would be necessary to prevent the tipping phenomenon in which projects shifted gradually from all white to all black occupancy. Such a quota system had been called for by a Judgment Order (*Gautreaux* v. *Chicago Housing Authority,* 1969) to end the segregated housing pattern which the courts said emanated from the Chicago Housing Authority's unconstitutional site selection and tenant assignment procedures.[17]

By 1970, however, the Nixon Administration had replaced the Johnson Administration, and integration was no longer a priority. In addition, the pressure from civil rights groups and the minority community had diminished. One black HUD official expressed the feeling that if the assignment plan resulted in all-black occupied projects rather than mixed projects, it was a reflection of the greater need of black families. Moreover, the financial plight of large authorities was worsening. The 1972 special audit of the BHA, for example, was initiated out of a concern not for integration but rather for the solvency of local housing authorities. One of its main recommendations was that the BHA select a cross section of income groups so that it could increase its income. As a result of this shift in emphasis, HUD neither modified the 1–2–3 rule nor adopted an alternative strategy to replace it. The 1–2–3 rule simply died quietly.

---

[17]Lazin, "Public Housing in Chicago." *Yale Law Journal,* "Public Housing and Urban Policy: *Gautreaux* v. *Chicago Housing Authority,*" in *Housing Urban America,* ed. Jon Pynoos, Robert Schafer, and Chester Hartman (Chicago: Aldine, 1973), pp. 108–113.

HUD'S POWER

Some commentators have argued that even when HUD supported policies such as first come, first serve, it did not effectively insure compliance because its sanction powers were limited. Under its regulations, HUD had the power to recover title or possession of projects. However, HUD resorted to this strategy infrequently and only on occasions of bankruptcy or financial scandal. According to one HUD official, "HUD doesn't want to run projects—our managers are even worse than local personnel." HUD has the option to deny uncooperative authorities funds for new projects, modernization, or subsidies for the elderly, displacees, and very poor tenants. In 1969, as discussed in Chapter 2, HUD threatened to cut off such funds if the BHA did not accept the priority and assignment plan. This sanction, however, was infrequently used because, as one staff member said, "If you cut off funds, it only hurts the tenants and the projects get more rundown." Nevertheless, as one student of grant programs has observed, the federal ability to withhold funds "lies at the foundation, as a weapon in reserve, of all federal enforcement activity."[18] Still, HUD cannot continually threaten to invoke this power without actually acting because it would lose much of its credibility.

Given their hesitancy to employ legal powers, HUD officials relied instead on more informal techniques. According to one HUD official:

> The best method of enforcement is through personal contact and the writing of heavy-handed letters. You have to assume that most people are rational and will go along. In a small authority, enforcement is easier because there are fewer people to deal with. In a place like the BHA, however, enforcement is compounded by size and lack of leadership.

HUD's most effective compliance method appears to have been the presence of its own personnel at the authority. For example, during the regular occupancy audit of 1971, the HUD auditor gave the Tenant Selection Department staff the impression that he was literally poring over the cases. When he found abuses, such as inadequate documentation of special circumstances necessary to allow a single person under 62 years of age to live in a federal project, he would pull the folder and go over it item by item with managers and tenant selection staff. One immediate effect was

[18]Martha Derthick, *The Influence of Federal Grants*, p. 209.

that while he was there staff members became extremely hesitant to send out exceptional assignments that were not adequately documented.

The 1972 special audit created even more pressure on the Tenant Selection Department. According to one staff member, "You could feel the antagonism. The auditors, many of whom were black, were going through records, which were terrible, seeing the way cases were handled, and accusing the staff of discrimination."[19] Moreover, because the department did not have a clear system for priority and assignment of applicants, staff had difficulty answering the charges of HUD staff. Even though conflict characterized the investigation, the actual report was a compromise second draft arrived at through negotiations between HUD and the BHA and was a private, not a public, document. Such reports, however, can be used by outside parties with access to them for their own purposes. For example, when the mayor attempted to remove the tenant board members (see Chapter 5), he cited as evidence parts of the audit report that stated that over-income tenants should be evicted. Even though HUD officials played no part in the hearings, the potential political impact of their reports was heeded by the authority. According to one staff member, the mayoral hearings resulted in

> an insane preoccupation with the book. The director wanted the staff to be able to explain its behavior. If you received a phone call you were supposed to write it down and then pass it on to the appropriate person. It was the accompanying publicity more than what HUD could do that caused the response.

Still, the effect was short-lived. The same BHA staff member commented, "In the end, what does HUD do? Not much. HUD makes its report and everyone gets nervous and is glad when the auditors leave. But there is usually no carryover." Even one HUD official agreed:

> HUD as a supervisory agency has let local authorities go their merry way. Even our occupancy audits occur only every two years. To accomplish results we should have someone in Boston all the time. Moreover, there should be a follow-up of findings.

As a result of its weak enforcement powers, HUD was generally able to reach accord with the BHA on matters in which HUD's findings provided either the impetus or the legitimization for policy changes which

---

[19]*Ibid.* Derthick, on the other hand, suggests that, in the long run, federal enforcement is characterized by diplomacy rather than confrontation because of the mutual interests of the two governmental parties.

upper-level HBA officials supported.[20] For example, the BHA reformers were willing to recall pool cases from projects because that strategy fit in with their goals for centralization. However, in situations in which there was substantial disagreement between the BHA and HUD or in which the BHA was unable to carry out reforms because of inadequate resources or internal problems, HUD had little influence. For example, although HUD called for the elimination of pool cases, it objected to other BHA policies to strip managers of their power and to centralize operations. Since HUD recommendations, such as returning the power of intraproject transfers to the managers, were not based on any statutory requirements, the BHA viewed them as they would suggestions that came from a consultant: they could either accept or reject them. In this case they rejected them.

CONCLUSION

Although HUD had limited surveillance capacity, through a combination of its own monitoring system and unsolicited feedback, it had enough information to know that the BHA was not following the priority and assignment rules. In light of these findings, HUD began to reevaluate its strategies for insuring equity and integrating projects. By that time, the political climate had changed and a new national administration, less committed to the original goals, had come into power. Instead of either modifying the rules or creating a new strategy to meet the integration goals, HUD simply put the 1–2–3 rule aside. Yet, because of HUD's limited enforcement powers, it still had difficulty in securing compliance with other objectives it supported. HUD's power was limited to getting the authority to agree to changes which upper-level BHA management considered in the agency's best interest; but, as has been noted in other chapters, even BHA officials had problems in carrying out their own policy.

[20]A Detroit study similarly concluded, "The Detroit Housing Commission follows the mandates of a circular only if the application of the circular would be feasible for the Detroit Housing Commission." Portia Hamlar, "HUD's Authority to Mandate Effective Management of Public Housing," *Journal of Urban Law*, 50 (1972), 78–127.

George Lefcoe states that "the policy of local control in the public housing program serves as a continual constraint upon HUD's authority to manage local housing authorities from Washington." George Lefcoe, "HUD's Authority to Mandate Tenants' Rights in Public Housing," *Yale Law Journal*, 80 (1971), 463–514.

CHAPTER EIGHT

The Later Years
Court-Initiated Reform Efforts

In the late 1970s and early 1980s tenant selection and assignment issues again came to the fore as outside parties began to play a larger role in promoting change at the BHA. However, unlike past years, during this period the major force was neither HUD nor politicians; it was the courts. Following suits brought by legal service attorneys representing BHA tenants to improve general operations and conditions, a master was appointed by the court to plan and monitor BHA activities. Later, when progress was judged inordinately slow, further suits resulted in the court's actually taking over the BHA through an appointed receiver. As a result of the court's involvement, issues which had lain dormant for several years suddenly gained new attention and several major new thrusts in tenant selection and assignment emerged.

LIMITED INTERVENTION

In February 1975, public housing tenant Armando Perez and eight other tenants filed suit against the BHA, seeking to have the Massachusetts Department of Community Affairs correct alleged widespread violations of the state sanitary code. In response, Housing Court Chief Justice Paul Garrity held hearings and toured a half-dozen of the city's sixty-seven public housing projects. Walking through Mission Hill, he observed:

> that in every building almost every pane of glass joining common area stairways was broken out from the first floor to the roof, that most

incinerators were erupting flames a few feet into the open air of the
height level of small children, that smoke and soot from incineration
permeated the air, that sidewalks and streets were cracked with
entire sections missing, that automobiles were speeding through play
areas set aside for children . . . and . . . most apartments were without shades.[1]

In March 1975, Judge Garrity issued an order requiring the State of
Massachusetts to correct substandard conditions. These repairs were estimated to cost up to $105 million. He also ordered the BHA to draw up
plans to rehabilitate substandard apartments, reduce the level of crime
and vandalism, and desegregate all projects.

However, in July 1975, the Massachusetts Judicial Court reversed
the Boston Housing Court's decision concerning the state's responsibility
to correct the BHA's substandard public housing. The court ruled that
Garrity had exceeded his authority in naming as defendents any of the
parties except the BHA. Acknowledging the seriousness of providing
decent housing as well as reducing crime, violence, and racial segregation
in BHA projects, the court ordered the case sent back to Garrity for
further proceedings against the authority as he deemed appropriate in the
circumstances.

To oversee the improvements, Judge Garrity appointed Robert
Whittlesey, a local housing expert, as the courts special master. Whittlesey was given broad authority to prepare plans for correcting conditions in BHA-run developments and to report back to the court on progress. The Housing Court's strategy was to have the master and his small
staff oversee specific orders to rectify conditions and to produce a comprehensive analysis of the BHA.

The master's 1,500-page report, released in July 1976, called for
sweeping reforms of the BHA, including elimination of political patronage, return of responsibility for management and maintenance to local
project managers, and a hiring policy that depended on job expertise and
experience.[2] In the area of tenant selection and assignment, the Master's
Office reviewed previous reports and studies and interviewed a range of
groups and individuals with concerns regarding policies and procedures.
The report identified four basic principles to form the basis of a revised

[1]*Perez* v. *Boston Housing Authority*, 368 Mass. 333; 331 NE 2d 801 (1975), p. 13.
[2]Robert B. Whittlesey, *Report of the Master in the Case of Perez v. Boston
Housing Authority*, (n.p.: mimeographed, July 1, 1976).

tenant selection and assignment system: clear and consistent standards and procedures for treatment of applicants; recognition of the most urgent needs of applicants; fair and simple priority ranking by chronological order—in cases wherein urgent needs or other special requirements of the system were not applicable; and fair and consistent screening of applicants to avoid the admittance of destructive persons whose acceptance would render the BHA unable to adequately serve its tenants. These four general principles formed the basis for six primary areas of tenant-selection recommendations adopted by the Master's Office:

1. improving the tenant selection, assignment and transfer system
2. improving efficiency
3. desegregating developments
4. marketing public housing
5. increasing managerial discretion
6. increasing screening

Improving the Tenant Selection, Assignment, and Transfer System

The Master's Office found that three written plans influenced the handling of tenant selection, assignment, and transfers: the 1965 plan which had been posted as recently as 1975; a 1974 plan submitted by the BHA and approved by HUD; and a plan adopted by the BHA board in November 1975 but rejected by HUD in March 1976. All three plans were found to be seriously inadequate by the standards of the Master's Office. The 1965 plan was considered outdated and lacking in sufficient detail for implementation; the 1974 plan called for assignments without consideration of project preferences and was judged incomplete; and, finally, the 1975 plan was judged to be based upon inappropriate priorities for two-parent families and upper-income households.

Similar to general findings reported earlier concerning operations (see Chapter 3), the Master's Office found that the Tenant Selection Department did not carry out selection and assignment according to any one of these plans, which again resulted in a great deal of inconsistency and arbitrariness in decision making. Some written procedures were followed whereas others were not; and, although the majority of the procedures were unwritten, nonetheless some were followed consistently. Others, however, were handled on an *ad hoc* basis through "individual and sometimes inconsistent responses to specific situations."[3] The assignment of emergency cases, for example, represented both types of unwritten policies. Although not stipulated in any written plan, this priority rating was used in approximately ten percent of all assignments. However, assignments among emergency applicants were not based on any consistent standards for priority ranking. Instead, assignments were based on department staff's opinion of the most urgent emergencies.

Lacking any consistent written plan, departmental staff, who at this point were primarily low-grade employees, hesitated to exercise discretion and instead often turned to the departmental head to handle individual cases. This situation also left applicants poorly informed regarding the tenant selection process. In line with earlier HUD suggestions, the Master's Office recommended that the BHA develop and implement a revised and complete tenant selection, assignment, and transfer plan that better defined priorities and procedures.

Improving Efficiency

Problems of backlog, inefficiency, and excessive demands on staff time continued to plague tenant selection in the middle 1970s. The waiting list had not been updated for over three years, leading to problems in assigning applicants to units. In addition, because of recent policies that required the authority to provide applicants with information on their status, an enormous amount of staff time was consumed talking with applicants on the phone and administering the waiting list. These problems were compounded when the waiting list shifted from a community-wide to a project-preference system. Not only were applicants now calling to change their preferences, but each project had its own turnover rate, making it difficult to inform applicants accurately how long it would take before they would be offered an apartment. The recommendations of the Master's Office included better provision of information to applicants about such matters as waiting lists and turnover rates and computerization of the waiting list. It even went so far as to suggest closing applications for all but emergency situations so as to limit their volume.

Desegregating Developments

Among the original findings of the Perez case was that occupancy by race in BHA developments "reinforces and exacerbates segregated hous-

[3]Whittlesey, pp. ix–51.

ing patterns in Boston's neighborhoods."[4] Although according to a HUD
official the judge's finding was based on impressions, it was substantiated
in a regional HUD investigative report submitted to the BHA in March
1976 concerning BHA's compliance with Title VI of the Civil Rights Act of
1964. HUD claimed that BHA housing had intentionally been administered to maintain patterns of racial segregation, that minority applicants
waited longer for housing than whites, and that when minority applicants
did receive housing it was generally in worse condition than that received
by whites.

The Master's Office was instructed to prepare interim plans and draft
court orders to reduce segregation. A draft report and orders concerning
desegregation were submitted to the court by the Master's Office in
October 1975. These documents then became the subject of discussions
between the Massachusetts Commission Against Discrimination (MCAD)
and HUD, both of which were concerned that any actions taken by the
court also be in accord with their own guidelines and regulations. Three
major strategies emerged: racially integrated developments would be
maintained; voluntary desegregation would be encouraged; and a project-
by-project waiting list, based on the locational preferences of residents,
would be kept.

The initial effort to reduce segregation was a court order issued in
December 1975. This court order was designed to maintain racial integration in four family developments identified as having a *substantial racial
mix*, that is, a minority population at least proportional to the minority
residents in the city of Boston as a whole (approximately 23 percent), and
having a nonminority population of at least 30 percent.[5] The procedures
called for assigning a racially mixed group of applicants to each of the
projects. However, even though the BHA tried to market the projects,
the effort was undermined by the fact that only a small number of white
applicants on the waiting list were willing to move into these projects.
Nevertheless, the Master's Office recommended that the BHA continue
such a strategy through advertising, presentations to community organizations, and publicity about its efforts to achieve and maintain integrated
housing.

In the analysis of BHA tenant selection and assignment during 1975,
the Master's Office found that little effort was being made to encourage
voluntary desegregation of projects. The December 1975 court order

[4]*Perez* v. *Boston Housing Authority* (1975).
[5]*Perez et al.* v. *Boston Housing Authority*. Superior Court No. 17222, Suffolk,
s.s., Commonwealth of Mass., May 10, 1977. Order and/or Decree.

established procedures giving priority in assignments to applicants who would move into a project in which they were in the racial minority. Thus, a white applicant willing to move into a predominantly black development, or a black applicant willing to move into a predominantly white development would be given priority. Although over 1,000 letters were sent out informing applicants of the new priority system, only five applicants indicated that they wished to take advantage of it.

Although HUD supported the court's priority category for applicants voluntarily willing to accept placements which would help integrate developments, a major point of disagreement was that HUD wanted the BHA to drop its procedures for maintaining separate waiting lists for each development and permitting applicants to choose up to three projects. Instead, HUD wanted the BHA to adhere to the 1–2–3 rule, which did not allow for location preferences. The Master's Office argued that the elimination of all locational preferences by applicants was unrealistic given the fact that a substantial proportion of applicants were interested only in living in a specific development or section of the city. It further argued that if offered places other than those which they selected, these applicants would reject them.

The Master's Office attributed part of the problem in adopting a racially blind tenant assignment system to the fact that many BHA developments were unsafe for minority applicants. During the spring of 1976, racial tensions escalated in many sections of Boston, in part due to protests related to school busing. Both blacks and whites were attacked in various neighborhoods where they were in the racial minority. In many public housing developments, large numbers of children and teenagers were bused. This situation was accompanied by a great deal of racial animosity, and several projects experienced racial violence against blacks. In East Boston the violence became so fierce that over half of the twenty-three resident black families requested, and were granted, emergency transfers. The Master's Office concluded that, given BHA's severe financial problems, it could not provide extra security in all of its developments. Accordingly, they recommended marketing specific projects to underrepresented racial groups, a strategy requiring that applicants apply to specific developments.

Marketing Public Housing

When the Master's Office began its analysis of tenant selection, it was hampered by inadequate data on the racial composition of applicants, new tenants, or persons who refused public housing assignments. Without this information, the Master's Office found it impossible to understand the market for BHA housing or to analyze when and if it might be feasible to plan for desegregation. A survey of those on the waiting list coupled with an analysis of current residents revealed several major shifts in public housing demand. First, there were few applicants for family developments, such as Columbia Point, which had poor reputations. Consequently, such projects were experiencing increasing difficulty in filling vacant apartments. Second, the characteristics of families on the waiting list for public housing in Boston, as in many other cities, represented the poorest welfare-dependent families, the majority of which were one-parent families supported by AFDC. Third, although whites represented approximately 70 percent of Boston's income-eligible families for public housing, BHA housing was increasingly becoming viewed as a resource for black and Hispanic households, who represented almost 80 percent of the waiting list. Consequently, developments in all areas except those which were considered unsafe for minority families most likely would become segregated unless the BHA intervened. The Master's Office recommended that the BHA try to reactivate the market for BHA housing by expanding the waiting list for those projects without effective demand and increasing the number of white applicants from all parts of the city.

Increasing Managerial Discretion

As reported earlier, at one time managers had a number of pool cases at their developments from which they could choose tenants for apartments when they became available. The BHA eventually considered this practice subject to abuse by managers who were not accountable to the central office for their assignments. As a result, in 1975 a system was designed to minimize managerial discretion. When an apartment became vacant, the project manager forwarded a vacant notice to the Tenant Selection Department, which then assigned that unit to an applicant and then forwarded the applicant's case file to the development. The manager then tried to contact the applicant.

The process, however, still suffered from inherent flaws. For example, because the waiting list had not been updated for several years, case files sent to the projects were often inaccurate. Sometimes tenants had moved or were no longer interested in public housing or the family's composition had changed, making the designated unit inappropriate. As a result, operating income was lost or, in the worst case, a unit might be vandalized while another applicant's file made its way through the system. In addition to recommendations on updating the waiting list, the Master's Office suggested that the Tenant Selection Department pre-assign a specified number of cases in proportion to the number of vacancies reflecting both the need to minimize time lag and the need for central control of files and assignments. In order to insure equity at the project level and to avoid the problems described earlier at Columbia Point, the Master's Office also recommended that detailed procedures be established for managers to follow in contacting applicants assigned to their developments. These procedures included both telephoning the applicants and sending them letters. Finally, it was recommended that the Tenant Selection Department allow managers some flexibility in assigning applicants within their developments, for example, in cases wherein the unit to which they were assigned was not ready or to balance the density of children.

Increasing Screening

During the late 1960s and early 1970s screening of applicants came to a virtual halt in the face of legal decisions restricting the types of records available from the police, the lack of staff to investigate potential problem tenants or conduct hearings, and an overall liberal philosophy that the BHA should provide housing to all those in need. In the mid 1970s, however, a movement toward more careful screening resulted from a perceived need for greater security in the projects, deteriorating physical conditions, and the lack of resources for adequate security, maintenance, and social services. At that time, the small amount of screening done was carried out by the Tenant Services Department, to which about 4 percent of all applicants were referred; on the basis of loose standards, only about 5 percent of those applicants referred were denied housing. Although managers could also refer applicants to Tenant Services, only a few exercised that option.

The lack of screening resulted in part from the minimum amount of useful information collected on new applicants. Although the BHA could request credit and character references as well as names of landlords, welfare workers, and employees, such information, even when recorded, was usually not pursued. Additionally, the BHA's practice of letting applicants fill out forms at other agencies resulted in a great deal of incomplete information.

Although the Master's Office noted that screening was easily subject to abuse and was not a panacea for the problem of destructive tenants, it nevertheless recommended that some applicants should be barred from housing. Identified as such were those applicants who had a record of (1) failure to pay rent, unless residing in substandard conditions or paying in excess of 35% of income; (2) disturbance of neighbors, destruction of property, or housekeeping habits that affected the health, safety, or welfare of other tenants; (3) criminal activities; and/or (4) having been evicted from BHA housing in the last two years. The process designed to evaluate applicants in this regard included better collection of information, telephone contact with references, personal interviews with all applicants, and special investigation of the background of applicants considered to be potential problems.

Outcomes of Limited Intervention

The master's report formed the basis for a number of orders issued by the court to improve conditions. These directives, however, failed to satisfy the plaintiff; and in August 1976 the court moved to place the BHA in general receivership. Instead, Judge Garrity involved himself, the Master's Office, the Boston Public Housing Tenants Policy Council, the BHA, and attorneys for the plaintiff in lengthy negotiations and courtroom procedures over an eight-month period, the result of which was a constant decree agreed to by all the parties.

The decree, which fell short of receivership, was a 250-page blueprint for change that contained myriad requirements and timetables for plans and subplans. It required the BHA to reorganize extensively and develop long-range planning over a three-year period. It called for many personnel positions to be eliminated and others to be created. The master, who continued to be responsible for overseeing the plan, was also given a direct role in all personnel appointments. The decree contained a number of highly detailed plans for new procedures and policies in such areas as maintenance, management, security, purchasing, and finance. In terms of tenant selection and assignment, the consent decree translated the major points discussed in the master's report into a set of carefully worded standards and procedures entitled the Tenant Selection and Assignment Plan (TSAP). In addition, it created a timetable for implementing the TSAP, a reorganization plan for the department, and a series of directives for position changes.

According to a senior staff member, the TSAP, a detailed document of 38 pages, represented a laborious attempt to create fairness through a very tight system of chronological ordering and control of applications as well as a variety of checkpoints by which staff reviewed decisions for adherence to that system.[6] It attempted to solve many of the past problems through the elimination of discretion. And, in fact, tenant selection appears to be one of the areas in which the Master's Office felt it had some success, as indicated by computerization of the waiting list, a tightening up of emergency status, increased screening, and even the promotion of a modicum of racial integration in several developments. The implementation of the TSAP, with its written policies and defined ends and procedures, also appears to have relieved the tenant selection staff of pressure to respond to outside third parties.

The period following the consent decree was one of considerable turmoil within the BHA and friction between the BHA and the Master's Office. The BHA board, four members of which had been appointed by the mayor, still operated the agency and was considered by the court to be harassing the master through delaying tactics and obstruction. And, in spite of many personnel changes, the Master's Office was faced with an increasingly hostile, uncooperative, and sometimes abusive attitude on the part of BHA staff. The master reported substantial noncompliance with scheduled changes in financial forecasts and programs, budgets, maintenance organization, work orders for repair, and security.

For fourteen of the final eighteen months of the consent decree, the agency had only an acting administrator. In July 1979 Garrity ordered the Housing Authority to be placed in receivership, stating that "throughout the four-year history of this case the BHA has shown itself to be capable of nothing more than gross mismanagement."[7] Instead of improving, he found that conditions at BHA projects had worsened. He added that "the unabated mis- and non-feasance of the board necessitates the extraordinary action of appointing a receiver at this time."[8] Garrity's order was upheld by the State Supreme Court in February 1980. The Supreme Court noted:

[6]Boston Housing Authority, "Tenant Selection, Assignment and Transfer Plan" (Boston: BHA, mimeographed, 1978). The emphasis on a centralized system was similar to the one operating in New York City visited both by the author and the staff of the Master's Office.

[7]Quoted in Joseph Harvey, "Court to Run BHA," *Boston Globe*, July 26, 1979, p. 8.

[8]Quoted in Harvey, *Boston Globe*, p. 8.

No Judge or court could enjoy the prospect of interfering with local authority and assuming a measure of supervision over a large outside enterprise, least of all one sliding downhill. Nevertheless, the violations of the law are there and on the facts remedial efforts cannot stop short of receivership.[9]

Garrity appointed Lewis (Harry) Spence as the receiver to administer the agency. Spence, a graduate of Harvard Law School, had previously run the Somerville and Cambridge Housing Authorities. A Yankee by background, he had a reputation as a bright, energetic, high-principled liberal professional administrator who would get things done. Along with Garrity, an Irish Catholic known for his hands-on, no-nonsense, action-oriented approach, Spence began an almost five-year effort to reform the BHA. This move represented the first time a court had taken charge of a publicly financed independent authority. Through his receiver, Garrity had the power to hire, fire, transfer, and create positions for all employees. Garrity's order also gave the court the ability to change "any internal rule, regulation, by law, policy, custom, or practice."[10]

THE RECEIVERSHIP

In spite of some who viewed the purpose of the receivership as the liquidation of a problem-ridden housing stock, Spence set out as his overall goal the preservation of public housing as a resource for low-income people. Although the vacancy rate in Boston's public housing was the highest in the country, amounting to almost 23% of its 17,000 units, he saw public housing as a critical resource for Boston's low-income citizens who were faced with rising rents and gentrification of many city areas. Given these circumstances, Spence decided that his highest priorities were the reconstruction of 4,000 vacant units in the worst developments and the conservation of the rest of the BHA's housing stock.

Spence identified three main objectives necessary to achieve reconstruction and conservation: stability and security, restored building sys-

---

[9]Quoted in Alan Sheehan, "State High Court Backs BHA Receivership," *Boston Globe*, February 4, 1980, p. 1.
[10]*Perez et al.* v. *Boston Housing Authority*, Order of Appointment of Receiver (n.p., 1980), p. 7.

tems, and improved maintenance.[11] Security problems were manifested by the condition of vacated units in distressed developments which were not simply empty but were destroyed as a result of fires having been set, plumbing stolen, and windows smashed. Spence identified four underlying causes of security problems: adolescents who harassed other tenants; violent groups of youths engaged in criminal actions such as breaking and entering and assault and battery; the drug industry, some of whose entrepreneurs operated out of several developments; and those opposed to integration. Failures in building systems were sometimes related to security problems but also had their own roots. Plumbing, electrical, roofing, heating, and elevator systems had simply worn out in many developments, and outdated electrical systems constantly failed due to overloading of modern conveniences. Although the structural elements (that is, the actual buildings) were sound, in large developments the subsystems were too expensive to replace in piecemeal fashion and required major capital investments. Maintenance problems arose primarily because almost no preventive maintenance was performed to extend the useful life of building systems; instead, work was aimed at immediate code violations. In some developments, even emergency maintenance requests remained unanswered for several days due to lack of manpower, inadequate supervision, inappropriate work rules, and hiring practices which were based more on political affiliation than ability.

In order to restore security, building systems, and maintenance, Spence pursued an overall strategy of "reconstruction" based on reallocating operating and capital resources to existing public housing developments rather than new projects. Specifically, resources were first targeted at mid-sized projects in bad condition and next at larger projects in the most dire circumstances. The one exception was Columbia Point, which was planned to become a privately developed mixed-income model because of its location near the recently constructed John F. Kennedy Library and the Boston branch of the University of Massachusetts. In order to improve overall conditions, Spence secured additional capital from both HUD and the state, decentralized management authority to developmental-level supervisors, deployed security forces paid for through Community Development Block Grant funds, and reduced the

---

[11]Spence's strategy is outlined in Boston Housing Authority Receivership, *Second Semi-annual Report to the Suffolk Superior Court (August 6, 1980–February 1, 1981), February 13, 1981.*

density of some projects. More amorphous goals—such as developing stronger relations between public housing projects and adjacent neighborhoods, increasing residents' roles in management, and civil rights— also received attention, but fewer resources were allocated to their achievement.

Spence viewed tenant selection and assignment as an integral component of his plan, and an original goal of the receivership was to review and update the TSAP. However, this plan was placed on the back burner, partly because many of the issues were so fundamental that Spence considered them extremely difficult and because their success depended on improving security and physical conditions. In the meantime, he organized a committee of senior staff and representatives of several departments who were assigned to deal with conceptualizing policy plans and strategies for implementation. The receivership identified the following five areas as its priorities: (1) management reorganization, (2) increased screening, (3) implementation of fair housing initiatives, (4) broad range of income selection policy, and (5) tenant empowerment.

Management Reorganization

In spite of the plans of the Master's Office and perhaps as a result of them, systems problems continued to provide barriers to an efficiently operating tenant-selection process. As a senior staff member commented, the TSAP had introduced a highly rational plan into an irrational system. A review of the department in 1982 concluded that its structure was still not conducive to its role of assuring a flow of eligible applicants who were prepared to move into BHA units as they became available. For example, the team found that the intake process consumed a disproportionate share of the department's resources.[12] On the one hand, this led to unrealistic expectations and frustrations among applicants unlikely to be housed for several years. On the other hand, it invested significant resources in some applicants who, because of changing family needs and/or interest, would never be housed.

In the intake process, an admissions counselor interviewed each prospective applicant; filled out a lengthy application form; explained the tenant selection process, priorities, and housing opportunities available;

---

[12]Boston Housing Authority, "Occupancy Department Reorganization" (Boston: BHA, mimeographed, n.d.).

requested and reviewed documentation as it was received; and determined program eligibility (i.e., that the applicant qualified for public housing on the basis of family composition, income, age, and citizenship or equal residency). As in the past, the walk-in service approach resulted in the department's major activity being at the mercy of how many people decided to apply on any given day.

Since most of the effort was spent on initial intake, very few resources were left to devote to other activities considered to be just as important, such as keeping the waiting list up to date, marketing, and screening. Consequently, according to one senior staff member, the system was still not allowing the BHA to meet its objectives. One year after the receivership took over the BHA, the plaintiffs were still complaining that the waiting lists remained long and inaccurate. They noted:

> Tenant selection is the first and often most significant encounter of low-income persons with the BHA. Sadly, this contact accurately reinforces the prereceivership perception of an inefficient BHA unresponsive to human needs.[13]

In addition, the system still did not allow managers to fill vacancies in developments in an efficient manner. For example, in 1982 the BHA embarked on a strategy to rehabilitate Beach Street, a racially mixed development in a white area. In order to expedite occupancy of six vacant units, the Tenant Selection Department sent the manager twelve cases that indicated an interest in moving into the project on initial intake. However, the applicants had not been contacted in more than a year, and none of the cases had been screened. Some of the applicants had moved, and most of the applicants whom the manager was able to contact either did not want to move into the development or were now ineligible. Since the process required that the manager wait at least a week before making an offer to another applicant, it was enormously time consuming. Not only did the BHA lose valuable income, but units were vandalized in the meantime. After a considerable amount of effort, only one of the eligible applicants wanted to move in, a built-in disincentive to screen this applicant since the manager's performance evaluation to a great extent was based on his ability to fill vacancies.

---

[13]*Perez et al.* v. *Boston Housing Authority,* by Its Receiver, Lewis H. Spence, Commonwealth of Mass., Superior Court Department No. 17222, Suffolk, s.s., (1980), p. 7.

In order to improve the tenant selection process, the receiver re-organized the office procedures. For example, fewer of the department's resources were invested in the intensive application process. Instead, applicants filled out a simpler form and participated in group briefing sessions in which the process was outlined, the waiting time at various projects highlighted, and the priority system explained. Not until their names had risen almost to the top of the waiting list were applicants called in for more intensive interviews in which an occupancy specialist checked their eligibility, screened them for acceptance by checking references, and conducted a home interview if necessary.

Screening

The staff of the receivership attributed great importance to security in their efforts to build stable development communities and preserve the housing stock. This emphasis clearly signaled a shift away from the BHA's role as the houser of last resort concerned primarily with the needs of individuals and toward its role as a protector of the public interest. One aspect of this new role was protecting the welfare of those residents already living in BHA developments; therefore screening became one of the highest priorities in tenant selection.

The BHA's increased screening procedures actually began with efforts to reestablish the credibility of evictions in cases in which tenants were engaged in acts of violence against other residents. Through a series of court actions, several of which it initially lost, the receivership finally gained acceptance of a modified "fast-track" eviction procedure. Yet, once having established procedures for evicting tenants who were terribly destructive, the staff member in charge of reforming tenant selection indicated that the receivership had come to the conclusion that they were letting in equally troublesome replacements:

> We're not screening people, so those who have been bad tenants, irresponsible or criminal, are getting into BHA housing and ruining the lives of people around them. We also have the question of de-institutionalized mental health patients. We have to decide what is acceptable behavior and what is not.

In order to beef up its screening capabilities, the initial reorganiza-tion of the tenant selection department included the assignment of two staff members whose reponsibility it was to conduct credit checks, contact previous landlords, carry out home visits when needed, and investigate applications for which the accuracy or reliability of the information was in question. Although the reasons for rejecting an applicant were spelled out in the TSAP, in order to avoid some of the abuses of the past, a committee of high-level BHA staff was created to review applicant acceptances and rejections. This reorganization, however, was judged ineffective because there were weak links between the interviewers, the screeners, and the project managers.

Later reorganization resulted in each applicant's coming in for an interview as his or her name came close to the top of the waiting list. This process created personal contact with the BHA occupancy specialist assigned to handle tenant selection in particular projects. This staff member then contacted personal references and past landlords, asking them a set of standard questions. If there was some doubt or disparity in the information, a home visit was made. If the occupancy specialist made an unfavorable ruling or if the manager, upon receiving the information and interviewing the applicant, judged the applicant inappropriate, the case was then reviewed by the assistant director.

The end result of the reorganization and increased emphasis on screening was a higher proportion of rejected applicants. Although previously only a handful of applicants had been found ineligible, approximately 10 percent were rejected after the new screening procedures took effect. Out of 120 applicants judged ineligible by the screening process during the period January 1, 1983 through June 30, 1983, the breakdown of reasons other than too high an income included the following: criminal activity (5); inability to function independently (13); poor housekeeping habits (13); failure to meet financial obligations (13); other reasons such as inability to relate to others (19). The screening process also identified 65 applicants who were former BHA tenants and had terminated their prior tenancy with a rent balance.[14] In addition, Spence felt that at least another ten percent of applicants dropped out because they thought they would be rejected: "They got the message—once the credibility of the screening process was restored a large number of people deselected themselves."

[14]Boston Housing Authority Receivership, *Seventh Semi-annual Report to the Suffolk Superior Court* (Boston: n.p., June 30, 1983), p. 27.

Promoting Fair Housing

The BHA and the Master's Office had negotiated fair housing initiatives, which became part of the TSAP, with HUD and the Commonwealth in 1977. However, as of February 1980 the agency had no plans, staff, or other capability to address fair housing concerns.[15] As a result, the authority made only sporadic attempts at integration in the case of individual tenants. These attempts were characterized by little or no planning and a lack of support services such as adequate police protection. Furthermore, they sometimes included inadequately screened persons whose mental health or physical incapacities made them inappropriate candidates for placement. Consequently, few placements were attempted and some conspicuous failures occurred. In the meantime, explosive situations developed at some projects while others were becoming rapidly less integrated.

In 1980 the receivership moved to address racial issues structurally by creating a Civil Rights Division. This division was designed to plan and oversee integration efforts in such areas as employment and tenant selection. At that time, a fair housing task force, composed of BHA employees who represented diverse job categories and levels (including tenant selection and project management), was also created to advise on racial integration issues. Strategies to improve the racial integration of projects differed depending on whether a project was considered to be racially troubled, integrated but not in racial crisis, or in an area historically resistant to racial change.

At the outset of the receivership, the BHA considered itself to have little capacity for addressing issues of racial integration. In fact, racial conflict associated with school busing was so prevalent, both in the city at large and in specific developments, that the BHA decided to focus its limited efforts on maintaining desegregation at several of the most troubled projects. These areas—Brighton, Hyde Park, and East Boston—were the scenes of several firebombings, shootings, and harassment. In each case, the BHA increased security, discussed the new security measures with tenants, and met with community leaders to elicit strategies to increase racial harmony in the neighborhoods. When the situations calm-

[15]Lewis H. Spence, letter to Joseph Vera, HUD Regional Office, May 31, 1983.

ed down, the BHA gave priority to minority applicants to bring their percentage back up to previous levels in these projects.

Once it had tried its hand at stabilizing crisis projects, the BHA attempted to address integration in less volatile projects. Its objective was to target developments most amenable to efforts toward racial balance and to create open housing subplans designed either to maintain the existing racial mix or to increase the representation of specific racial groups. The plan was to select housing applicants of designated races from the standard waiting list in proportions that either maintained or promoted racial balance in developments. The criteria for identifying projects included the racial demography of the community surrounding the project, the presence or absence of diverse racial groups already in the development, and an assessment of whether members of underrepresented racial groups would be accepted without violence. Depending upon the circumstance at particular projects, the task force recommended maintaining the racial percentages at current levels, increasing the percentage of whites or nonwhites, or no action because of the possibility of racial violence.

The subplans consisted of several elements, a key to which was a placement strategy. For example, one subplan called for the placement of two white families and one nonwhite family to fill every three vacancies in the project. Additional strategies sometimes included placement by building or entry way. The basic principle was that, at a minimum, the racial mix of residents in BHA developments as a whole should approximate the racial mix of all those eligible for public housing in Boston. However, most subplans went much further and their goals took into consideration the current racial mix of the development and of the surrounding neighborhood. In contrast to many other cities, such as New Haven, which primarily had minority projects in minority areas, Boston had projects located in most of its neighborhoods.[16] This included the existence of predominantly minority projects in mixed areas, a condition which seemed conducive to balancing such developments by attracting white applicants.

The overall ratios for each project were often negotiated with local task forces. For example, at several projects in white neighborhoods

[16]Ellen Gessmer, "Discrimination in Public Housing Under the Housing and Community Development Act of 1974: A Critique of the New Haven Experience," *Urban Law Annual*, 13, No. 49 (1977), 49–80.

where blacks represented almost 60 percent of the residents, plans called for reversing the ratio so that whites comprised 60 percent. However, in some cases blacks argued that they were fearful because they had only just begun to feel reasonably safe against racial violence and some of that sense of safety came from their majority standing within the project. According to Spence, "they were afraid that if the number of whites increased again they would be victimized on the streets." In this case, the BHA altered its goal to 50 percent black, 50 percent white.

The willingness and ability of applicants to reside in a given project where they were the minority represented major constraints on the effectiveness of the subplans. A primary strategy used to overcome the reluctance of the applicants and the resistance of residents was to use rehabilitation as an incentive. For example, Orient Heights, a project in East Boston occupied overwhelmingly by whites, was slated for major modernization subject to an agreement that 25 percent of the rehabilitated units go to minorities. Such a public-housing modernization strategy was similar to the concept of magnet schools—make the housing so desirable that all persons, regardless of race, will desire to live in it. According to a senior-level BHA staff member, the tenants participated in developing the plan because the project was in physically poor condition and the vacancy rehabilitation program would improve living conditions. Moreover, he felt that since the goal was to increase the proportion of minorities to 13 percent, fears were abated that it would "tip" toward becoming a minority-dominated development. The creation of these goals, however, was an imprecise science as was the theory underlying the tipping point phenomenon on which it was based. Moreover, this strategy was not necessarily effective in projects which had a history of intense racial violence.

As discussed earlier in this chapter, during the 1970s several attempts to place black families in areas such as South Boston and Charlestown resulted in threats of violence or actual violence, harassment, and the departure of the families in question. According to Spence, these failures reinforced "the community's sense that it could prevent integration by such actions." Consequently, the BHA's strategy was different in such projects. Spence and his staff concluded:

> The *aggressive placement of black and Hispanic families,* such as takes place under open housing sub-plans, is *not* feasible in develop-

ments with *such surroundings at least in* the *absence of forceful and effective local, state and federal support.*[17]

Lacking such support, Spence instead embarked on a strategy of slowly integrating BHA work forces at such developments as a positive sign for the future housing of minority applicants. As black and Hispanic families came to the top of BHA's chronological waiting list for such projects as Charlestown, they were screened carefully with regard to their disposition and how they would stand up if violence broke out. Black applicants with teenagers were rejected to avoid friction with white teenagers in the area. Staff also communicated with a broad range of tenants, other individuals, and groups emphasizing that the black families were not displacing Charlestown residents and had been on the waiting list for several years. They made the applicants' status as well as BHA's intention to house them clear to quell misconceptions or rumors about the BHA's plans for occupancy of the development by indicating that the process would be gradual and the eventual black population would not exceed 15 percent. As Spence recalled, "People said simply, 'It's impossible. Given the recent history, it will blow up.'" But Spence, in turn, told them: "Then we've got a real problem, because it's impossible for me to tell them that I can't give them a place to live because of their color."[18] Spence continued to meet with the community and eventually secured the support of Humberto Cardinal Medeiros, the Archbishop of Boston, who instructed his parish priests to get out the message that resistance was "un-Christian, un-Catholic and un-American." At the same time, Spence asked the blacks to delay moving to these projects for one year to give Charlestown enough time to prepare. In March and April of 1984, five black families moved in without any incident.

In its assessment of the promotion of integration, the receivership concluded it had made progress. Even though only a few minority tenants lived in Charlestown, it considered that a remarkable achievement, given the previous racial hostility. Moreover, it had a fair amount of success in implementing its subplans so that a number of projects now more closely mirrored the racial composition of those considered eligible for public housing. For example, the BHA had increased the percentage of non-

[17]Lewis H. Spence, Letter to Joseph Vera, May 31, 1983.

[18]Quoted in "Boston Housing Project Is Peacefully Integrated," *The New York Times*, March 18, 1984.

white families at the Orient Heights development from 3 percent in 1980 to 14.5 percent at the end of 1982. Nevertheless, serious problems remained. Because over 70 percent of the families on the BHA's waiting list were minority, if often was easier to attract nonwhites to predominantly white projects than to attract whites to minority projects. The continued presence of whites on the waiting list, however, was a testimony to the tight housing market in Boston, accentuated by the gentrification of several working-class white neighborhoods. The success of the subplan approach was also somewhat dependent on the modernization of projects which required additional funds from the state or federal government. In the early 1980s the BHA had been able to secure funds to rehabilitate small and medium-sized projects, many of which happened to be in white areas. Yet to be tackled were some of the larger projects housing minorities such as Mission Hill, which would be extremely costly to modernize. Finally, the issue of benign quotas hung over the authority as a thin cloud. This issue had been raised in the mid-1980s in relation to a private development in Starrett City, New York, which was settled out of court. The BHA had thus far been able to avoid such attacks by claiming that its subplans reflected not quotas but goals and that because it had many developments, applicants had considerable choice.

Broad Range of Income

The Housing and Community Development Act of 1974 set as a major goal the establishment of communities composed of persons with a wide range of incomes. Under this act, each local public housing authority was required, as part of its contract with HUD, to pursue "tenant selection criteria designed to assure that, within a reasonable period of time, projects will include families with a broad range of incomes and will avoid concentrations of low-income and deprived families with serious social problems."[19] Two major assumptions appear to have formed the basis for this new policy. First, Congress believed that public housing faced an economic crisis and, since higher-income tenants payed higher rent, income mixing would create a "healthier social environment," the unstated assumption being that the mere presence of higher-income tenants would create a more socially viable housing project. Although recognizing that these regulations set forth reasonable tenant selection goals, the Master's

[19]See Gessmer, p. 19.

Office had earlier rejected granting higher-income applicants priority because such a policy would cause the large number of lower-income applicants who had been waiting for BHA housing for as long as six years to wait an additional period of time.[20]

During the receivership, however, the BHA began to reconsider its stance on income mixing. Earlier proponents of income mixing had argued in its defense that social incentives are created when upward mobility can be observed within a community.[21] Spence, an early opponent of the idea, eventually came to much the same conclusion. However, his support was not based so much on the idea of role models but rather on the opportunity for employment: "If public housing projects are to offer hope and opportunity, rather than entrapment and despair, their residents have to come into contact with the larger world and especially the world of work."[22] Spence noted the common-wisdom idea that to learn of job opportunities, and thereby to get work, one must know someone who has a job. More broadly, he came to believe that the isolation issue was fundamental, both as a consequence of the symptom and as one cause of the powerlessness of residents in the sense that lack of engagement beyond the project offered residents no forum in which to learn the skills for surviving on the outside. Therefore he argued that projects turned into places of exile as well as places of dependency because they did not promote development of skills for surviving in a competitive outside world. On the other hand, Spence considered that the work context provided endless continuing education in goal setting, group problem solving, negotiating, and mediation.

Spence also believed that, in addition to creating opportunities for individual residents to enter the working world, the addition of greater numbers of the working poor as residents would serve to strengthen community institutions within public housing. He observed, for example, that the working poor took a disproportionate interest in serving on tenant task forces. He speculated that their experience at work encouraged them to participate in project activities. Even though he had observed nonworking people who had superb organizing skills, Spence felt that the likelihood of having enough residents of this kind within a project com-

[20]Whittlesey, pp. ix–73.
[21]Gessmer, p. 53.
[22]Quoted in Kirk Scharfenberg, "BHA to Favor the Working Poor," *Boston Globe*, August 6, 1983.

posed of almost all nonworking residents was small. Since he had concluded that the only hope for the program was to build its own political constituency, Spence saw the strategy of including the working poor as a necessary step to increase the political clout of public housing tenants.

The new income criteria were planned as a "two-tier" system.[23] The first tier would consist of applicants with incomes below 25 percent of the area's median income and would include a maximum limit. The range for a family of four was $0 to $7,700. The second tier would consist of applicants with incomes equal to or above 25 percent of the median income, with a maximum limit. The range for a family of four in tier two was from $7,701 to $17,400. Applicants were to be selected at a ratio of two in the second tier to one in the first tier until the ratio within a development was 1:1. A similar plan had been adopted by other housing authorities such as St. Louis.

Spence considered his economic integration proposal the most difficult policy decision during his tenure at the BHA. It became a hotly debated issue opposed by many of the groups that supported the receivership in general. For example, a letter to the editor of the *Boston Globe*, circulated to local and state officials by the Coalition for Basic Human Needs, attacked Spence's assumptions that public housing residents were isolated and that income mixing would solve the problems of single-parent women who try to work: "Lack of day care, inequitable wages, discrimination, and lack of training are problems which are not going to be solved with a little 'networking.' "[24] They also attacked the argument, also raised by Spence, that more "male-headed households" would be better able to control teenage boys as representative of a sexist philosophy based on the false assumption that women were inherently incapable of handling their own families. Finally, the coalition argued that, given overcrowding in some projects, the introduction of higher-income households would only result in those families most in need being left homeless: "To displace these families would mean taking away one of the few housing resources that they have at their disposal."[25]

The Massachusetts Coalition for the Homeless also voiced their opposition to this policy both through a demonstration at BHA offices and

---

[23]Boston Housing Authority, "Broad Range of Incomes Program," (Boston: BHA, mimeographed, 1983).

[24]Coalition for Basic Human Needs, Letter to the Editor of the *Boston Globe*, May 21, 1983.

[25]Coalition for Basic Human Needs, Letter, p. 2.

through the issuance of a position paper outlining the seriousness of the housing situation in Boston for minorities and for households headed by single women. An editorial written by a coordinator of the Homeless Coalition said, "Underlying the BHA's move to thin out the number of welfare recipients in public housing are belittling assumptions about women and the poor: that what women do in the home is not valuable, that it is not "work," and that the poor are responsible for their poverty."[26]

Spence had his supporters in the governor's office and at the *Boston Globe*. In an editorial, the *Globe* described the policy proposal as a "bold and welcome step toward strengthening the political clout and social stability of public housing."[27] And Spence tried to head off some of the opposition by targeting BHA Section 8 leased-housing subsidies to low-income tier-one applicants. Therefore, in spite of the opposition, Spence received both HUD and state approval. However, the Governor's Executive Office of Communities and Development added the stipulation that the BHA specify how the Section 8 rental assistance programs would work and how they would increase the stock of low-income housing.

Tenant Empowerment

Most of the efforts of the receivership focused on making the centralized system work better. However, after several years, Spence became disenchanted with the merits of creating a system based solely on clearly defined rules administered by BHA bureaucrats. Instead, he began to turn his attention towards tenant involvement in selection at the project level.

Spence's belief in this approach was based on three problems he associated with the bureaucratic system of tenant selection: (1) its arbitrariness, (2) its secondary side effects, and (3) its inhumaneness. He saw the arbitrary nature of the system as a natural outcome of its need to categorize people. In the case of the BHA, applicants were slotted into either emergency or standard categories, easing the decisions of the lower-paid employees who were not expected to exercise discretion. The problem was that some cases did not fall neatly into either category, and some distinctions probably should have been made, one result being that

---

[26]Monica Hileman, "Wrong Way to Select Tenants," *Boston Globe*, April 28, 1984.

[27]Editorial, "Housing Boston's Poor," *Boston Globe*, April 26, 1984.

those who barely missed qualifying as an emergency even though their situation was urgent went to the bottom of the chronologically ordered list.[28] However, given the variability of misery and need as well as the inherent problems of measurement, such judgments were beyond the capacity of the organization as it was presently composed. The secondary side effects issue existed because the tenant selection system ignored the influence of new tenants on existing residents: for a resident already living in a development, who moves in makes an enormous difference both in the short and the long term. But, even if the bureaucracy and the legal system were perfectly designed and able to work well, Spence viewed them as dehumanizing. Applicants came in, described their difficult situations, and the staff explained why the BHA could do little to help them.

Spence's alternative was to create a process that allowed discretion at the project level. Other staff again wanted managers to play a greater role in tenant selection. Interestingly, now that the housing authority had come full circle with the reintroduction of screening at the central level, managers' concern over tenant selection issues greatly diminished. Although not opposed to increasing manager discretion still further, Spence believed that such a strategy did not go far enough and that managers would always be biased because of their class. Instead, Spence wanted tenants to become the major decision makers in tenant selection. Spence's proposed structure was an elected tenants' organization at each project which would then appoint a tenant selection committee with the condition that it include racial representation. Initially, to avoid racial discrimination the plan could be used only in developments where there was potential for integration and where the tenants' committee agreed on an integration plan. Eventually, Spence hoped that it would provide an incentive for integration, in return for which the project residents would get much better control, not over race, but over the character of who moved in.

Spence hoped his plan would result in the selection of tenants more on the basis of need but that applicants likely to cause problems would be screened out. He also foresaw that the plan would result in more flexibility and responsiveness to project conditions, such as the need for a certain type of family in a particular location. Although he had little sense of how far it would go, Spence envisioned a system whereby two residents of a

[28]See Kirk Scharfenberg, "Home Rule Test," *Boston Globe*, October 17, 1981, p. 11.

project, rather than a white-collar worker from BHA's central office, might visit a prospective tenant in his or her home. On the basis of that evaluation and other information, the tenant selection committee might decide that the applicant should be bypassed for the time being in favor of another prospective tenant who better met the perceived needs of the particular areas in that project.

In addition to helping tenants mold the communities in which they lived, Spence also hoped the new plan would involve them in a political process important in their daily lives. It would build the political capacity of the community by opening up two types of patronage. First, it could create a reward system and a greater stake in the project for a good tenant who might, for example, want a relative or friend to move into the development. By having something to hand out, it would also provide the tenants with some political patronage with groups such as the city council. For example, if they directly helped out members of the city council, then when the allocation of funds such as Community Development Block Grants came up, the tenants could make some demands on the council. Spence felt this type of influence would aid the tenants in gaining political astuteness and power. While he acknowledged that some abuse might result from their misuse of discretion, Spence came to the conclusion that such a community system might be less abusive than one in which no discretion was exercised or bureaucrats made decisions. He also thought it preferable to "use the democratic process to prevent abuse than the regulatory one." And, given its legal implications, although the BHA might surrender some of its direct control, it would have to keep oversight in such areas as eligibility and race.

The End of Receivership

On October 18, 1984, four months before it was to have come up for formal reevaluation, Judge Garrity ended the receivership. In announcing his decision, Garrity noted that the BHA had made an important stride in upgrading living conditions. The end of receivership followed soon after Kevin White, Boston's mayor for four terms, did not run again for office and was replaced by Raymond Flynn, a populist candidate. Even though earlier in his career Flynn had been strongly opposed to school busing, his campaign was marked by more moderate stands on other racial issues and his commitment to insure access of all races and ethnic groups to housing in Boston's neighborhoods. Garrity noted that his decision was based in part on his endorsement of Mayor Flynn's plan for governing the authority. When the receivership ended, under the new plan BHA administration would report directly to the mayor; and public housing tenants would hold five seats on a nine-member monitoring committee.

The overall impact of the court's intervention on tenant selection is difficult to assess. Certainly the receivership itself insulated the BHA from Boston's political patronage system, thereby allowing it to hire a number of new staff at all levels with no strong outside attachments. This provided the context within which tenant selection could evolve from a very loose ad hoc operation with a great deal of discretion to a centralized system in which chronological order and stated priorities controlled the flow of applications. The court was also a force for new efforts to integrate projects. And it was a strong advocate for reintroducing screening and eventual decentralization of tenant selection to the project level, practices that had been commonplace up until the 1970s.

Thus, in some ways, the 1980s brought the BHA full circle. As one senior staff member commented, "A lot of the problems haven't changed but the parameters of the problems have changed. Some lead you in new directions and others lead you back to where you started." Moreover, the tugs and pulls in tenant selection were related. For example, without the backing of the court, increased screening might have been more strongly opposed by liberal civil rights organizations; and racial integration would probably have remained a lower item on the BHA's agenda given Boston's racial problems.

Although the receivership permitted the BHA to increase the rate of change, reincorporate several old procedures, and head in new directions, several initiatives barely got off the ground and some of the changes created their own dilemmas. For example, the incoming mayor, whose supporters included the coalitions opposed to the plan, refused to endorse the broad-range-of-income policy and it therefore died. Similarly, the project-level tenant selection experiments, a response to concerns that the rational system had gone too far, even though judged successful, took hold only at a few projects. And finally, the efforts to integrate developments were highly restricted by the needs of minorities for housing, the diminishing number of white applicants willing to move into minority-dominated projects for low-income tenants, and the reluctance of minorities to move into developments in hostile white neighborhoods such as South Boston.

CONCLUSION

Only the unprecedented intervention of the court as receiver and the Herculean efforts of a dedicated group of reformers over a five-year period saved, at least for the time being, the BHA from disaster in the 1980s. In their attempts to improve the situation, reformers tore apart and rebuilt the very core of the agency by hiring new staff, redefining tasks, and securing additional resources. One result of these changes was a more rational tenant selection system.

For all the reform efforts, however, the future of the BHA and other housing authorities remains in doubt. Although the situation had somewhat stabilized, conditions in many projects were still bad and the number of vacant units still high. Spence always viewed the bad conditions of Boston's housing developments as evidence of the poor population's repudiation of the system intended to purchase their acquiesence in being excluded from the broader social fabric. Therefore, the problems of the BHA indicated not only the failure of a housing program, but also a larger distress eroding the life of low-income communities. Hence, at their basis, Spence's efforts to reform public housing always involved not only the provision of decent housing but also the resolution of problems of race and class: the provision of jobs, the creation of order and security, the integration of projects and neighborhoods, and access to political power.

Although many projects were modernized during this period, the underlying fiscal crisis of the authority still continues to threaten its ability to improve the quality of its dwelling units and provide security. Family public housing is particularly vulnerable in this regard because of adverse publicity and the difficulty its supporters have had in lobbying for a program which, in the long run, has ended up serving a welfare-dependent population at a time when potentially less expensive alternatives, such as housing vouchers, have gained popularity. In addition, solutions to the large dilemmas of the general poverty, lack of education, and limited employment opportunities in this population are beyond the scope and capability of the authority.

It is little wonder, given these conditions, that the federal government and individual authorities have considered the disposal of projects to tenants, private management, or private developers with the hope that improvements will occur or, at least, that they will become someone else's problems. However, such an approach will not solve the problems of poverty and race that underlie the current crisis in public housing but rather will accentuate them by reducing the stock of housing for low-income people, an increasing number of whom are Hispanic and Asian. These problems should remain high on the public agenda.

CHAPTER NINE

Summary and Implications

A major purpose of this study has been to examine attempts to introduce predictability and fairness into the allocation process of a major public bureaucracy. In order to do this, the experiences of the Boston Housing Authority were examined. One must be careful in generalizing policy implications which arise out of a specific case study. However, to the extent that generalizations can be made, the BHA is a valuable example because of its representative structural and historical characteristics.

The initial strategy of the BHA's attempts at equity was to set up rules such as allocation on a first come, first serve basis and a specified procedure governing the selection and assignment of public housing applicants to projects. This rule-based decision-making strategy is typical of many public housing authorities. It is based on the theoretical assumption that a bureaucracy should function in a manner which treats like cases alike through the application of general rules to particular cases. Still, up until the early 1980s, despite many reports highlighting its inadequacies and recommending improvements, tenant selection remained a rather loose, ad hoc operation.

This is in direct contradiction to the characterization of bureaucracies as rule-bound and rigid, although in accord with criticisms of inefficiency. As seen in the case of the BHA, many of the barriers to reform arise from lack of acceptance of some rules as valid decision-making constructs as well as disagreements about whom public housing should serve. In this context, maintenance of the status quo in developments along racial and class lines undermines implementation of such efforts as the 1–2–3 project assignment rule.

Continued failure to implement an effective rule system appears also to have roots in a number of other external and internal factors. For

example, in the case of the BHA, a modified patronage system made the
bureaucracy accountable to the mayor's office both in terms of employment and tenant selection and assignment. Because many of the
politicians were advocates of particular applicants, their efforts undermined the effectiveness of the rule-based system. Although politicians
lost some interest in preferential assignments when the projects eventually housed more welfare-dependent tenants, social workers and other
agency staff took their place as advocates, continuing to undermine the
equity system. In addition, the multilayered nature of the housing authority allowed project managers, a form of street-level bureaucrat, to
exercise discretion in selecting applicants whom they felt would make
good tenants. Both of these pressures for discretion rather than rule
adherence were compounded by the lack of resources and generally low
morale that made it difficult to run an efficient tenant selection and assignment operation. Such low quality services are endemic in programs
that cater to groups that society views as unproductive or undeserving.
Taking these problems as a point of departure, as demonstrated by the
case history of the BHA, eight major issues important to the allocation
process in public housing become evident: (1) conditions for reform, (2)
whom public housing shall serve, (3) regulatory justice, (4) federal–local
relationships, (5) the influence of third parties, (6) the power of street-
level bureaucrats, (7) client empowerment, and (8) the privatization of
public housing.

CONDITIONS FOR REFORM

Robert Yin, in a book examining change in urban bureaucracies, has
hypothesized that key factors exist which are facilitators to routinization of
innovation.[1] Following his lead, this study suggests that certain key conditions can be identified as facilitating the routinization of bureaucratic
reform, which in the case of the BHA was the implementation of a tightly
centralized, rational management system in which chronological order
and stated priorities controlled the flow of applicants.

First, the deficiencies and need for reform are reported by outside
groups important to the agency's survival, in this case HUD, the funding
and monitoring agency of the BHA. These reports add legitimacy to

[1]Robert Yin, *Changing Urban Bureaucracies: How New Practices Become Routinized* (Lexington, MA.: Lexington Books, 1978).

reform efforts. Second, the agency itself must become sufficiently insulated from politics so that it can pursue a rational tenant selection system based on rules and procedures. Court intervention, in the BHA's case, reduced political patronage to a minor element in securing jobs or promotions, thereby eliminating most of the outside pressures on staff and allowing new staff to be hired in place of those who opposed reform. Third, the clients, in this case tenants, can be a force for change when they collectively band together in lawsuits or tenant actions. Fourth, inefficiencies which cause economic problems for the agency may arise which in turn cause reduced revenue and thereby set reform as a high priority. For example, in the case of the BHA, the department could not insure an adequate flow of applicants interested in the projects to which they were assigned; therefore income was lost and apartments vandalized. Thus, reform which promised payoffs to the agency in terms of needed increased revenue became a high priority. Fifth, changes need support from top administrators who are not only committed to them in principle but provide additional resources to ensure their implementation. In the case of the BHA, top administrators observed the results of such rules in similar agencies and decided that the creation of an improved tenant selection and assignment system had a high enough priority so that additional resources, including the assignment of senior-level personnel as consultants, were brought to bear on it. Sixth, the routinization of change requires a long enough gestation period so that implementation problems can be ironed out and the system may take hold. Often such endeavors fail because reformers leave before changes become the accepted way of doing things. In the case of the BHA, the receivership lasted almost five years, a period long enough so that problems could be analyzed, goals and objectives set, staff recruited and trained, procedures established, and feedback obtained. Seventh, there must be little outside opposition to the implementation. In this case, the rational system took pressure off central office staff; and, once they realized that tougher screening was being conducted, project managers also accepted it more readily.

Clearly, the ability to initiate and carry out reform is extremely difficult to secure in a complex bureaucratic system that serves a poor clientele.[2] It is dependent on the presence of a number of key factors.

[2]Lisa Peattie suggests that public housing is a complex system, the output of which is system-determined—that is, "not truly planned or intended, much less controlled, by any individual or group, but rather the outcome of the regular

Furthermore, even after the the mandate and the means to do so have been established, many other controversial issues can arise which complicate and undermine the effectiveness of the most serious efforts.

WHOM SHALL PUBLIC HOUSING SERVE?: THE INFLUENCE OF SOCIOECONOMIC CONDITIONS

Effective reform is dependent on the acceptance of certain underlying principles such as some agreement as to whom a program should serve. In the case of public housing, much of the controversy concerning tenant selection and assignment policies and practices, and therefore much of the interference in their implementation, has been about whom public housing should serve. Over the years, family public housing has experienced a shift from poor white tenants, either temporarily unemployed or working, to primarily welfare-dependent minority tenants. A major cause of this shift has been the rising numbers of public-welfare recipients among the general population of those who need affordable housing.

In the BHA as in other public housing authorities these changes were supported by civil rights advocates, including legal service attorneys who worked to convince the courts and government agencies such as HUD that public housing must assure fair treatment to all applicants by not denying eligibility to certain classes of tenants. In their view, public housing must serve as the housing of last resort for those who have no other viable options. In the case of the BHA, these advocates pushed the authority to take positive steps to end racial discrimination and segregation in accord with their views concerning the responsibility of a public agency using government funds.

At about the same time that poor and minority applicants were increasingly occupying public housing, central city authorities began to be plagued by security, maintenance, and financial problems. Some analysts viewed this outcome as a consequence of the overconcentration of lower-class residents in high-rise public-housing developments. In such dense

---

interrelations of a number of components or subsystems." Lisa Peattie, "Public Housing: Urban Slums Under Public Management," in *Race, Change and Urban Society,* P. Orleans and W. Ellis, eds. (Los Angeles: Sage Publications, 1971), p. 285.

environments where there is a low ratio of adults to adolescents, problems such as poverty, poor education, lack of job opportunities, drug addiction, and hostility of neighbors undermined a sense of community and led to vandalism and property destruction.[3] Other analysts instead emphasized failure in local practices and federal policy. For example, Eugene Meehan laid part of the blame for the demise of St. Louis's Pruitt Igoe project on poor design, inadequate bidding practices, and cheap construction which led to inferior units requiring excessive maintenance.[4] In addition, he noted that federal policies, such as the one which limited the accumulation of financial reserves to a maximum of 50 percent of one year's rental, contributed to the problem because they undercut the ability of authorities to secure funds to modernize physically aging projects.

The financial problems of public housing which surfaced in the late 1970s placed some reformers in a difficult position. For the most part, these reformers had been the ones arguing for equity and fairness—applicants eligible for public housing should have access regardless of race, class, or income. On the other hand, faced with limited ability to improve environmental conditions in public housing, let alone do much about the underlying conditions of poverty that contributed to the problems, many found themselves retreating from the stance that public housing should be the housing of last resort. Instead, given the government's movement away from providing additional new public housing units, their pragmatic approach became one of trying to preserve the existing public housing stock for low-income people. At this level, reformers were faced with what they perceived as a dilemma between the rights of individuals who needed public housing and the rights of the larger community, including existing tenants of public housing, to have safe communities. As was demonstrated at the BHA, many reformers eventually became strong proponents of more intensive applicant screening as well as speedier and easier eviction proceedings for tenants who caused problems. Thus the rights of certain individuals for access to a scarce commodity such as public housing may be overridden by the desire to preserve the community. This swing toward a more conservative position seems to have been related as well to cutbacks in federal funding and plans to sell off projects, both of which threatened the survival of public housing as a continuing resource for poor persons.

[3]See Roger Starr, "Which of the Poor Shall Live in Public Housing?"
[4]Eugene Meehan, *The Quality of Federal Policy Making: Programmed Failure in Public Housing* (Columbia: University of Missouri Press, 1971).

The dilemmas involved in whom to house are perhaps nowhere better exemplified than in the area of squatting. As noted earlier, during the mid-1970s and early 1980s, the BHA experienced severe problems in accounting accurately for vacant units as well as renovating and renting those that it knew about fast enough to keep them from being vandalized. This situation provided an opportunity for squatters, who were often living doubled up with relatives or were homeless, to illegally occupy units that might otherwise remain vacant. Many of these squatters reportedly came from Puerto Rico where there was more of a tradition of taking over a vacant unit or unoccupied land and through a process of self-help, making it liveable. On the other hand, many applicants on the waiting list had needs that were just as great but rather than break the law they waited until it was their turn to be legally housed by the authority. Because squatters later advocated that their units be brought up to standard conditions and the authority felt compelled to reduce overcrowding several times over a 10 year period, the BHA evicted squatters from projects, arguing that their presence violated the principles of the waiting list, bypassed the elegibility requirements, and would otherwise result in squatters occupying unsafe units. While still upholding those principles, the BHA under the receivership introduced a program of sweat equity, giving applicants on the waiting list preferential treatment if they agreed to help fix up their unit.

The issue of whom to house also raised the dilemma of racial integration versus housing for the neediest. For example, Boston like many other northern cities has been known as a city of strong ethnic neighborhoods, and early in its history the BHA clearly had projects designated by race. The civil rights movement in the 1960s put an end to the most blatant racial discrimination policies of the previous period. Nevertheless, many projects remained segregated and, as discussed above, federal rules to change the situation had limited impact. During the 1980s, however, the BHA, like several other authorities, began to take a much more activist stance in relation to racial integration. This was accomplished through its general plan of giving preference to applicants willing to be housed in developments in which their race was substantially in the minority as well as its specific plans to create and/or maintain racial balance in projects.

However, in most housing projects throughout northern cities, the racial integration strategies appeared to be most effective in insuring the access of minorities to white projects in nonhostile neighborhoods. In some cases, such as that of the BHA, marketing efforts were begun in order to attract white applicants to minority projects. Some staff justified this approach on the basis that there were many whites in the community who had just as great a need for public housing as minority-group members but who chose not to apply because of a project's poor reputation and concern about living in a minority-dominated setting.

However, housing need was a difficult concept to define. In Boston a larger number of whites than minorities had low incomes; yet they represented a smaller proportion of their respective racial group. Furthermore, if the BHA's waiting list data collected in the early 1970s were still valid later, a greater proportion of racial minorities compared to whites on the BHA's waiting list lived in poor housing conditions. Moreover, many felt that whites were reluctant to apply because they had many more housing options in the private sector than minorities who were still subject to racial discrimination. Therefore, attempts either to retain or attract whites might deprive minorities who, when all is considered, may be in greater need of public housing.

While acknowledging the possible inequity involved in retaining or attracting whites, both the court and senior-level BHA staff strongly felt that BHA projects had to include whites with the additional proviso that projects be integrated as thoroughly as possible. Their arguments related in part to the political survival of the authority in a city in which whites were still dominant, the obligations of an agency using federal funds to guarantee equal access for applicants to all areas, and the appropriate role of public housing in providing a model for the rest of society. Thus, in some situations broader societal or organizational goals may override need as criterion for allocation. But the wisdom of placing the responsibility for residential integration on an institution that serves only the poor and which is experiencing serious economic hardship is extremely questionable. Although outright discrimination in programs such as public housing should be prohibited, it would make more sense to focus integration efforts in suburban areas. Although the suburbs may have disadvantages such as inadequate public transportation its residents are not already burdened by poverty and dilapidated housing conditions. A broader view of the residential integration issue is especially important given that many central city housing authorities have waiting lists consisting of only minority applicants. Still, only a few court cases have concluded that the achievement of residential integration needs to be the responsibility of the wider society that has an obligation to provide housing for low income families in a variety of locations including the suburbs. And, to date, few concrete results can be attributed to such decisions.[5]

REGULATORY JUSTICE: USES OF DISCRETION

This study supports Lipsky's contention that public service reform is a dialectical search for the appropriate balance between compassion and flexibility (responsiveness), on the one hand, and impartiality and rigid rule adherence (equity), on the other.[6]

The theoretical assumption of a strategy based on rules is the Weberian notion that a bureaucracy, like a machine, can and should function in a predictable manner which treats all cases equally.[7] A bureaucracy can be made to apply general rules to particular cases without succumbing to political pressures, personal biases, and other external influences which are specifically excluded from its specialized calculus. Lawrence Friedman has argued that a welfare program such as public housing is the ideal context for simple allocation of rules to be effective because in principle the staff have no personal reason to favor some applicants over others.[8] In addition, in a client-oriented bureaucracy, rule adherence protects the staff from charges of discrimination and unfairness.

However, even though simple rules were acknowledged to have their advantages, throughout the period of this study bureaucrats expressed ambivalence about strict rule adherence, a reaction typical of many bureaucracies. For example, the first come, first serve rule was theoretically an easy equity principle to administer. However, even once obstacles to its implementation, such as an inefficiently operating system, were finally overcome, many senior staff members considered it unfair

---

[5]Irving Welfeld, "The Courts and Desegregated Housing," *The Public Interest*, 45 (1976) 123–35, and Paul Davidoff, "Decent Housing for All: An Agenda," in Chester Hartman, ed., *America's Housing Crisis: What is to be done?* (Boston: Routledge & Kegan Paul, 1983), pp. 186–201.

[6]Lipsky, *Street-Level Bureaucracy.* See also James Q. Wilson, "The Bureaucracy Problem," *The Public Interest*, 3 (1967), 3–10.

[7]Max Weber, "The Essentials of Bureaucracy," in Robert K. Merton, Aisla Gray, Barbara Hockey, and Hanan Selvin, *Reader in Bureaucracy* (New York: Free Press, 1952) pp. 18–20.

[8]Lawrence Friedman, "Public Housing and the Poor," p. 687.

because of its lack of responsiveness to client needs. For this reason, the status of *emergency applicant*, which indicated a special need and a high priority, was developed. This status was constantly being redefined as outsiders pushed to expand it and inside staff both tried to respond to special conditions and to keep the principle of equity under control. One of those control measures was that final judgements about emergency status were made by upper-level professionals rather than lower-level clerical staff. However, given its limited resources in terms of funds and level of staff as well as inherent measurement problems, the Tenant Selection Department did not go much beyond emergency status to further define special need; therefore, it eventually adopted the first-come first-serve criterion as its standard. This policy took some pressure off lower-level staff who could now fall back on the rules, but created criticisms of indifference and unresponsiveness.

FEDERAL-LOCAL RELATIONSHIPS: CLARITY OF RULES

Theodore Lowi has argued that client equity can best be achieved through congressional passage of clear statutes followed by the promulgation of specific agency rules.[9] However, as this study indicates, problems may arise in the case of public housing when rules from Washington are imposed on localities with their unique and special problems. Federal agencies face major obstacles to the formulation of clear and specific rules, particularly when the rules are designed to change values which are firmly held by large and powerful segments of the society. For example, Martha Derthick has suggested that federal grant programs conspicuously fail to deal with issues of major substantive importance because the federal government is unable to formulate policies that are precise and internally consistent.[10] The reasons for this failure lie in the nature of the agency system. Since the federal government must reconcile very diverse interests, it leaves difficult allocation choices to state and local agencies. Federal agency stipulation of value-laden conditions is also constrained by the necessity to "buy" program participation; lower-level governments might refuse grants if locally unacceptable conditions are known to be strictly enforced. Therefore, federal agency policy statements, as a prac-

[9]See Lowi, *The End of Liberalism.*
[10]Derthick, *The Influence of Federal Grants.*

tical matter, tend to be general and ambiguous, leaving a great deal of latitude to local agencies, whereas from Lowi's point of view the opposite would be more desirable.

The more than 30 years of federal noninvolvement in public housing tenant-selection and assignment policies corroborates Derthick's observations. The federal Public Housing Administration left decisions to housing authorities at the local level partly because it could not formulate one set of rules that would apply to the diverse conditions in the over 2,400 agencies that ran public housing programs and, more importantly, because of its instinct for survival: public housing has always been an unpopular welfare program. Whatever success the program had in Congress was in large part dependent on southern legislators who were likely to withdraw their support if the federal agency actively pursued integration. Moreover, the existence of public housing units required the voluntary initiative on the part of local governments. If the federal agency pursued integration, many communities would be reluctant to participate in the program and the agency would face the prospect of smaller budgets and continual struggle with its client agencies. Acquiescence to the environment in the interest of survival was therefore the federal agency's watchword.

Furthermore, this study casts serious doubts on the ability of a federal agency to implement a single national rule to achieve objectives such as equity and integration even when such a rule is attempted. Rules related to such volatile issues as race and even simple rules such as first come, first serve are not self-implementing, and a great deal of discretion is still available at the local level in this regard. For a long period of time, instead of strictly adhering to the rules, the BHA central staff exercised a fair amount of discretion through interpretation of these rules and thereby responded in a number of cases to key elements in their work environment such as pressure from third parties.

In spite of the limitations of its rule strategy, the federal government should still be considered a potentially important force in promoting change and insuring fairness in the practices of local agencies. For example, HUD was the major agency which provided oversight of BHA operations and feedback on its performance. Even though HUD itself had difficulty enforcing change because for a long period its major sanction of withholding funds was so heavy-handed, its reports on problems in tenant selection served as useful information to those staff and outsiders who desired to change the system. In addition, when HUD itself began to disburse special discretionary funds to authorities for modernization and to base some of its funding on agency performance, its power increased *vis à vis* agency operations. Just as importantly, such agencies represent the federal government's voice on issues of national significance. For example, when HUD backed racial balance plans, it added a moral force to efforts of the BHA reformers.

Thus, clarity of rules affects the extent of the federal government's ability to regulate local agencies. The relationship of specific government agencies to the local bureaucracy in terms of feedback and support can influence the degree of adherence to those rules as well as to the overall direction the local group chooses to take.

THE INFLUENCE OF THIRD PARTIES

Faced with complicated written policies and rules that never completely eliminate discretion, as well as a number of more informal operating procedures, applicants for services are often in a weak position to advocate for themselves. But allocation decisions are not based only on interactions between clients and agency bureaucrats. They often also involve third-party sponsors such as social workers and politicians who can influence outcomes. Traditionally, the literature has examined the roles of such groups through their involvement in rights of appeals and hearings.[11] But as this study has demonstrated, social workers and politicians can also act as advocates for individual applicants in the more routine application process. On the one hand, their protectionist role is based on making certain that their clients are treated fairly in terms of procedures; hence, they can be a force for equity. On the other hand, they are often proponents of the special needs and circumstances of individual clients; in this sense, they can be a force to stretch the rules in terms of responsiveness.

The effectiveness of third party-sponsors emanates from sources such as their access to information and continuing relations with agency staff. For example, since admissions procedures are often complicated, outside parties who interact frequently with an agency are more likely to understand than individual applicants how both formal and informal processes work better than individual applicants. During the 1980s the BHA oper-

---

[11]Handler, *Protecting the Social Service Client.*

ated what might be considered a tightly centralized rational admissions and assignment system governed by a complicated 38-page document explaining eligibility requirements and priority categories. And, even though emergency status was defined in the procedures, it remained a somewhat elusive category in which outsiders continued to apply pressure. In such cases, advocacy by an outside sponsor might tip the balance for an applicant but perhaps at the expense of a needy person who does not have such an advocate.

THE POWER OF STREET-LEVEL BUREAUCRATS

It was hypothesized at the beginning of this study that public housing managers, a type of street-level bureaucrat, might have different roles and respond to different incentives than staff at the central office who are not as concerned with which applicants are housed. For example, as long as BHA project managers responded to goals such as maintaining project conditions and maximizing rent collection, they had a strong incentive to resist or subvert central office applicant assignments that would increase problems in their projects, even though such applicants might have been selected on the basis of equity rules. Because project managers were felt to have abused the wide discretion available to them at the expense of equity and other objectives such as racial integration, their discretionary authority was ultimately reduced through tight central control of assignments.

Once having virtually eliminated project manager discretion, however, upper-level staff realized that they had gone too far; the manager's degree of control was closely related to the project's success or failure. This finding was supported by an Urban Institute study of 119 public housing authorities which demonstrated that one aspect of organizational structure that led to high rather than low performance was decentralization—that is, more authority delegated to the project level rather than kept at the central office.[12]

In spite of the findings cited above, rather than returning to the situation in which managers exercised wide discretion, the BHA embarked on a strategy of setting certain conditions under which managers

---

[12]Robert Sadacca and Suzanne Loux, *Improving Public Housing Through Management: A Technical Report* (Washington, D.C.: The Urban Institute, 1978).

could exercise limited discretion.[13] First, managers did not always have to adhere strictly to such rules as first come, first serve; instead, they were encouraged to select applicants whose profile might fit the needs of a particular part of the development. Second, strict objectives were set in relation to factors such as race which previously had been troublesome. Since these objectives were usually agreed to by both managers and tenants, some of the heat was taken off project staff. Third, objectives were set for each project so that upper-level management could compare one manager to another. And finally, through the power of the court, the BHA acquired incentives and sanctions to discipline managers through promotions, demotions, transfers, or termination. Such a prospect was made feasible through court actions that allowed the BHA to hire new managers more sympathetic with its overall philosophy. Nevertheless, in recognition of the different roles of street-level bureaucrats, there was tight upper-level monitoring of assignments.

Therefore, as is evident in the case of the BHA, street-level bureaucrats often make policy through their behavior. It is clear that some level of input from this group is important if upper-level management is to be cognizant of issues related to the establishment and implementation of rules. However, because of the degree of personal investment of street-level bureaucrats in how the rules affect the community, subjective discretion becomes an important issue. Therefore equity and rule adherence are somewhat dependent upon choosing employees at this level who are at least sympathetic to the principles of the rules and upon careful monitoring of the decisions of such employees. The complete elimination of discretion at the project level, however, can undermine the manager's achievement of other objectives, such as community building, that in the end may be as important as equity in the life of projects and the survival of public housing as an institution. The challenge therefore becomes how to provide conditions in which street-level bureaucrats can exercise circumscribed discretion.

Public housing managers have more limited discretion in selecting and evicting tenants than their counterparts in the private sector whose role expectations are not overlaid with complex and often contradictory public purposes. In addition, the rundown condition of many projects, the poverty and associated problems of their residents, and the general lack of resources to improve the situation make the job of a housing

---

[13]See Lipsky, *Street-Level Bureaucrats.*

manager in a central city housing authority a challenge even to the most gifted administrator. Unfortunately, housing management remains an aspect of housing that has received the least attention. Although such organizations as the National Center for Housing and Management encourage more professionalism in the field through educational materials and training, housing management is a field in which most incumbents find themselves by happenstance; in other words, it is not a deliberate career choice for which they are professionally prepared. In the late 1970s the BHA opted for change when recruiting new managers, by clarifying their roles and by defining the performance expectations in such areas as rent collection and maintenance. A manager's success in meeting such objectives, however, is dependent not only on his knowledge of the physical plant and his ability to get tenants to pay rent on time, but on skills in advocacy, tenant relations, community organizing, tenant development and linkages to the surrounding community. The critical role of the manager suggests the need for careful recruitment, upgrading of skills, and adequate compensation to insure not only high performance but, as the BHA later discovered, to keep qualified managers from being lured to the private sector where salaries may be higher and jobs easier.

CLIENT EMPOWERMENT

Most efforts at reforming bureaucracy focus on controlling staff behavior through such strategies as tightening rules, changing incentives, hiring more professional staff, and improving efficiency. An alternative approach is empowering clients.

In the case of the BHA, attempts were made to open up central office tenant selection by writing clear rules and procedures, computerizing the system, and letting applicants know where they stood on the waiting list. Such changes made staff much more accountable because certain applicants could not be easily skipped over in favor of others without justification. In addition, the availability of more accurate project turnover rate statistics allowed applicants to be better informed about how long they would have to wait before being housed in specific developments.

At a different level, it is possible to turn over actual management responsibility to tenants in order to reduce excessive bureaucracy and to increase residents' stake in a project as occurred at the BHA's Bromley-Heath development. Bromley-Heath had been designated a pilot tenant management corporation (TMC) in the late 1960s with support from the federal Office of Economic Opportunity. A large project with 1230 units occupied primarily by blacks, Bromley-Heath consisted of 38 apartment buildings on 25 acres of land in a rundown neighborhood of southwest Boston. The Bromley-Heath TMC operated almost as a miniature local housing authority with responsibility for maintenance, rent collection and hiring staff. Under this delegate model its budget was negotiated with the BHA from which it also purchased some services.

The success of the Bromley-Heath TMC and other similar experiments in cities such as St. Louis are difficult to judge because of inadequate comparative data. An evaluation of the Bromley-Heath TMC noted on the positive side that rent collections had increased, more jobs went to residents, tenant participation as judged by TMC meetings was strong and security had improved. On the negative side, vacancies continued to increase, vandalism was still a major problem and many tenants were apathetic about the TMC. Such mixed results are not surprising, however, given that the tenants took over one of the most problem ridden projects without adequate resources to upgrade it and without sufficient management and maintenance training or experience to run it. However, one should not conclude from Bromley-Heath's experience that a tenant management corporation should be rejected out of hand. In St. Louis, several tenant managed projects significantly improved conditions and expanded their activities into other community development projects. Instead, it suggests that such new forms of cooperative management should be tried in projects with fewer problems or in places at least clearly on the way up as indicated by increased resources and improved living conditions. Simply to hand over projects in bad condition to inexperienced tenant managers is only likely to increase resident frustration and disillusionment.

Another model is to turn over select management functions to tenants. For example, in several projects, including Bromley-Heath, tenants took over tenant selection and assignment responsibilities. In the few places where this was tried, tenants were generally considered tougher than housing managers in terms of screening prospective applicants. There were also reports that the TMC transferred active tenants to better apartments rather than providing them to new applicants, a policy that seemed like a reversion to previous practices when managers similarly rewarded good tenants. The backers of the tenant selection plan hoped that such discretion would lead not only to tighter screening and more sensitive placement of applicants in particular locations but also to build a political power base among tenants. But despite such apparent advantages, tenants seemed more comfortable setting standards and procedures for admissions, preferring to leave the difficult decisions to staff. The impact of tenant involvement in decision making on selection and assignment procedures therefore remains a question for further investigation. It seems clear, however, that given limited resources to improve the situation, tenants take on many of the attitudes and viewpoints of more traditional managers.

THE PRIVATIZATION OF PUBLIC HOUSING

Public housing has been subject to intense criticism over the last decade for its alleged inefficiency, bad design, poor management and inadequate maintenance. Although such problems are not universal, they certainly apply to some large authorities such as the one in Boston. A recent response has been the proposal to privatize public housing through the divestiture of projects to tenants or private developers. Similar proposals have been the subject of much debate in other countries such as France, West Germany and Sweden. During the 1980s the conservative government in Britain actually privatized a significant proportion of its government-owned housing stock.[14]

Privatization has several potential positive attributes. For example, divestiture may be a means for tenants to exercise more control over their residential settings or to escape their roles as renters and enter the world of home ownership. On a broader scale, privatization may reduce the oppressiveness of large bureaucracies and better control fiscal expenditures.

But in spite of the arguments that support the privatization of public housing, a great deal of caution should be exercised before embarking on a course that might serve to reduce the only part of our housing stock that remains out of the speculative profit-making sector and is accessible to low income persons. Smaller suburban projects or those in gentrifying areas within central cities are likely to be the most attractive ones for

[14]Ray Forrest and Alan Murie, "Marginalization and subsidized individualism: The sale of council houses in the restructuring of the British Welfare System," *International Journal of Urban and Regional Research*, 1986, vol. 10, pp. 46–66.

privatization. However, with adequate protections, such as a stipulation that such projects only be turned over to groups committed to housing low income persons, and continuing income and operating subsidies, such developments may no longer remain housing for the poor. In a continuing attempt to decrease government expenditures and public responsibility, officials will also be tempted to pass off less attractive and more rundown projects in inner city areas to unsuspecting community organizations or tenants. In the search for solutions, our government should not be allowed to walk away from its responsibilities to upgrade public housing and provide decent and affordable living conditions for its residents.

GENERAL IMPLICATIONS

Rules by themselves are somewhat insensitive allocation procedures. They exist partly because to operate without them in large bureaucracies would mean leaving enormous amounts of discretion in the hands of staff. But, as Handler points out,[15] the dichotomy between rules and discretion should not be taken literally: what we should focus on is degrees of discretion.

What can be done to encourage rule adherence? First, agencies must have the technology as well as the resources to create and maintain efficiently operating systems; inefficiency breeds discretion.

Second, just as important as the need to protect the rights of clients to fair and impartial treatment is the need to recognize and handle situations in which strict rule enforcement is an ineffective means to implement policy. For example, there are situations in which bureaucracies should differentiate among needy applicants beyond the capacity of rules, such as in cases where families are without housing of any form. However, it would appear to be more appropriate for professionals rather than less well-trained staff to make individual decisions about the needs of such clients. Another strategy in this regard is to take such cases out of the regular process by designating a specified percentage of the total resources for them.

In other situations the achievement of objectives may be beyond the ability of simple rules. For example, nondiscrimination rules proved to be

[15]Handler, *Protecting the Social Service Client.*

ineffective mechanisms to promote racial balance in projects. Instead, performance-based systems which set goals and recognize concepts such as tipping points may be more effective, but in truth we know very little about this process or the threshold points that may provide guidelines for such policies. But even more amorphous goals exist such as assigning specific applicants to projects in order to build a community. Again, our knowledge of who is likely to make a good tenant, let alone how to build a successful community, is extremely limited. Such lack of knowledge makes it difficult to design policies and procedures to guide the decisions of bureaucrats.

It does appear to make sense to encourage attempts to create communities in projects by decentralizing decision making, thus empowering project managers and/or tenant organizations. However, this must be subject to the broader constraints that these groups do not discriminate against applicants on the basis of such criteria as race or marital status. At issue is whether bureaucrats, in fact, have any special knowledge about community building or whether this task is better placed in the hands of tenants themselves who have more of a stake in the outcome.

Third, in situations where it is deemed important, multiple channels must be created and sustained to control discretion. For example, insuring client access to information about rules and procedures is one way to make these clients more effective advocates for their own rights. But because many procedures are informal and unwritten, assigning advocates to clients may also provide a source of control, although clients without such support may be unfairly disadvantaged. Fourth, appropriate incentives and sanctions must exist to encourage adherence to the rules among staff. Fifth, outside organizations must monitor overall activities to determine deviations and prescribe remedies. Finally, rules, and procedures to implement them should be periodically reviewed to insure that they are appropriate to changing socioeconomic conditions.

Bibliography

Abrams, Charles. *The City is the Frontier*. New York: Harper & Row, 1965.

Almond, Gabriel, and Harold Lasswell. "Aggressive Behavior by Clients Toward Public Relief Administration." *American Political Science Review*, 28 (1934).

Ascher, Charles. *The Administration of Publicly Aided Housing*. Brussels: International Institute of Administrative Sciences, 1971.

Bailey, Stephen, and Edith Mosher. *ESEA: The Office of Education Administers a Law*. Syracuse: Syracuse University Press, 1968.

Bardach, Eugene. *The Implementation Game: What Happens After a Bill Becomes a Law*. Cambridge: M.I.T. Press, 1980.

Bellin, Seymour, and Louis Kriesberg. "Relations Among Attitudes. Circumstances and Behavior: The Case of Applying for Public Housing." *Sociology and Social Research*, 52 (1967).

Bernstein, Julius, Doris Bunte, and John Connelly. "Statement of Objectives." Mimeograph. N.P.: n.p., April 26, 1971.

Blau, Peter. *Dynamics of Bureaucracy*. Chicago: University of Chicago Press, 1963.

Boston Housing Authority. "Resolution Establishing Policies and Standards Governing Occupancy of Federally Aided Developments." Boston: BHA, 1965.

———. Department of Tenant and Community Relations. "Follow-up Study of a Selected Group of Tenants Identified During Application Process as Potential Problem Families." Mimeographed. Boston: BHA, 1967.

———. *Annual Report*. Boston: BHA, 1970.

———. "Occupancy Department Reorganization." Mimeographed. Boston: BHA, n.d.

———. "Broad Range of Income Program." Mimeographed. Boston: BHA, 1983.

———. Chief of Tenant Selection. "Proposal to Abolish the Tenant Selection Scoring System." Mimeographed. Boston: BHA, July 29, 1971.

———. "Compliance Agreement Between the United States Department of Housing and Urban Development and the Boston Housing Authority." Boston: BHA 1972.

———. Director of Management Services. "Administrative Reorganization: Tenant Selection." Mimeographed. Boston: BHA, 1973.

———. "Tenant Selection Assignment and Transfer Plan." Mimeographed. Boston: BHA, 1978.

———. Director of Management Services. "Report to the Board—Vacancies." Mimeographed, n.p., September 25, 1972.

Boston Housing Authority Receivership. *First Semi-annual Report of the Boston Housing Authority Receivership to the Suffolk Superior Court.* (Aug. 6, 1980–Feb. 1, 1981.) Part III: Exhibits. Boston: n.p., 1981.

———. *Second Semi-annual Report of the Boston Housing Authority Receivership to the Suffolk Superior Court.* (August 6, 1980–Feburary 1, 1981). Boston: n.p., February 13, 1981.

———. *Third Semi-annual Report of the Boston Housing Authority Receivership to the Suffolk Superior Court* (February 1, 1981–June 30, 1981.) Boston, MA: n.p., 1981.

———. *Seventh Semi-annual Report of the Boston Housing Authority Receivership to the Suffolk Superior Court.* Boston: n.p., June 30, 1983.

Bryan, Jack. "What's Happening at HUD?" *Journal of Housing,* 27 (1970).

Citizens Housing and Planning Association. *A Struggle for Survival: The Boston Housing Authority 1969–1973.* Boston: Citizens Housing and Planning Association, 1973.

Coleman, Richard. "Explorations in the Contemporary Images of Housing." Mimeographed. Cambridge, MA: MIT–Harvard Joint Center for Urban Studies, 1972.

Cullingworth, J. D. *Housing and Local Government.* London: George Allen & Unwin, 1966.

De Leeuw, Frank. *Operating Costs in Public Housing—A Financial Crisis.* Washington, D.C.: Urban Institute, 1970.

Derthick, Martha. *The Influence of Federal Grants.* Cambridge: Harvard University Press, 1970.

Deutscher, Irwin. "The Gatekeeper in Public Housing." *Among the People,* Irwin Deutscher and Elizabeth Thompson, eds. New York: Basic Books, 1968.

Donnison, D. V. *The Government of Housing.* Harmondsworth, Middlesex, England: Penguin Books, 1967.

Downs, Anthony. *Inside Bureaucracy.* Boston: Little, Brown, 1966.

Fisher, Robert. *Twenty Years of Public Housing.* New York: Harper & Brothers, 1959.

Freedman, Leonard. *Public Housing: The Politics of Poverty.* New York: Holt, Rinehart & Winston, 1969.

Friedman, Lawrence. *Government and Slum Housing.* Chicago: Rand McNally, 1968.

Friedman, Lawrence. "Public Housing and the Poor: An Overview." *California Law Review,* 55 (1966).

Galm, Sharon. Welfare—An Administrative Nightmare. *Issues in Welfare. Studies in Public Welfare.* U.S. 93rd Congress, 2nd sess. Washington, D.C.: U.S. Government Printing Office, 1972.

Genung, George, Jr. "Where Have We Come With the Brooke Amendment?" *Journal of Housing,* 27 (1970).

Gessmer, Ellen. "Discrimination in Public Housing Under the Housing and

Community Development Act of 1974: A Critique of the New Haven Experience." *Urban Law Annual*, 13, No. 49 (1977).

Glaser, Barney, and Anselm Strauss. *Awareness of Dying*. Chicago: Aldine, 1965.

Glazer, Nathan. "Housing Policy and the Family." *Journal of Marriage and the Family*, 29, No. 1. (February 1967).

Goldfeld, Abraham. *The Diary of a Housing Manager*. Chicago: National Association of Housing Officials, 1938.

Greater Boston Committee on Racial Equality (CORE). "Report on CORE's Public Housing Survey." Mimeographed. N.P.: n.p., 1963.

Greater Boston Committee on Racial Equality (CORE). "Segregation in the Boston Public Housing Projects." Mimeographed: n.p., 1963.

Hamlar, Portia. "HUD's Authority to Mandate Effective Management of Public Housing." *Journal of Urban Law*, 50 (1972).

Handler, Joel. *Protecting the Social Service Client: Legal and Structural Controls on Official Discretion*. New York: Academic Press, 1979.

————. *Social Movements and the Legal System*. New York: Academic Press, 1978.

Handler, Joel, and Ellen Hollingsworth. *The "Deserving Poor": A Study of Welfare Administration*. Chicago: Markham Publishing Co., 1971.

Hartman, Chester, ed. *America's Housing Crisis: What Is to Be Done?* Boston: Routledge & Kegan Paul, 1983.

Hartman, Chester. "Social Values and Housing Orientations." *Journal of Social Issues*, 19 (1963).

Hartman, Chester, and Gregg Carr. "Housing Authorities Reconsidered." *Journal of the American Institute of Planners*, January (1969).

Hartman, Chester, and Margaret Levi. "Public Housing Managers: An Appraisal," *Journal of American Institute of Planners*, 39 (1973).

Hipshman, May. *Public Housing at the Crossroads: The Boston Housing Authority*. Boston: Citizens Housing and Planning Association, 1967.

Hirshen, Al, and Vivian Brown. "Too Poor for Public Housing: Roger Starr's Poverty Preferences." *Social Policy*. May/June (1972).

Howitt, Arnold. "Strategies of Governing: The Executive Behavior of Mayors in Philadelphia and Boston." Ph.D. Dissertation, Harvard University, 1974.

Huttman, Elizabeth. "Stigma and Public Housing: A Comparison of British and American Policies and Experience." Ph.D. Dissertation, University of California, Berkeley, 1969.

Joint Center for Urban Studies of MIT and Harvard. *America's Housing Needs: 1970 to 1980*. Cambridge, MA: Joint Center for Urban Studies, 1973.

Katz, Daniel, and Robert Kahn. *The Social Psychology of Organizations*. New York: John Wiley & Sons, 1966.

Kaufman, Herbert. *Administrative Feedback: Monitoring Subordinates' Behavior*. Washington, D.C.: Brookings Institution, 1973.

Lazin, Frederick. "Federal Low Income Housing Assistance Program and Racial Segregation: Leased Public Housing." *Public Policy*, 24 (Summer 1976).

————. "Public Housing in Chicago, 1963–1971. *Gautreaux* v. *Chicago Housing Authority*: A Case Study of the Cooptation of a Federal Agency by Its Local Constituency." Ph.D. Dissertation, University of Chicago 1973.

————. "The Failure of Federal Enforcement of Civil Rights Regulations in Public Housing, 1963–1971: The Cooptation of a Federal Agency by Its Local Constituency." *Policy Science,* 4 (1973).

Lefcoe, George. "HUD's Authority to Mandate Tenants' Rights in Public Housing." *Yale Law Journal,* 80 (1971).

LeGates, Richard. *Can the Federal Welfare Bureaucracies Control Their Programs: The Case of HUD and Urban Renewal. Working Paper No. 176.* Berkeley: Institute of Urban and Regional Development, University of California, 1972.

Lempert, Richard, and Kiyoshi Ikeda. "Evictions from Public Housing: The Effects of Independent Review." *American Sociological Review,* 35 (1970).

Levin, Jack, and Gerald Taube. "Bureaucracy and the Socially Handicapped: A Story of Lower Status Tenants in Public Housing." *Sociology and Social Research,* 53 (1970).

Levin, Sol, and Paul White. "Exchange as a Conceptual Framework for the Study of Interorganizational Relationships." In *A Social Reader on Complex Organizations.* Amitai Etzioni, ed. 2nd ed. New York: Holt, Rinehart & Winston, 1969.

Lipsky, Michael. *Protest in City Politics.* Chicago: Rand McNally, 1970.

————. *Street-Level Bureaucracy: Dilemmas of the Individual in Public Services.* New York: Russell Sage Foundation, 1980.

————. "Street-Level Bureaucracy and the Analysis of Urban Reform." *Urban Affairs Quarterly,* 6 (1971).

Lowi, Theodore. *The End of Liberalism.* New York: Norton, 1969.

Lucas, Keith Allen. *Decisions About People in Need.* Chapel Hill: University of North Carolina Press, 1957.

Luttrell, Jordan. "Public Housing and Integration: A Neglected Opportunity." *Columbia Journal of Law,* 6 (1970).

————. "The Public Housing Administration and Discrimination in Federally Assisted Low-Rent Housing." *Michigan Law Review,* March (1966).

MacDonnel, Philip: "The Process of Change at the Boston Housing Authority." Unpublished undergraduate thesis, Harvard College, 1971.

McEntire, Davis. *Residence and Race.* Berkeley: University of California Press, 1960.

McGuire, Marie. Memo to Donald Hummel, Assistant Secretary, HUD. Policy Governing Equal Opportunity in HUD Operations and Programs. February 8, 1967.

Mayer, Albert. "Public Housing Architecture." *Journal of Housing,* 19 (1962).

Mayhew, Leon. *Law and Equal Opportunity: A Study of the Massachusetts Commission Against Discrimination.* Cambridge, MA: Harvard University Press, 1968.

Mazmanian, Daniel A., and Paul A. Sabatier, Ed. *Effective Policy Implementation.* Lexington, MA.: Lexington Books, 1981.

Meehan, Eugene J. *The Quality of Federal Policy Making: Programmed Failure in Public Housing.* Columbia: University of Missouri Press, 1979.

Meyerson, Martin, and Edward Banfield. *Politics, Planning and the Public Interest.* New York: Free Press, 1955.

Mollenkopf, John. "Community Organization and City Politics." Ph.D. Dissertation, Harvard University, 1973.

Moore, Wilbert. *The Professions: Roles and Rules*. New York: Russell Sage Foundation, 1970.

Morris, R. N., and John Mogey. *The Sociology of Housing*. London: Routledge & Kegan Paul, 1965.

Muir, William Kenneth, Jr. *Police: Streetcorner Politicians*. Chicago: University of Chicago Press, 1977.

Mulvihill, J. "Problems in the Management of Public Housing." *Temple Law Quarterly*, 36 (1962).

National Committee Against Discrimination in Housing. *How the Federal Government Builds Ghettos*. Washington, D.C.: National Committee Against Discrimination in Housing, February 1967.

National Commission on Urban Problems. *Building the American City*. Washington, D.C.: Superintendent of Documents, 1969.

Nenno, Mary. "Housing and the Urban Development Act of 1969." *Journal of Housing*, 27 (1970).

_____. "Housing and the Urban Development Legislation of 1970." *Journal of Housing*, 28 (1971).

Nordlinger, Eric. *Decentralizing the City: A Study of Boston's Little City Halls*. Boston: Urban Observatory, 1972.

Orfield, Gary. *The Reconstruction of Southern Education: The Schools and the 1964 Civil Rights Act*. New York: Wiley-Interscience, 1969.

Peattie, Lisa. "Public Housing: Urban Slums Under Public Management." In *Race, Change and Urban Society*. P. Orleans and W. Ellis, eds. Los Angeles: Sage Publications, 1971.

Perez v. *Boston Housing Authority*. 368 Mass. 333 and 331 NE 2d 801 (1975).

Perez et al. v. *Boston Housing Authority*. Order of Appointment of Receiver, n.p., 1980.

_____. Superior Court Department No. 17222, Suffolk, s.s., 1980.

Pesso, Tana. "Local Welfare Offices: Managing the Intake Process," *Public Policy*, 26 (1978).

Peters, Guy D. "Insiders and Outsiders: The Politics of Pressure Group Influence on Bureaucracy." *Administration and Society*, August 1977, pp. 191–218.

Philadelphia Housing Authority. "Recommended Tenant Selection Policy." Mimeographed. N.P.: n.p., 1970.

Popper, Lewis. "The Boston Housing Authority: A Study of Conflict in Bureaucracy." Unpublished undergraduate thesis, Harvard College, 1968.

Pressman, Jeffrey, and Aaron Wildavsky. *Implementation*. Berkeley: University of California Press, 1972.

Prottas, Jeffrey Manditch. *People Processing: The Street-Level Bureaucracy in Public Service Bureaucracies*. Lexington, MA: Lexington Books, 1979.

_____. "The Power of the Street-level Bureaucrat in Public Service Bureaucracies." *Urban Quarterly*, Vol. III (I) March (1978), p. 285–312.

_____. "Techniques of the Weak in Bureaucratic Conflict. The Case in Public Housing." Discussion Paper 078-6, Department of City and Regional Planning. Cambridge, MA: Harvard University, April 1978.

Rein, Martin, and Francine Rabinowitz. "Toward a Theory of Implementation."
   Mimeographed. Cambridge: Joint Center for Urban Studies, 1974.
Report of the Regional Realignment Working Group. Washington, D.C.: N.P.,
   n.d.
Riker, William. *Federalism.* Boston: Little, Brown, 1964.
Scholnick, Michael. "Organizational Change at the Boston Housing Authority."
   Master's Thesis, Harvard University, 1970.
Scobie, Richard. "The BHA's Department of Tenant and Community Relations,
   1964–1968." Mimeographed. Boston: BHA, n.d.
———. "Family Interaction as a Factor in Problem-Tenant Identification in Pub-
   lic Housing." Ph.D. Dissertation, Brandeis University, 1972.
———. *Problem Tenants in Public Housing: Who, Where and Why Are They.*
   New York: Praeger, 1975.
Shefter, Martin. "City Hall and State House: State Legislative Involvement in the
   Politics of New York and Boston." Ph.D. Dissertation, Harvard University,
   1970.
Schermer, George Associates and Kenneth Jones. *Changing Concepts of the
   Tenant Management Relationship.* Washington, D.C.: National Association
   of Housing and Redevelopment Officials, 1967.
Silverman, Abner. *Selected Aspects of Administration of Publicly Owned Hous-
   ing.* Housing and Home Finance Agency. Washington, D.C.: U.S. Govern-
   ment Printing Office, 1961.
Simon, Herbert. *Models of Man.* New York: John Wiley & Sons, 1957.
Sjoberg, Gideon, Richard Brymar, and Bufford Farris. "Bureaucracy and the
   Lower Class." *Sociology and Social Research,* 49 (1966).
Solomon, Arthur. *Housing the Urban Poor.* Cambridge, MA: M.I.T. Press, 1974.
Starr, Roger. "Which of the People Shall Live in Public Housing?" *The Public
   Interest,* 23 (1971).
Sternlieb, George *et al.* "America's Housing: Prospects and Problems." Bruns-
   wick, N.J.: Center for Urban Policy Research, Rutgers University, 1980.
Struyk, Raymond J. *A New System for Public Housing: Salvaging a National
   Resource.* Washington, D.C.: Urban Institute, 1980.
Taube, Gerald. "The Social Structural Sources of Residential Satisfaction and
   Dissatisfaction in Public Housing. Ph.D. Dissertation, Brandeis University,
   1970.
U.S. Bureau of the Census. *Measuring the Quality of Housing: An Appraisal of
   Census Methods and Procedures.* Washington, D.C.: U.S. Government
   Printing Office, 1967.
U.S. Department of Housing and Urban Development. *Check List of Activities
   Involved in Conducting Occupancy Audits of Local Housing Authorities.*
   Washington, D.C.: U.S. Government Printing Office, 1967.
U.S. Department of Housing and Urban Development. *Manual for Low Rent
   Housing.* Washington, D.C.: U.S. Government Printing Office, 1968.
U.S. Department of Housing and Urban Development. *Occupancy Audit Report
   of the Boston Housing Authority.* Housing Services and Property Manage-
   ment Division, Washington, D.C.: U.S. Government Printing Office, June
   8, 1971.

U.S. Department of Housing and Urban Development. "BHA Audit Report." Washington, D.C.: U.S. Government Printing Office, March 3, 1972.

U.S. Department of Housing and Urban Development. *Statistical Yearbook.* Washington, D.C.: U.S. Government Printing Office, 1974.

Van Duesan, Richard. "New Federalism." *Journal of Housing,* 26 (1969).

Weaver, Robert, Secretary, U.S. Department of Housing and Urban Development. "Statement." Mimeographed. N.P., February 8, 1967.

_____. *The Negro Ghetto.* New York: Harcourt Brace Jovanovich, 1948.

Weber, Max. "The Essentials of Bureaucratic Organization." In *Reader in Bureaucracy,* Robert K. Marton, Aisia Gray, Barbara Hockey, and Hanan Selvin, eds. New York: Free Press, 1952.

Welfeld, Irving. "The Courts and Desegregated Housing." *The Public Interest,* 45 (1977).

Whittlesey, Robert B. "Report of the Master in the Case of *Perez* v. *Boston Housing Authority.*" CA 03096. Boston, MA: n.p., July 1976.

Wilensky, Harold, and Charles Lebeaux. *Industrial Society and Social Welfare.* New York: Russell Sage Foundation, 1958.

Willis, Dorothy. "Briefing Paper on Tenant Selection and Assignment Policies." Mimeographed. Washington, D.C.: Department of Housing and Urban Development, 1969.

Wilson, James Q. "The Bureaucracy Problem." *The Public Interest,* 3 (1967).

_____. *Political Organizations.* New York: Basic Books, 1973.

_____. *Varieties of Police Behavior.* Cambridge, Mass.: Harvard University Press, 1968.

Wirt, Frederick. *Politics of Southern Equality.* Chicago: Aldine, 1970.

Wolf, Eleanor. "The Tipping Point in Racially Changing Neighborhoods." In *Urban Planning and Social Policy,* Bernard Frieden and Robert Morris, eds. New York: Basic Books, 1968.

Yale Law Journal. "Public Housing and Urban Policy: *Gautreaux* v. *Chicago Housing Authority,*" Jon Pynoos, Robert Schafer, and Chester Hartman, eds. *Housing Urban America.* New York: Aldine, 1980.

Yin, Robert K. *Changing Urban Bureaucracies: How New Practices Become Routinized.* Lexington, MA: Lexington Books, 1978.

Zald, Mayer. *Organizational Change: The Political Economy of the YMCA.* Chicago: University of Chicago Press, 1970.

Author Index

Subject Index

Boston Housing Authority staff
circumvention of 1–2–3 plan, 62–65
discretion, 67–70
morale of, 49–50
norms of, 8
See also Managers
Boston Housing Court
discipline of managers, 199
interventon by, 157–185
political patronage and, 189
Boston Redevelopment Authority, 18
relocation division advocacy, 95
Brighton project
racial integration of, 173–174
Bromley-Heath development, 200–201
Brown v. Board of Education of Topeka,
25–26
Bunte, Doris, 34
Bureaucrats. *See* Street-level Bureaucrats
Bureaucratic discretion. *See* Discretion
Bureaucratic goals, 71n
Bureaucratic types
discretion and, 70–87

Catholic Church
racial integration and, 23
Centralization, 118–121, 155, 183, 198
Chardon Street missionary, 131
Charlestown project
racial integration of, 15, 176
Chicago Housing Authority, 13
assignment procedures, 152
Citizens Housing and Planning Associa-
tion study, 33–34
Civil Rights Act of 1964, 27
Civil Rights Division, 173
Client empowerment. *See* Tenant
empowerment
Coalition for Basic Human Needs, 179
Columbia Point project, 90, 136, 138, 168
applicaton for, 163
influence of situation at, 131–134
profile, 124–129
racial integration of, 15
Community Development Block Grants,
168–169
Congress on Racial Equality (CORE),
16n, 29n
NAACP–CORE agreement, 140
reform and, 16, 18–19

D Street project
racial integration of, 23
Department of Housing and Urban Development (HUD), 45n, 52n, 107,
161–162, 196
desegregation and, 28–33
monitoring of BHA, 139–150
1–2–3 plan, 29–33
powers of, 139, 153–155
reform and, 19–25
Desegregation. *See* Racial integration
Detroit Housing Commission
assignment procedures of, 155n
Discretion
definition and uses of, 5–6
managerial, 163–164
outcomes of, 82–87, 203–204
project-level, 113–138
race and, 83–87
regulatory justice and, 3–4, 194–195
rule interpretation, 196–197
situations as a determinant of, 123–134
staff types and, 70–87
street-level bureaucrats and, 7
third-party sponsors and, 95
Division of Civil Rights
desegregation and, 28
Division of labor
applicant processing and, 47

East Boston project
racial integration of, 173–174
Economic integration, 178–180
Efficiency, 160, 163–164, 169–171, 187,
189
Elderly
assignment of, 58–60
Columbia Point project, in, 126
discretion and assignment of, 85–87
Mary Ellen McCormick project, in,
125
political advocacy for, 104
Emergency status, 37, 48, 73, 95–96,
160
discretion in determining, 68–69
HUD audit of, 148–50
regulatory justice and, 195
English council housing
advocacy in, 77n
applicant scoring procedure, 41n